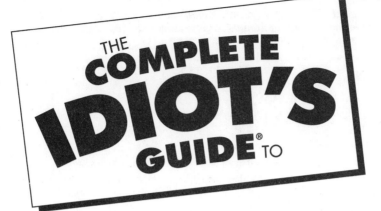

THE COMPLETE IDIOT'S GUIDE® TO

Social Media Marketing

by Jennifer Abernethy

ALPHA

A member of Penguin Group (USA) Inc.

This book is dedicated to all those who have dreams. Dreams to make a difference in the world. Dreams to grow their business and brands so that they can do more to contribute, share information, and help others.

ALPHA BOOKS

Published by the Penguin Group

Penguin Group (USA) Inc., 375 Hudson Street, New York, New York 10014, USA

Penguin Group (Canada), 90 Eglinton Avenue East, Suite 700, Toronto, Ontario M4P 2Y3, Canada (a division of Pearson Penguin Canada Inc.)

Penguin Books Ltd., 80 Strand, London WC2R 0RL, England

Penguin Ireland, 25 St. Stephen's Green, Dublin 2, Ireland (a division of Penguin Books Ltd.)

Penguin Group (Australia), 250 Camberwell Road, Camberwell, Victoria 3124, Australia (a division of Pearson Australia Group Pty. Ltd.)

Penguin Books India Pvt. Ltd., 11 Community Centre, Panchsheel Park, New Delhi—110 017, India

Penguin Group (NZ), 67 Apollo Drive, Rosedale, North Shore, Auckland 1311, New Zealand (a division of Pearson New Zealand Ltd.)

Penguin Books (South Africa) (Pty.) Ltd., 24 Sturdee Avenue, Rosebank, Johannesburg 2196, South Africa

Penguin Books Ltd., Registered Offices: 80 Strand, London WC2R 0RL, England

International Standard Book Number: 978-1-59257-989-1
Library of Congress Catalog Card Number: 2009937010

12   11   10   8   7   6   5   4   3   2   1

Interpretation of the printing code: The rightmost number of the first series of numbers is the year of the book's printing; the rightmost number of the second series of numbers is the number of the book's printing. For example, a printing code of 10-1 shows that the first printing occurred in 2010.

Printed in the United States of America

Note: This publication contains the opinions and ideas of its author. It is intended to provide helpful and informative material on the subject matter covered. It is sold with the understanding that the author and publisher are not engaged in rendering professional services in the book. If the reader requires personal assistance or advice, a competent professional should be consulted.

Publisher: *Marie Butler-Knight*
Editorial Director/Acquisitions Editor: *Mike Sanders*
Senior Managing Editor: *Billy Fields*
Development Editor: *Ginny Bess Munroe*
Senior Production Editor: *Janette Lynn*
Copy Editor: *Amy Borrelli*

Cartoonist: *Steve Barr*
Cover Designer: *Bill Thomas*
Book Designer: *Trina Wurst*
Indexer: *Brad Herriman*
Layout: *Chad Dressler*
Proofreader: *John Etchison*

Contents at a Glance

Contents

Introduction

Overwhelmed by all this social media talk? Maybe you are feeling as if it's just too much and you will never understand it. Well, you are not alone—many people feel the same way. Here's some good news, though: this book was written just for you! Whether you know enough to be dangerous and want to learn more, or are just a beginner and want to join the social media revolution, I guarantee you will discover something new to help you with your social media marketing efforts. Ready to go? I raise my glass to your success!

How This Book Is Organized

To make this easy to read and not too complicated, you'll find tons of screen shots to help you navigate the social media websites. I've divided this book into five key parts:

Part 1, "The World of Social Media and Social Networking," is a breakdown of what I refer to as the Big Seven in social media marketing. You get the lowdown on each of them, including how to get a good feel for the types of people using these platforms and why you need to strongly consider them for marketing you and your business. You will learn about having the right mind-set and why it's critical to your success on these social media platforms. You'll also come away with a good grip on the basics of what you need to get started.

Part 2, "Let's Begin Marketing Your Business on Facebook," is where we begin rolling up our sleeves and getting you into that savvy social networker mind-set. You will learn how to create an amazing Facebook profile, learn about applications to use on Facebook, and get the details on how to customize your Facebook experience. And all this is done by taking you step by step through each process.

Part 3, "Twitter," shows you what all the chirping buzz is about and why the world is suddenly all a-Twitter. In this part, you'll learn how to set up an amazing marketable Twitter profile. And when you're finished with this part, it's my hope you will run (not walk) to your computer to set up your Twitter account and incorporate the amazing applications and tools. If you follow the recommendations in this part, you will become a Twitterer worthy of millions of fans and followers.

Part 4, "LinkedIn and Other Social Network Options," gives you so much more additional information to put into your social media strategy. You'll go from the more professional site, LinkedIn, to examining the power and possibilities of MySpace. You'll also gain a better understanding of how online video and .tv are taking over the social media marketplace. This part provides the tools, the knowledge, and the comprehensive fundamentals of LinkedIn, MySpace, and video marketing strategies. By the time you finish this part, you'll be ready for your online close-up.

Part 5, "Streamlining and Expanding Your Program," shares with you the incredible tools and processes you can incorporate into an effective social media marketing strategy. After reading this part, you'll no longer feel overwhelmed as you add social media marketing to your day. You will learn ways to make this process easier to manage, and you'll even have fun implementing these techniques. This part also introduces more tools and strategies to help you streamline your social media marketing as you reach out to more prospects and clients.

Extras

To help you get the most out of this book, you'll find sidebars covering different facets of social media marketing. You'll find tips, tricks, and interesting facts to further educate and empower you and your team.

def•i•ni•tion
Terms you need to know to navigate the world of social media.

Try This
Simple and quick social media marketing ideas to try online.

Netiquette
Tips that help you know what to do—and not to do—online to stay popular.

Online Cautions
These boxes give you warnings about what to watch out for while engaging in social media.

Did You Know?
These are interesting statistics and projections about the world of social media marketing.

Note from the Author

In writing a book on a topic that is so rapidly changing, I was well aware that most social media programmers and designers are busy working and developing the next generations of tools. This means it is likely that some of the screen shots and functionality described in this book could be a bit different by the time the book's in your hands. I still trust that by reading and understanding the techniques and strategies that I recommend, you'll become a savvy social media marketer.

Acknowledgments

A virtual applause and tremendous thank you goes to a number of people who helped me put this book together. First, I want to thank an incredible coach and person, Anne Byrd, for calling me early one morning as I was walking out the door to vacation, and telling me that her literary agent was looking for someone with my expertise and that she had recommended me to her agent. Anne, we are going to do great things together! Also, I'd like to thank that agent, Marilyn Allen, for recommending me to the Penguin/Alpha Team and signing me. Marilyn, this is just the beginning.

I'd like to also especially thank Tom Stevens, who not only is a great acquisitions editor at Penguin, he just knows a lot about a lot of stuff and I enjoyed talking to him throughout this process. I will look forward to your trip to Virginia, Tom! This book could not have happened without my personal editor and now Twitter friend, Beverly Blair Harzog. Beverly, you were such an incredible source of inspiration and motivation for me to keep writing even when my hands were numb. Your positive enthusiasm and savvy editorial decisions made this a great experience. Thank you, and I can't wait to see you in Atlanta for our martini! Follow Beverly on Twitter: @BeverlyHarzog.

Heartfelt and sincere thanks to those peers and friends who have championed me along the way: My Coach and Mentor extraordinaire, Simon T. Bailey @BrilliantTweet. Mentor Friends Cynthia de Lorenzi, Kristina Bouweiri, and Mary Doherty. All The SITC Divas! My Mastermind group, Meredith Liepelt, Barbara Wayman, Ruth Sherman, Nika Stewart—thank you, ladies. I'm so happy we are growing together! Dr. Michael Mercer and friends Evelyn Heitman and Tina Hamet for your incredible support. Dr. Fern Beu for always being there and watching all of this happen and being an inspiration and true pillar of support. Dr. Gary Frankel and the Thursday Gang—you guys are the best! To all my Twitter followers and fans on Facebook and LinkedIn who have always cheered me on. For book content expert assistance, a warm thank you goes to Denise Wakeman (blog tips), Lesley Bohm (photography tips), and Sam Horn (book marketing). Thanks to Daniel Davis (Tinkernut) (technical advice), Susan Wight (E Women Network), and NSA DC. Shout out goes to Pete Prodoehl of 2XL Networks for designing the book's blog site! Thanks to Ginny Munroe and Janette Lynn for your expert editorial help! High 5 to A. J. Pomery, my Summer 2009 intern, for his amazing assistance. And to my Insiders Success Circle and Sales Lounge Alumni and Club members, thank you all! This book is for you to continue growing, building, and reaching your dreams. Make a difference!

On a personal note, I would like to extend a sincere heartfelt thanks to my family—in particular, my partner in crime, my incredible creative designer husband, Michael Abernethy, who ran the household during the writing of this book and helps me tremendously behind the scenes at The Sales Lounge. And our amazing children, Natalie and Brayan, who are already savvy social networkers after watching me tweet, Facebook, video, and podcast over the past few years. Thank you for putting up with me writing away in summer 2009. To my parents, Eddie and Bing Edwards, and brothers, Eddie and John, and sisters-in-law, Linda and Gina. Thank you for being you!

Special Thanks to the Tech Editor

The Complete Idiot's Guide to Social Media Marketing was reviewed by an expert who double-checked the accuracy of what you'll learn here, to help us ensure that this book gives you everything you need to know about marketing using social media. Special thanks are extended to Gina Schreck.

Gina and I met on Twitter and she is just too fun (and knows her stuff, too). Gina, thank you for your support and assistance and, most importantly, your friendship. I look forward to getting our families together and working with you more in the future (and in Second Life!) Follow her on Twitter @GinaSchreck.

Trademarks

All terms mentioned in this book that are known to be or are suspected of being trademarks or service marks have been appropriately capitalized. Alpha Books and Penguin Group (USA) Inc. cannot attest to the accuracy of this information. Use of a term in this book should not be regarded as affecting the validity of any trademark or service mark.

Part 1

The World of Social Media and Social Networking

The concept of social media can be overwhelming to the novice or first-time participant. This part takes away the confusion and highlights the seven most popular social media sites and platforms. You learn in detail what they are, who uses them, and why they are important to consider for marketing your business.

The first part of this book also explores one of the key components to successful social media marketing: your mind-set. You are introduced to mind-set strategies to help you become a savvy social media marketer.

What Is All This Social Media Stuff Anyway?

In This Chapter

- ◆ What is social media?
- ◆ The scoop on social networking
- ◆ The big seven social media sites
- ◆ Social media and its effect on business marketing

Everyone is talking about it. By now, you've at least heard or seen the term "social media," and that's most likely why you are reading this book. Big companies are getting involved with it, and entrepreneurs and business professionals are using it. Many people feel they *need* to use it, but they're not quite sure how to use it or exactly why they need to. If that is you, then you're not alone. And you're in the right place to find the answers you seek to your questions.

Why should you use social media? Well, if you are in business for yourself, it's something to consider because social networking is free and millions of other business owners are using it. Because so many are using it, it is a great way to reach your prospects, customers, strategic partners, and the media to get information to grow and enhance your business.

In this chapter, we briefly explore the concepts of social media and social networking. By the end of this book, you will be a savvy social media marketer.

Social Media

Are you ready to learn about how combining social media with your small business marketing efforts is probably something worth your time? I know you aren't quite sure how to begin wrapping your mind around all this, but don't worry. I lay it all out for you and show you how to get started. First, let's get you on your way by looking deeper into just what social media is. Then you'll understand how that ties into social media networking and social media marketing.

A simple way to view social media is in layperson's terms: social media enables you to socialize through the Internet; the Internet is the "medium" through which this socializing is accomplished. So you're socializing via the Internet with your current clients, future prospects, and *business champions*. What makes it so effective? It's an interactive way to communicate.

def•i•ni•tion

Business champions are people who will always give you a great reference and are high-powered networkers who will sing your praises. They can also serve as your strategic partners so that no matter who they are talking to, when the opportunity arises they will bring up your name. For example, if you are a real estate agent, build a circle with a loan officer, an interior decorator, an insurance agent, a house inspector, a banker, a painter, and so on. And of course, this is a circle you create, so you'd also recommend them to your own network.

Social media is revolutionizing the way entrepreneurs and small business owners market their businesses. To put these changes in perspective, let's take a brief walk through the past.

When people started a business in the late 1990s, they would build Flash websites. Everyone ran to web developers and asked for Flash, hoping to get a beautiful opening page with music, movement, and an integrated sound. And then you would click to open the website and see changing art or words on the screen. People thought if they invested in that new software development, their phone lines would ring off the hook. As it turned out, the web hosting sites just couldn't handle the speed of this technology back then and consumers got frustrated at the long loading times on their computers.

Also, in the 1990s, most small businesses would usually buy a yellow page ad or phone book listing, and purchase ads in the local newspaper to become more visible. Perhaps they'd also distribute flyers, network, and have an open house at their business storefront. Maybe they'd find a local PR person who would help write some press releases. And if they were really savvy, they would buy some local radio spots.

Well, times have certainly changed. People aren't reading newspapers like they used to. The yellow pages are, for the most part, obsolete as far as entrepreneurs and small business owners are concerned, or people are opting for their "yellow page listing" to appear on the Internet only. Why? Because most people search the Internet before they use a telephone book. In fact, most 20-something adults use Google as their primary search engine for research. Now, a small business is so eager for business that one has to ramp up marketing efforts in a hurry. Entrepreneurs and business owners have to quickly tune in to how prospects (and your customers) are getting information or your business will not succeed.

It is exciting now to imagine the number of people you can reach by going to your computer and simply logging on to several social media platforms that have millions of people participating on them, networking with them, and getting the word out about your expertise and your business. It's really an entrepreneur and small business person's dream come true. Think about it: free platforms to meet, connect, and share with people who might be your future clients, customers, or business champions! It is also important to realize that your customers are most likely using social media (or will be soon). You want to be there, too, right along with your customers and potential clients.

I often say that in a world where we are so connected with things like e-mail, instant messaging, texting, Bluetooth wireless technology, cell phones, and social media, people are feeling more disconnected than ever before, because they find it hard to directly "reach" anyone and they want to feel a part of a community. The more connected you can make your prospects and customers feel with you and your business, the more successful you are likely to become. People want to do business with people who make them feel good about doing business with them.

> **Did You Know?**
>
> The average user on Facebook has 130 friends. There are more than 55 million status updates each day. More than 10 million users become fans of pages each day. The average user spends 55 minutes online. (Source: Facebook.com statistics Jan. 2010)

Social media gives you, as a business owner, the platform to reach people directly and make them feel a part of your community online. At the same time, it also gives your prospects and customers a platform to engage with you and for you to get to know them. In the past, consumers talked about their purchasing experiences with their friends, family, and neighbors. Now, they are more likely to write about it in their blog or share their experience on one of the social media networks. Keep reading, and before long you will be a part of the conversation loop, too.

Social Networking

In the previous section, we took a trip to the recent past. Now, let's go much further back. How much further? Way back to the 1800s.

In the 1800s, networking was by word of mouth. This was the way small business owners and, in those days, socialites or those who wanted to raise their status in society got the word out about themselves and their services. After all, the phone wasn't invented until the 1870s. If you wanted to expand your status and grow your business and connections, you needed to network with the well-connected, affluent folks, such as those in high society.

During this time, "calling cards" were used. An individual would carry his card when he went out on a stroll. And he would leave a card (imprinted with his name on it) at the home of a specific "card receiver." If the receiver wasn't home, the individual would leave the card with the housekeeper or family member so the resident would know he had stopped by. Then, as the card receiver got to know this individual—and if they got along—the receiver would make appropriate introductions and acquaint the card holder with the receiver's circle of friends.

Now, back to the future—specifically, the late 1980s to the early 1990s, when AOL created chat rooms with member communities and profiles. Soon, everyone was running to get a PC into their home so they could hear those glorious words: "You've got mail." People would spend time searching online AOL chat rooms in an attempt to find folks who had similar interests. Additionally, you've probably seen Classmates. com when you're on the Internet. This site reconnected us with our high school peers, which jump-started reconnections and socializing. At this point, online conversations were in full throttle.

Now, let's fast forward. This time, the destination is the present, 2010. Many of us are getting too much e-mail, and our e-mail relentlessly follows us on our iPhones,

BlackBerries, and texting devices. We can't even relax while watching TV because the people we are watching are asking us to join their Facebook Fan page or follow them on Twitter. Then, when we go online, we see videos—live video streaming of people connecting through webinars and teleseminars.

People are also making goofy videos that are getting millions of viewers. These every-day online celebrities are popping up everywhere. Maybe even your average neighbor, Joe, has become a cyberstar? Maybe he did one of these silly videos a few months ago, and now he suddenly has thousands of Twitter followers and raving Facebook fans online? And you're shaking your head because you know Joe isn't exactly fan-worthy. Or is he? That's the power of the Internet.

But wait, put on the brakes! Let's forget about the 1800s, the 1990s, and even Joe, and just take notice that social networking isn't new. Really, just the delivery mechanism is new. After you get to know social media marketing and networking, you will see that there are many similarities to old-fashioned Victorian-era networking. Today's social networking simply involves different mediums in which to leave one's calling card.

The Big Seven

The social media platforms are evolving at such a quick rate that it's hard to know which services will be a "must-have" in your marketing arsenal by the time we go to print with this book. I've seen one list that showed more than 100 social media platforms.

However, my guess is that the top seven I'm going to introduce you to won't be too different by the time this book is published. What you see listed here could have easily included more sites, but I've chosen seven that I think you, at the very least, need to become aware of. You should know from the start that each of these sites has its own "netiquette" rules and culture and many allow you to incorporate your "status update" within them to keep your audience up-to-date with your goings on. As you go through this book, we get into all these sites (and many others) in much greater detail. This will include listing the big do's and don'ts for growing your audience on each of these platforms.

For now, let's just get comfortable with the basic concepts of each site. The following is my quick breakdown of the big seven components that entrepreneurs should include in their social media marketing campaigns.

Facebook

You can find Facebook at www.facebook.com. I refer to Facebook as "the television network of social media" because it skews far and wide, including 17- to 75-year-olds and both males and females.

Here are a few interesting Facebook facts:

- The average age of the Facebook user is 39, but that number is rising.

- The average income is $89,000. Surprised? Many still think of Facebook as a site for college students, because that's where it started. However, now baby boomers use it for socializing and for business.

- While still using Facebook, college kids are also using other devices (such as mobile texting and video chat).

- Facebook has become the place to engage in business networking for 30- to 60-year-olds.

- Entrepreneurs, small business owners, and independent professionals are using this site with a high level of sophistication.

- Each month, more business applications on Facebook are emerging.

- Facebook has nearly 350 million users.

Does this begin to paint a clearer picture of the possibilities of social media marketing? You can network, have a *status update*, have a fan page, grow your client list, and have all kinds of fun connecting with old collegues and new friends all while marketing your business and brand.

We cover Facebook more in Part 2 of this book, but for now just keep in mind that it merges well with LinkedIn, Twitter, blogs, and podcasts.

def•i•ni•tion

Status updates are given on social media sites. Your status update answers the question: "What are you doing right now?" or "What is on your mind?" Think of your status update as your marketing message on Facebook or Twitter (or LinkedIn, which we cover next). Now, don't take the questions literally. Savvy marketers will use the update to share expertise, trust, and credibility, and drive traffic to their website.

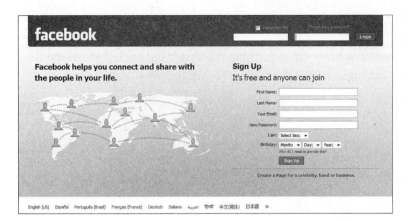

Here's what the Facebook Login page looks like.

Twitter

You can find Twitter on www.twitter.com. I call Twitter the "online cocktail party." Twitter is another incredibly popular place to shout out to the world your expertise and how it's different from other businesses. All types of organizations, companies, entrepreneurs, and independent professionals are using this social media site to do amazing things with their business. Demographics are hard to confirm, but 33 to 50 years old is the basic age range, with females slightly outnumbering males.

After you experience Twitter's potential and learn a few applications on Twitter (we'll cover Twitter starting in Chapter 8), you will find this to be another fantastic tool to broadcast your message to your business prospects and fans. You really have to experience Twitter, and after you try it, you will understand how this popular platform works. Check out the Twitter Login page!

Here's the Twitter Login screen.

LinkedIn

You find LinkedIn at www.linkedin.com. I call this "the cable channel of social media." Here are some facts about LinkedIn:

- ◆ LinkedIn has a white-collar audience. Executives from every Fortune 500 company are members.

- ◆ LinkedIn has approximately 53 million users.

- ◆ The average age is 49, and the average income is $104,000.

LinkedIn is a bit more serious than the other sites, but if you want to become a savvy marketer, you must include this in your marketing toolbox. It's a definite must if you want to network with business executives, C-level executives (for example, CEOs and CFOs), Fortune 500 executives, and other sophisticated professionals. Entrepreneurs and small business owners network here and often benefit from having a profile on LinkedIn. And there is much more to this site than just serving as an electronic Rolodex.

In fact, the LinkedIn team appears to be working on adding more interactivity to the platform by incorporating more *sticky* applications to the site to make it more fun and engaging for the users. Take a look at the LinkedIn Login page.

This is the LinkedIn Login screen.

def•i•ni•tion

Sticky refers to a social media site where one can easily write, post, or paste information on the page and then replace it with something else. As of now, the trend is the more sticky the site is, the more engaging and popular the site becomes. Facebook, for example, is extremely sticky because you can frequently replace your status update with something new.

MySpace

You can find MySpace at www.myspace.com. MySpace is a popular site for the younger audience and for entrepreneurs targeting the younger (say, 14- to 26-year-old) age group. It has millions of users. It is one of the most popular platforms for music and video collaboration.

Although MySpace lost popularity with the baby boomer crowd to Facebook, Twitter, and LinkedIn, many professionals such as speakers, realtors, and entrepreneurs have a presence on this site. This site is a must if you are targeting a young/hip audience with an innovative product, service, or other type of offering. Take a look at the login screen.

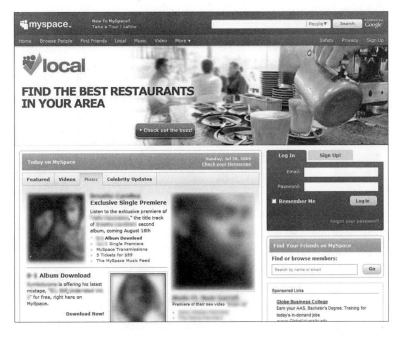

This is the MySpace Login page.

YouTube and Online Video

Video marketing is going to become a must-have in your business during the next few years. With video phones and small handheld video cameras made specifically for the Internet, just about anyone these days can be a producer. The great news is that you don't have to have a degree in acting or take Film 101 to participate.

In fact, trends are that while slick, well-rehearsed videos are good, viewers want to see the real you in an authentic and transparent way. People love the immediacy of getting to see and hear you. It's okay for the camera to move a bit and your words don't have to be read off of a cue card. You only have to be yourself.

With over 1 billion views per day on YouTube (October 2009 YouTube Blog), you can see that video is extremely popular and by all signs here to stay. There are entrepreneurs and business owners uploading speaking engagements, videos of their seminars, and client testimonials. There are even many who are just "talking" to the camera and are attracting a loyal following to their businesses by just being visible and interesting to listen to.

Here's a screen shot of YouTube.

Blogs

A blog is a contraction of the word "weblog." A blog is usually maintained by an individual who makes regular posts of commentary, descriptions of events, or other material such as graphics or video. Entries are commonly displayed in the reverse chronological order—that is, the most current post is at the top of the blog. The term "to blog" means you plan to maintain or add content to your blog, which is the act of blogging.

Blogs are a great way to continue to build a following, share your expertise, and get better at communicating with your readers and followers. Although blogs are not a must-have, most regular bloggers say the benefits of having a blog are tremendous, not only to the business but for the writer as well. Many different types of blogs exist, and wonderful applications are available to incorporate into your blog to further inspire and educate your readers.

Blogs can help your business bottom line, and it can drive readers to your website and ultimately to your phone or online shopping cart (the modern-day cash register) or even to your brick-and-mortar business storefront. These days, new blogs are incorporating other components of social media marketing such as Twitter, Facebook, and video. We review what you can do with blogs in Chapter 16.

Ning

You can find Ning at www.ning.com. This site enables users to create their own social network. Imagine having a platform to send information back and forth—all within one portal. As of June 2009, Ning has more than 1.8 million social networks created and more than 39 million registered members.

The site's popularity is expanding so quickly that, as of this writing, more than 4,000 new Ning networks are created *each day.* Members are from all walks of life—from dog owners to activists. In May 2009, Ning added 90 new applications to further enhance the user experience.

This is the Ning Login page.

Create a New Social Network

Create your own!

Name your social network

For example, Paris Cyclists

Pick a web address

.ning.com

At least 6 letters. For example, pariscyclists

Create >

or find one!

Discover New Social Networks

What are you interested in?

Online Video

In later chapters, you learn more about some online strategies and get additional tips to support you in your online video marketing efforts. Although some might be shy about putting themselves out there on the Internet, studies show that people want to watch online videos. ComScore, a digital media research firm, found the following for August 2009:.

◆ 161 million Internet users watched an online video in August 2009.

◆ The average viewer watched 157 videos during the month of August 2009.

◆ 81.6 percent of the total U.S. Internet audience viewed online video, with the largest majority viewing on YouTube.

◆ 44.9 million viewers watched 340 million videos on MySpace. The duration of the average online video was 3.7 minutes.

For the entrepreneur or small business owner, getting started with online video can seem a bit daunting. But don't fret. Later in this book, you will learn about sites to bookmark to publish your videos, products you need to begin shooting video, and most importantly, the right mind-set and strategy you need to begin video marketing for your business. Who knows? You might just become the next Internet star.

Try This _____

To avoid feeling overwhelmed by all these social media choices, take a deep breath and keep reading. When you finish this book, just decide which social media platform you'd like to explore first. You don't have to jump into all of these at once. Take your time and get comfortable.

Social Media Is Impacting Marketing Strategies

Social media is an incredible way to market your business, your cause, and yourself. It's also a great way to connect, interact, teach, help, deliver, inspire, and engage with your customers, prospects, members, friends, advocates, and business champions. Social media is still in its infancy, but it's already changing the face of business marketing and personal branding. Most experts agree that the potential and the impact of social media marketing are extraordinary. We cover this topic in more detail throughout the book.

The Least You Need to Know

- Social media is not just a trend, so it's worth your time to become familiar with its potential.

- Social media refers to the mediums that people use to socialize on the Internet.

- Social media networking is the process by which people network with those they know and those they are meeting for the first time on social media sites.

- Although hundreds of social media sites exist, you should familiarize yourself with the handful of popular sites that seem to have the most staying power.

- Although social media marketing and networking are still in the early stages, they will continue to evolve, and you want to be sure you're included.

The Right Mind-Set

In This Chapter

- Having the right mind-set
- Investing your time
- Networking online
- Building celebrity status
- Protecting your business reputation
- The unwritten rules of social media

What do you think is the most important aspect of successful social media marketing? Well, it isn't having the know-how to effectively use all of the available platforms. Sure, it helps, but that's something just about everyone can learn. You'll find that the most important aspect to successful social media marketing is having the right mind-set.

Think about this: there are millions of people on Facebook, Twitter, and LinkedIn, but only a few thousand are actually using it to its fullest potential. In this chapter, you'll learn what it means to have the right mind-set. When that happens, you'll become one of the few who use social media marketing to its fullest potential.

Attracting Clients

I know from my own social media workshops that the people who enter the program with an open mind, a positive attitude, and a determination that this is going to help them are the ones who are ultimately successful using the platforms.

It's natural to worry about learning a new way to market your business. Change can be stressful. But try to avoid starting out with thoughts like the following on your mind:

- ◆ "I just don't get it. I don't care if someone just purchased a cup of coffee. I really don't think this will help me."

- ◆ "I really don't have time for this."

- ◆ "If someone doesn't buy from me within the first month, forget it."

If you enter into social media marketing with one or more of these negative thoughts, then your social media efforts just won't work. You'll have a hard time making a commitment to master the techniques in this book.

However, start out with the right mind-set and you'll be amazed at what you accomplish! So what's the right mind-set? It's a combination of things. Keep reading and you'll get a few ideas about how to get off on the right foot in social media.

Keep an Open Mind

Most early adaptors to Facebook or Twitter didn't know how it would impact their businesses. Yet today, those same people are now successful social media marketers and are gaining thousands of followers and champions for their businesses. By keeping an open mind, early social media adaptors found that people from all over the country and the world referred their businesses to their own networks.

Early adaptors also didn't know how many strategic alliances they would make or how many products they would sell. However, they had a hunch that social media would pay off and so they kept an open mind. They reached out to people and treated them with respect. They offered great customer service and follow up—and violà!—they ended up with raving fans and followers.

Be Yourself

You are probably wondering how you can stand out in a crowd of millions. Is it possible? After all, you might think you aren't the most outgoing person out there. Here's the good news: you don't have to be an extrovert! In fact, many introverts actually like social media because they can write easily and network online, and it's more comfortable for them. And for the extroverts, well, they just love this stuff, and it enables them to communicate in another way to potentially millions of people.

How do you stand out on a platform that has tens of millions of people? Believe it or not, the secret is to just be yourself. That's what participants in social media look for. They are seeking a new voice and a unique perspective. If you begin copying someone else's style, that won't feel right to you. And you won't keep up your efforts to participate because it will be too much of a struggle. Be yourself and you'll find it easy to keep engaging in social media. Express your thoughts—your way. Share links that *you* believe will be of interest to your audience, not links that everyone else is posting. Don't worry about the number of followers you have, just focus on quality. Follow those you want to follow and your unique voice and brand will begin to emerge.

Energy Attracts Followers

We've all had that consumer experience where we go to buy something in a store and an unenthusiastic clerk makes us wonder if we really want to buy the product after all. However, when you go to a store and the staff is helpful, you have the opposite reaction. When the staff asks you questions or wants to know if you need help with anything, you have a great customer experience. You feel important, right? And you feel good about buying the product.

It's really the law of attraction: good energy attracts people and, ultimately, followers. The same concept holds true on social media. If people find you friendly, engaging, and authentic, and they need what you have to offer, they will continue to read your posts. They might even go a step further and recommend you to their networks.

Know Your Ideal Client

Successful social media marketers who have the right mind-set also have a clear sense of who their ideal client is. As you begin to engage on social media platforms, a good practice is to write and converse as if you are talking to your future client base.

If you are having a hard time visualizing this, try this exercise: imagine that your ideal client is reading what you are posting. Then ask yourself some of these questions:

◆ Who is my ideal customer?

◆ What would they need to hear to make me a trusted expert in their mind?

- What are they looking for when seeking someone like me to work with or buy a product from?
- Why do they need what I have to offer?
- When searching for similar products and services to mine, what keywords would they typically use when searching online?
- Where would they participate online?
- What keywords would attract them to my business?

Answering these questions now helps you later as you put together your social media strategy. As you write to your ideal client, be conscientious of your tone and what you are saying or posting. Although you want to be yourself, you also need to remember who you are talking to at the same time. By incorporating the previous ideas, you begin to attract the types of followers you want to attract, which, ultimately, should match the profile of your ideal customer.

Marketers used to use the "push" mentality. This means they would push their ideas or products in front of us so often that we would end up buying what they're selling. But now, savvy social media marketers use the "pull" or attraction mentality. You put out the right information with the right tone to the right types of users, and you begin to pull prospects and customers to your business. You or your offerings attract them, and they will become clients, followers, or champions of your business. Maybe even all three!

Networking Online

Think of social media marketing as the largest and biggest networking event you can imagine. It's one that operates 24/7 and it's accessible to you anywhere, anytime, right at your fingertips. In a society where we are all busy and pulled in many directions (and watching our budgets), this really is an entrepreneur's dream.

Netiquette

Just like you would do with in-person networking, don't try to sell people your products and services the first time you meet them online. Build rapport, earn credibility, and gain trust. Eventually, your business and brand will benefit from the supportive followers you build, and ultimately it will lead to sales.

By utilizing social media, you can now network not only with people from your town, but with people from other states and countries. You never know who your next customer will be or where your next referral source will come from, so treat everyone as a prospect or referral source.

As you begin your journey into social media, apply the following traditional networking strategies:

◆ Be interested in others versus worrying about being interesting.

◆ Don't constantly be in selling mode.

◆ Follow up consistently.

◆ Be helpful, give information, and bring great energy to conversations.

◆ A great networker stays involved, so don't just appear once or twice and then disappear.

Remember, just because your social media contact might not be a potential customer, they just might be connected to someone who *is* looking for your services. Treat everyone with courtesy and respect. You never know where your next client will come from.

Building a Network of Followers

One of the beneficial things about social media marketing is that you can build a great community of followers. This should clearly be one of your goals. Whether it's on Facebook, Twitter, your blog, or your YouTube video channel, new followers equal prospects. And prospects equal customers, customers equal referral partners, and referral partners lead to business champions.

Twenty percent of your core followers provide 80 percent of your business. Think of popular musical stars and where they'd be without their loyal fans. Their fan clubs serve as their base; it would be much more difficult to continue to sell out venue after venue without their base supporters. The musical star is loyal to his or her fans and that loyalty gets reciprocated.

This is similar to the way it works with social media. You will build your follower base over time. It won't happen overnight. Remember, you must build trust, they must like you (or at least your products and services), and they must have reasons to stay connected with you. In this book, you will learn strategies to keep people connected to you by incorporating a strategic plan using various social media platforms. You will then continue to grow and shift to maintain your "star appeal" with your followers and fans.

Building Online Celebrity Status

For many people, thinking of themselves as a celebrity type is very uncomfortable. However, a unique phenomenon is happening on social media platforms. Every day, entrepreneurs and small business owners just like you, who are working from home or other locations, are garnering tens of thousands of followers and fans through social media marketing. In the past, you could not collect tens of thousands of followers without having huge marketing budgets or hiring a PR or ad agency to help spread the word about your business.

Do you feel self-conscious when you try to think of yourself as a star in your business? If so, try your best to get rid of this feeling. After all, if you don't think you are worth following or having others connect to you on LinkedIn or another social website, then no one else will. Good business owners roll out the red carpet for their clients and deliver exceptional customer service. Begin shifting your thinking to the fact that, like it or not, you are the star in your business. Tell yourself that no one does it quite like you do. The more confidence you project, the more people you'll attract to your blog or website. Sound good?

To begin creating your celebrity status, you have to show your readers that you have expertise in your area. In fact, you're not just another expert; you're the go-to person for what you do. Over time, you will build trust and your followers or blog readers will feel good about taking advice from you. How does this happen? Through your social media marketing, your followers will begin to develop an affinity for your brand and for you. This is how you build your celebrity-dom within the online social media universe.

Try This

As you develop a following on various social media platforms, begin engaging in dialogue, whether it's through direct messaging on Twitter, or writing on a follower's wall on Facebook. Listen to what people are saying online and show your support. You are building trust. Focus on giving.

Eventually, you begin to get testimonials from customers and clients. You guide your new clients to write online about the good experience they had with you and your business. Through writing online articles, sharing your expertise in your blog, participating on the top social media sites, and creating videos, you'll begin to elevate your online status.

I know it sounds a little overwhelming, but you'll learn how to do this quickly, and believe it or not, it will even feel natural. Remember this mantra: You are the expert in what you do, no one does it like you, and that's why they are following you. Are you ready for your close-up now? Say yes!

Guiding People to Your Business

You're already getting the picture that participating in social media for your business is a good thing. Meeting new people, finding old friends, and meeting strategic partners is a lot of fun, isn't it? However, at the end of the day, you are doing this to drive revenue to your business. To successfully "work" social media, you need to begin effectively networking and building your connections, just as you would do at live speaking events.

As we talked about in the previous section, over time sharing your expertise helps you build credibility and guides people toward your business or website. While participating online, one of your goals should be to build on your list of customers. You will see this repeated several times throughout the book, but it's worth repeating: your list is your gold mine. Don't ever forget that.

In the past, people would say, "I want to add you to my mailing list," and it meant, literally, the traditional mail that actually shows up in your mailbox (the one on the street, not on your PC). Today's social media marketers are building an e-mail list of their followers and fans along with attaining a cell phone list of their followers for future mobile (cell phone) marketing.

Did You Know?

By gathering cell phone numbers of your customers and prospects, you will be ready for future mobile marketing to your followers via their cell phones. Start planning now! Many people are also already obtaining the .mobi domain for their business; this domain is for the mobile service. Mobile marketing is expected to be huge in the near future.

From now on, in all of your marketing invite people to connect with you on Facebook, to follow you on Twitter, link with you on LinkedIn, and so on. After they are connected to you on these sites, invite them to get your newsletter or e-zine, subscribe to your blog, or look at your videos on your YouTube channel. This will drive more people to follow and connect with you, which in turn will guide people toward your business. The more people you have following you, the more people you are likely to have singing your praises and recommending you.

Remember, This Is Your Business Reputation

If I were your personal business Sales Stylist, I would sit you down and talk to you about your business reputation. This is a very important aspect of social media marketing. Everything that you write, tweet, podcast, video, respond to, or even say publicly is a reflection of your business and ultimately your business reputation. It might sound silly to even bring this up, but oftentimes on many social media platforms people get so caught up in the fast-paced typing and the quick responses, they often forget that after you hit that send button it is on the Internet forever.

One story out there in the media is about a Twitter user who went on a job interview. When he left the building, he updated his twitter status about how lame the interviewer was. Although he didn't mention the company's name, the company did a Google search on him and his Twitter status update (or Tweet) appeared in the search findings. Needless to say, he did not get the job.

Online Cautions

There is a new segment of the legal industry beginning to appear: social media liability. Although it's a fairly new industry, it's good to think about your social media policy, particularly if you have more than one person representing your business online. Many businesses are developing social media policies and crisis communication plans to manage online defamation issues and personal liability.

Another mistake people make is writing about their political or religious views. Although some might think it's not doing much harm to comment on this political person or that particular religious holiday or issue, it might offend enough people that it could hurt your business. A word to the wise: stay away from politics and religion and any other sensitive topics. You wouldn't approach these in traditional networking settings, so avoid it online. Of course, you will find the diehard political consultants or advisors writing about political views, but that is what they do. Stay focused on topics that are of interest to your ideal client.

Another danger is not thinking before hitting the send button. People may read or hear something and feel strongly about it. They immediately log on to a site, spill their guts, and hit send. In some instances this can be fine; however, in many other cases, it is most definitely not okay.

Fair warning: your social media entry just might pop up months or years later within a search engine (such as Google). You need to think about whether that will help or hurt your business reputation.

Some companies have hired people to help with *online reputation management (ORM)*, which is a new buzzword these days. As an entrepreneur or business owner, you might not be able to hire a reputation management team just yet, but you can manage your own online reputation by just becoming aware of what you are writing and posting on your social media sites.

It probably seems like a lot to think about, but maintaining the right mind-set will all come together for you as you read this book.

def•i•ni•tion

Online reputation management (ORM) is the process of monitoring online references to a person, brand, company, product, or service with the objective of minimizing the damage of online negative feedback and defamation.

The Unwritten Rules of Engagement

Although social media is still in its beginning stages, some unofficial unwritten rules of engagement exist. Many people do not follow these rules, but the crème de la crème of marketers and networkers do. Remember that the following rules can shift a bit as the social media landscape evolves, but these are good, basic rules to adhere to as you enter the world of social media marketing.

♦ Never post anything negative about your competition, or anyone else for that matter.

♦ Don't post when you are angry.

♦ Do not spam, because sending unsolicited marketing to unsolicited prospects is considered electronic abuse.

♦ Do not sell continuously.

♦ Share your expertise and tips to help others.

♦ Build relationships and trust.

♦ Share success stories that will help people.

♦ Don't write ego-driven posts or promote a personal agenda.

♦ Really listen to what people are saying.

♦ Organically grow your list of followers using the tips in this book.

♦ Don't buy programs or software that link you to thousands.

♦ Be your authentic self.

Looking Forward to Logging In

Two of the biggest objections people have before they even get started with social media marketing are that they just don't have time or they don't understand why they should start connecting to people they do not know. Here's a simple goal to start with: look forward to logging in to your social media platforms. Approach it without dread or fear.

This is where the mind-set again comes into play. All successful social media marketers look forward to logging in each day and reading the messages people wrote or seeing who their new followers are. To get yourself into the right mind-set, remember the following:

- This is efficient and inexpensive marketing.

- These social media platforms are marketing you and your business to potentially millions while you sleep.

- You never know who you are going to meet online that will change the destiny of your life and business for the better.

With all of these points in mind, you should look forward to logging in. Just keep the basic principals in mind: engage online regularly, tell everyone you know that you are now using social media platforms, and share your expertise. Before you know it, you'll be looking forward to logging in.

Some social media marketers who have built a large following have begun hiring either a virtual assistant, an intern, or an employee to help them with their social media efforts. We'll get into time management strategies later in the book, but imagine if you had so many followers and were gaining so much attention that you had to hire help to assist you in managing your social media. That would be a good thing, right? The more people who know about you, your expertise, and your business, the more likely your business will grow.

Investing Your Time

Although nearly all of the social media platforms are free, one cost does exist. That cost is your time. Business owners all know that time is money. However, the good news with social marketing is that now you're investing your time in something that can have substantial returns in the long run.

One mistake people make when they first get started with social media is thinking that the payoff is going to be immediate. They think that with a few Facebook postings or by starting a blog, business will start growing and loyal fans will start suddenly referring people to you.

You should know that this is not typically the case. It does take time to organically grow your online network of followers and fans. However, at a certain point, your network will expand faster and larger. When that happens, two followers grow into four, four grows to eight, eight to sixteen, and so on. Before you know it, you have 1,000 new connections.

A good strategy for beginning social media users is to invest 20 minutes in the morning and 20 minutes in the evening. Think of it as attending a networking event. First you log into Facebook, then LinkedIn, and next Twitter. Eventually, your time spent on social media platforms will expand. As you become comfortable, make some weekly goals. For instance, perhaps once a week you'll update your blog and upload a new video.

For some, the time invested online using social media has allowed them to cut back on some in-person networking events. While I don't recommend you cut back entirely on in-person networking, participating online allows you to have a regular presence to share information about your business or to learn about what others are doing. The value is in the conversations and the relationships you are building.

The Least You Need to Know

- The right mind-set is one of the most important aspects you bring to social media marketing.

- Think of social media as networking with the world, and spend time each day networking by getting to know others and sharing your wisdom.

- Social media marketing enables you to build your network of business champions, future referrals, and strategic partners.

- Think before hitting send because everything you post on the Internet stays there forever and affects your business reputation.

- Follow the unwritten rules of social media and you can create online celebrity status for yourself.

- Be ready to invest some time, because growing your business doesn't happen overnight.

Chapter 3

What You Need to Get Started

In This Chapter

◆ What you need to know about headshots

◆ Examples of great headshots

◆ Using cameras and video cameras in your business

◆ Thinking about your business strategy

◆ Determining who your target audience is

◆ Using social media to communicate with new and existing customers

Okay, so you are reading this book and you are ready to get started. Are you wondering what to do first or where to begin? If you've talked to other people about this, you've probably discovered that everyone has a different idea about where to start or what you need to get going. It's a bit confusing, isn't it?

Honestly, there is no absolute correct answer as to exactly what you should do first. However, in this chapter, I'll suggest a few things that you should put at the top of your to-do list to get you started on your way to building your social media marketing network. Are you ready? Okay, let's jump right in and talk about headshots first.

Your Headshot

Most social media platforms have a place for you to put your headshot—your pro-file picture. Other sites may ask you to upload your company logo or avatar. Which should you use? Consider using a logo if you're a national brand, an association, or if you represent a social community cause or network. A headshot (typically a picture of you from the chest up) is usually what most people go with, and in most instances a personal headshot is recommended. In fact, to be a savvy social media marketer, a headshot is usually required. As you begin connecting to people around the country and world, your headshot will be the image that reflects your brand and your business. Therefore, your headshot photo is extremely important.

If you can invest in a great personal photographer, be sure to tell him that you plan to use this for your social media marketing. Be sure to ask if the photographer has done headshots for this medium before, or if he is at least familiar with sites like Facebook, Twitter, and LinkedIn. Make sure to convey what kind of photo you are looking for, and that there is chemistry between you and the photographer so that your personality shines through.

Online Cautions

Social media identity theft is on the rise. Try to register your personal name (for example, John Doe) as a domain. Refrain from putting a lot of personal information such as home phone numbers, addresses, or a picture of your car with license plates on your social media platforms.

Also, Internet security experts recommend setting up a Google Alert (see www.google.com/alerts) for your personal name and your business name. The system will monitor the Internet for you and you'll get an e-mail every time your name or business name is mentioned online.

What's your goal with your headshot? To ensure it accurately represents your personality and brand. The typical headshot with the swirly gray/black background is no longer required, and frankly, no longer desired. In fact, you will look dated if you use that type of photograph. Remember, it's 2010 and you are now embarking into the world of *Web 2.0* social media marketing. This is your chance to stand out in a crowd of millions. Get creative with your photo, and let your personality shine through.

The following are some tips to keep in mind when making decisions about your headshot:

def•i•ni•tion

Web 2.0 does not refer to a new type of any technical specifications for your computer, but rather it refers to the cumulative changes in the ways Internet users "use" the web. Interactivity, information sharing, and user-centered experiences are all part of the Web 2.0 evolution.

- ◆ Have fun and be creative with your photo.

- ◆ There are no steadfast rules here.

- ◆ Laugh, tilt your head, use your hands, and bring your personality into the photo.

- ◆ Wear attractive clothing that either looks good on you or reflects your color scheme for your business.

- ◆ Solid colors work well and bright colors exude energy.

- ◆ Wear your company colors or have your photo taken while holding one of your products.

- ◆ Use an action shot if appropriate. For example, one photographer I know had someone take a picture of her taking a picture—right away you know she is a photographer.

Your main focus should be: Does the photo reflect what you want it to reflect? Whether you're an artist, writer, speaker, mompreneur, coach, or banker, have fun coming up with a photo that reflects who you are. The latest trends show that the social media audience likes not only out-of-the-box photos, but photos that reflect your true personality and business brand.

What's the bottom line? Don't be afraid to get creative. The whole idea is to attract people to you with the energy from the photo. You will see many people on social media sites with their headshots taken outdoors. The theory here is that you are bringing nature and life into a medium that is stagnant and one-dimensional.

If you don't have the funds to invest in a professional photographer, one way to get a good photo quickly is to go to your local mall and seek a family photo studio and get a decent headshot done in about an hour. In most cases, you can select the shots you want to keep, they will give it to you on a CD, and you can be on your way home.

However, if that isn't an option, at least have someone take a photo of you at your office, home, or outdoors. Many successful social media folks have great photos that were taken by friends.

And keep in mind, too, that you will be updating and changing your photo from time to time. So get your photo ready to upload on the social media sites and you can cross one thing off the top of your to-do list. More importantly, by getting the photo done, you are on your way to getting started with your social media marketing.

Your Virtual Business Suitcase

Social media marketing is a great way to socialize and network with friends and prospects, but again, you must remember that you're there to promote your business. So what should you have packed in your virtual suitcase?

Here are some business "supplies" you need to have in your virtual suitcase before you begin your first day of social media marketing:

> **Did You Know?**
>
> A PDF stands for portable document format. You create PDFs on the Adobe website by going to createpdf.adobe.com. A small monthly fee applies if you do not have Adobe Acrobat on your computer.

- A .jpg or .gif version of your business logo.

- A website address or URL. If you do not currently have a website domain (for instance, www.nameofyourbusiness.com), register the domain of your business before you get started. You will want to do this before others see your name and claim it as their own.

- Your business address and phone number. Note: if you run a home-based business, a good practice would be to not post your address.

- If you conduct business via cell phone, have that number ready to put on your site as well.

- A digital camera should become your new best marketing friend. Make sure you can easily download photos to the Internet. Carry it everywhere. You are now a marketer of your business and brand.

- A video camera that allows you to download easily to the Internet. The Flip Mino by Pure Digital (www.theflip.com) is one that most social media marketers use. (Hint: you can even get the camera branded with your name or company logo.) Remember, you are the marketing star now. Your digital camera and video are your new marketing best friends.

Online Cautions _____

Don't ask your young teenage niece or nephew to do your marketing for you. While they are quick on the keyboard, they typically don't understand how to market a business on social media.

Take a look at these headshots to get an idea of what works.

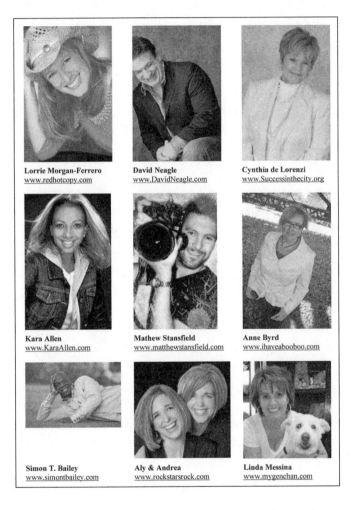

At this point, don't worry about where to place information on your website. In later chapters, you will learn how to place your website information on the social media sites.

Your Business Strategy

When starting social media marketing, it's easy to get caught up in the fun of finding old friends (or being the one who's found!). It's also fun seeing how many new followers and friend requests you get on a daily basis. However, in a medium where early adaptors weren't quite sure how social media would affect their businesses, recent adaptors have an advantage. You are going into social media with at least a basic business strategy.

Setting Goals

First, you want to have some clear goals in mind. Look at what your peers are doing. Look at your competition. Then do things differently. Put your own spin on your marketing. Remember, you want to stand out and be different. However, it's also important to be genuinely authentic in your approach.

As you get more involved with several social media platforms, you want to ensure your message is consistent across all platforms. Otherwise, your message will be interpreted differently on different sites. That wouldn't be very effective, would it?

Perhaps your initial strategy would be to drive traffic to your website. Let's examine a few different ways you can do that. Perhaps you want to market the benefits of visiting your website in all of your posts. Or maybe you want to offer a special that is only available on your website, so that all of your social media marketing is guiding people in that direction.

Or maybe you want people to read your blog. If this is the case, you will want to talk about your blog in the majority of your posts and messaging, along with providing links to your blog and recent entries. Maybe your goal is to build your golden list. (And it should be a goal!) If this is the case, your message should talk about the benefits of being on your list. Perhaps an advantage is that you will give them advanced notice of sales, special events, and allow them to garner VIP status in your business.

Maybe you just simply want another way to build relationships with your current clients and new prospects. Now, this is a great strategy as well. By doing this, you engage in more two-way conversations with your clients and prospects using social media platforms. It gives you an opportunity to listen more and understand what your clients and prospects are thinking about.

Do you get the idea now? By engaging in social media, you can create forums or message boards to have discussions and dialogue with your network. All you have to do is pick the direction that is right for you and your business. This is just a small sampling of great strategies you can use with social media marketing. We'll cover strategies in more detail later in the book.

For now, here are some good questions to ask yourself as you begin getting involved and setting goals:

- ♦ Why am I engaging in social media? Is it that I just want to learn the technology or do I want it to try to drive traffic to my website or business or blog?

- ♦ What message do I want to send to my customers and prospects?

- ♦ Do I want to handle this or will I delegate the social media marketing? Do I want to assign these duties to someone else in my business?

- ♦ What types of people do I want to attract to my business?

- ♦ What is the profile of my ideal customer?

- ♦ Am I willing to participate daily or at least regularly?

- ♦ Will I begin asking clients if they are using social media? How will I collect that information?

- ♦ Do I want to try to drive readers to my blog?

- ♦ Do I want to feature a client of the week or day? Would I want to feature a product of the week or day? Or maybe provide a tip for the day?

- ♦ Do I just want to get on the top social media platforms or am I ready to create an entire social media strategy using a blog, Twitter, Facebook, LinkedIn, video, and other social media?

Yes, the previous list is a lot of questions, but you really do need to narrow down your focus. At the beginning of the chapter, I said there is no right or wrong answer when it comes to effective social media business strategy. That's true, but it is important to consider the previous list of questions. If you begin social media marketing by randomly creating your accounts and occasionally posting comments, it isn't going to get you where you want to be. If you make it completely centered around you and your business, that won't work either. Social media is about participation; it should be a nice give and take.

Also, make sure you're not setting your expectations too high. I've said it before but it bears repeating: social media is not immediate access to millions of people who will gladly spend millions of dollars on your business. The potential is there, for sure, but set reasonable goals for your social media marketing so you don't get disappointed early in the process.

And rest assured, by answering the previous questions, you'll have a good initial strategy in place. It will help you know that you are on the right path for your business and to achieve your strategic goals. Over time, your plan and marketing strategy will continue to evolve, just as the social media networks and consumer-buying patterns evolve.

Know Your Target Audience

As with traditional marketing, successful social media marketing requires you to know your target audience. This might seem like a no-brainer, but some people do start businesses without a clear image of who they're selling to.

Even for the entrepreneur and small business owner, clarifying who needs your product or service and who wants it are key. To help you home in on your target market, answer these questions:

- Are your customers or readers men or women? Or both?
- What age group are you targeting?
- What are their income levels?
- Where do they live?
- Where are they when they go online—are they at home or in a corporate office?

After you answer these questions, you'll have a good feel for your customers. By doing this prework, you can begin to be seen and heard within the forums and sites where your target audience is participating as you get into social media marketing. And on the flip side, you'll know in a hurry if you're participating on a site that doesn't fit your target market. By knowing who your customer is, you save time and market your brand more efficiently.

Gaining New Customers

Millions of people have been flocking toward social media marketing for business to meet new people, network with new and current prospects, and share their expertise. One of the big outcomes of this might be that you will gain new customers.

However, I cautioned you in the last section about having unreasonable expectations. Don't make the mistake of thinking this will happen overnight. When you first begin, remember it's a social situation even though it's online. Take your time and get comfortable with how the sites work.

If you follow proper netiquette while participating, you will meet more new people from around the country (and globe) than you would have traditionally met had you not used social media. You'll begin to feel a momentum in your business, perhaps a momentum that's been missing. Realtors, for instance, join social media to network with their past clients, but they're also finding new ones. Recruiters use social media to post job openings, and they find people to fill the jobs.

Those who are involved in nontraditional areas are also using social media to find new clients. Artists, for example, share their photographs and artwork, often finding buyers for their work. Like all entrepreneurs and freelancers on social media platforms, they are practicing the art of patient persistence. By participating in social media, your name will be in front of hundreds, thousands, and perhaps eventually, millions.

After you take the plunge into social media marketing, you will remind people you encounter on these sites of what you do and who you are, and you'll connect to them on a regular basis. If you are offering a product or service that resonates with people, they might become your new customers or a strong referral source.

Talking to Existing Customers

Simply wanting to use social media as another medium to communicate with your existing customers is a great business strategy. Today, after they leave your store or office or after you conduct a phone meeting with them, you can share your positive experience with them online. You can also share some new information to help guide them back to your store or your website.

Throughout this book, you also learn many ways to talk to your existing customers, such as polling them electronically or surveying them online using various social media platforms. You can send a video message to them, post photographs, and interview them on a podcast or on Internet radio. Perhaps you can feature them on your Facebook page or in your e-zine or newsletter. When customers purchase

Try This _____

Show your clients how much you appreciate their talents and how happy you are when their lives are going well. For instance, when a client is promoted or runs a marathon, you can cheer him or her on using social media platforms.

products from you, send them a message on Twitter and ask how they like the products. After obtaining their reviews, then you can post the written testimonials. Better yet, after customers buy your product or service, ask them for permission to record a video testimonial and then publish it to your social media sites. It's one thing for prospects to hear from you, but when they hear from your happy customers, that's powerful! You can even record a video message from them as you hand them the product.

Do you see how much you can do with social media? You are a social media marketer now, so you get to be creative. The more you strengthen your relationships with your existing customers, the better you and your business will become.

Going Viral

In the days before social media, the business world relied on word-of-mouth advertising. Now, essentially the same thing happens with social media. No, really. It's called *viral marketing*. Viral marketing is like virtual word of mouth. It's done on the Internet and on a large scale; you can watch your message spread like wildfire.

def•i•ni•tion

Viral marketing is a marketing technique that encourages users to pass a marketing message to other users or websites, which can create an exponential growth in the number of people who see the message.

Today, with a few simple keystrokes from your clients, friends, followers, and online fans, your message can quickly and virally go out to worldwide networks. They can quote you, forward what you wrote, or retweet what you tweeted (you will learn about this in Chapter 8 when we discuss Twitter).

Your followers can also comment on your video or podcast. They might hit the Share button on some sites (I'm sure you've seen those buttons on websites and blogs) and share with their network of followers.

It's amazing how quickly the word can get out. You know what else is amazing? That when you hit Send on something you write in your office, you send it around the world in a flash.

However, going viral can have a dark side. In 1996, a national coffee chain offered a free iced coffee in an e-mail to a limited group of employees. The e-mail contained instructions on how to forward it to family and friends. The e-mail coupon was posted on the Internet and went viral, with the free iced coffee offer spreading around the country.

Can you guess what happened? The campaign became too successful. The chain had to end the campaign quickly because so many people were coming in to get the drinks and it was slowing service at all their locations.

Going viral can be a good thing, but just be prepared for the results. Throughout this book, you'll find ways to create a viral marketing effort for your business using each of the social media platforms.

The Least You Need to Know

- ◆ You should have a good headshot to get started in social media.

- ◆ Be creative with your headshot, but be sure it works with the image you want to project for your business.

- ◆ If you can afford them, a good digital camera and a video camera are useful for social media marketing.

- ◆ Carefully identify your target customers or readers.

- ◆ Social media is an effective way to obtain new customers, but it takes time to build momentum.

- ◆ Using social media to stay in touch with existing clients can be an effective marketing strategy.

Part 2

Let's Begin Marketing Your Business on Facebook

This part teaches you how to use Facebook in a step-by-step format. You see helpful screen shots and you learn how to use Facebook as a powerful networking and marketing tool for your business.

You also learn about powerful behind-the-scenes business applications and strategies to help you stand out in a crowd of millions. This part also gives you the inside scoop on what you need to have in your virtual business suitcase. And in the last chapter, you find instructions on how to customize Facebook so that it fits your needs perfectly.

Chapter 4

Facebook: The Television Network of Social Media

In This Chapter

- ◆ Facebook terms
- ◆ How to get started on Facebook
- ◆ How to build an amazing profile page
- ◆ Creative ways to add friends
- ◆ The one daily task you should do on Facebook

Although not everyone is using it, most people have heard of Facebook. Today, Facebook has more than 350 million active users, and more than 50 percent log on to Facebook at least once each day.

Facebook started out as a networking site for college students. Now, it's a worldwide household phenomenon. More than two thirds of the Facebook population is older than college age. The fastest-growing demographic? Those in the 35+ age group.

Introduction to Facebook Terms

Facebook has its own language. The following is a primer for you on terms you'll frequently come across while interacting on Facebook:

- **Wall.** The wall appears on every user's profile page. You can delete wall posts easily from your page if you do not like what you see (put your cursor to the right of the post and a pencil appears asking if you want to delete). If you are friends with someone, you can write on that person's wall. It's a great strategy for marketing; the Facebook culture loves the wall.

- **Add.** You will see the words "thanks for the add" or "please add me as your friend." Add is the Facebook term for adding someone to your Facebook friends list.

- **Friends.** These are your Facebook friends that you have added to your profile page. Some people accept only people they know. Others prefer to be what is termed "an open networker," meaning they accept just about anyone as their friend to expand their network and connections. People who keep their friend list open or who are "open networkers" believe that just about anyone can be a prospect or a good referral source or simply someone who is interesting to know.

- **Profile.** Think of your profile as an advertisement page for you. It summarizes who you are, where you've been, and, more importantly, where you want to go.

- **Status Update or What's on your mind?.** This is your chance to send targeted messages out to the world. Update this daily. This goes into friends' news feeds on Facebook. This is one of the single most important tasks you can do on Facebook to grow your brand.

- **News Feed.** Go to your Home page by clicking on **Home** and you will begin to see lists of updates from your friends. This is referred to as the news feed.

- **Home.** When you get lost on Facebook—go home. Among many things your Home page lists are your network's news feed, your friend requests, event requests, event highlights, and a birthday calendar. This is a great place to keep updated about what your friends are saying.

- **IM/Live Chat.** In the lower right part of your Facebook profile, you can chat live (Instant Messaging) with people online.

- **Events.** Create events by going to your Applications bar at the bottom left of your screen and click **Events.** Events range from open houses to seminars, classes, meetings, parties, book clubs, and gatherings both virtual and in person. You can also see birthdays on this page.

- **Post.** This is another term that is used for Status Update copy. You can post your update or you can write a post on a friend's wall.

- **Poke.** This is the equivalent of someone tapping you on the shoulder and saying hello. Find this on your Home page on the right-hand side. Note: the poke feature is not as popular with baby boomers as it was with the college crowd.

- **Groups.** Create groups on Facebook to further build community around your business and brand. Join groups to further network and market your business. When people join your group, your group name appears on their profile.

- **Link.** To create a live link, always put "http://" in front of the www to your website URL or website address. You can view links either you or your friends have posted by going to Applications and clicking **Links.**

- **Applications.** These are additional features that Facebook or third-party vendors have supplied to the Facebook platform. To view the thousands of applications, go to Applications and click **Browse Applications.**

- **Fan.** Anyone can become a fan of a person, business, or brand on Facebook if they have a Fan page. By becoming a fan, you agree to put that person's logo/photo on your Facebook page. This is an automatic process. As soon as you "become a fan," that person's photo or logo (whichever they have in their picture profile) will automatically transport to your profile page. It can be seen by clicking on the **Info** tab of your profile page and scrolling down to the bottom.

- **Tag or Tagging.** When uploading a photo or writing a note using the Notes application, you are given an option to tag someone. This means that the person is in the photo or mentioned in the note. When you tag them, the Facebook system sends them a note letting them know they have been tagged in a photo or note. Also, Facebook will ask you to identify people in the photo and then ask if you want them tagged. Tagging is very popular on Facebook. It's unpopular when people tag people who are not in the photo or note, which is considered a form of spamming.

- **Spamming.** A term that is used across all social media marketing, which refers to abusing social media channels for one's own interest or profit. This is something you should never do.

Creating a Powerful Personal Profile for Business

Again, I refer to Facebook as the television network because it has such broad demographics. Check this out: the age range is from 13 to 80, there are both male and female users, and there's a wide range of income levels. It's hard to nail down the exact income level of the average Facebook user, but one statistic places the average income at around $89,000 per year. I mentioned that the largest demographic is the 35+ user, but in July 2009, the largest-growing segment was women aged 55 and up. In fact, as of Fall 2009, many grandparents are getting onto Facebook to keep up with their baby-boomer children and grandchildren.

Here are some other interesting Facebook statistics (as of January 2010):

- The average user has 130 friends.

- Worldwide, more than eight billion minutes are spent on Facebook each day.

- Pages have generated more than 5.3 billion fans.

- More than 2.5 billion photos are uploaded to the site each month.

- More than 3.5 million events are created each month on Facebook.

- More than 65 million active users access Facebook through their mobile devices.

How do you stand out in a crowd of tens of millions? It does seem daunting, but you can begin by creating an amazing personal Facebook profile for your business networking and marketing. Remember, others want to connect with real people first.

Login page to Facebook.

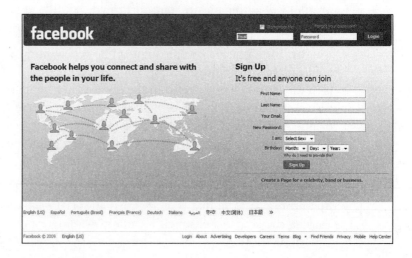

To get started, log on to www.facebook.com. First, you enter your name (make sure you spell it correctly). Some women question if they should give their married name or maiden name. Most savvy marketers use their business name. Thus, if you use your married name in business, go with that. However, you might want to use both your maiden and married name with hopes that you will connect to former friends and acquaintances; that's okay, too—it's a personal choice.

Next, enter your e-mail address and create a password. Enter your sex (male or female) and your birthday (don't worry about showing your birthday; I'll show you how to hide it in the next section). Facebook asks for this to identify you from the other people in the world that share your same name.

Facebook will send you a confirmation link to your e-mail inbox to verify that you have indeed opened an account with them. After you verify and click on the link in your inbox, you are ready to begin networking on Facebook. Next, you will be asked to enter information in a series of steps.

1. To avoid being overwhelmed right now, I suggest skipping the step of adding friends here. Take a look at the screen shot of this step and you'll see what I mean. Click **Skip** to move past this step.

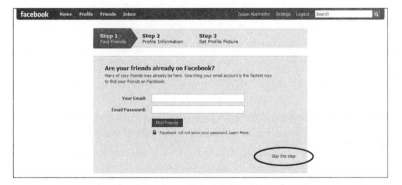

Here's Step 1 on Facebook.

2. The next screen asks about your high school, college, and current company. You can see **Step 2** in the figure. It's up to you whether you fill out the name of your high school or college, but many networkers feel it is a good thing to do because it makes you relatable and helps you connect with past friends and alumni. You definitely want to fill in the Company information with the name of your business. Then click **Save & Continue.**

Here's Step 2 on Facebook.

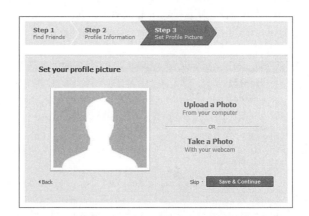

3. Next, you'll be asked to select people you know. As shown in the following screen shot, you might see some current and past friends here. If you connect, click Save **& Continue.** If you don't want to connect, you do not have to and no one will ever know. If you don't see anyone here at all, no worries, just click **Skip** and you'll skip this step.

Uploading your profile photo.

Now Facebook will officially welcome you. Congratulations!

Look at the right side of the next screen shot and you'll see that Facebook will suggest some friends you can connect to. You can click **Add** as friend or simply do nothing here. Other options you will see are Find People You E-mail and Find People You Know. I suggest you skip this part and continue to build and complete your profile first, then you can go back and add friends later. Click **View and edit your profile.**

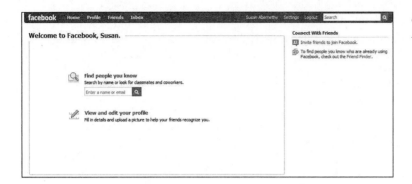

Seeing people you know on Facebook.

Here are some options as you're welcomed to Facebook.

Basic Information

Now your profile page will open up. You can see what this page looks like in the next screen shot. Let's begin to create your profile. Fill out the basic information that appears on the screen. Designate whether you are male or female, or you can simply opt not to show that in your profile, which is okay. If you don't fill it out, it won't show.

- ◆ **Birthday.** You can show Month/Date/Year, Month/Date only, or not show your birthday at all. Most people recommend giving your month and date only because as you build your friend list, they will be notified of your birthday and e-mail you. Most people put the town they currently live in. However, if you spent a large portion of your life somewhere else and want to put that down, do so.

- ◆ **Family Members/Relationship Status.** Because you are using this for business, it's recommended you keep these two fields blank. However, if you are comfortable with putting this information online, go ahead. It comes down to personal preference.

Netiquette

For business, I recommend that you keep most of your shared information 80 percent business and 20 percent personal—just as you would in a professional environment. You don't want to come across as a robot, so feel free to share some personal information. Just keep in mind this is business, so people want to get to know you professionally first .

- **Interested in.** Many people innocently check both boxes because they want to do business with both men and women. However, certain age groups might think that this is your sexual preference, so a best practice is to keep this blank.

- **Relationship Status.** It's a personal decision as to whether you include this or not.

- **Looking for.** Check Networking. Your clients and prospects don't need to know if you are interested in dating or seeking a relationship.

- **Political Views.** Keep blank. Some people show their sense of humor by typing "have those" or "will not share now" or "yes."

- **Religious Views.** Although you might be religious, religion and politics don't belong in the workplace. Again, you could use your sense of humor and put "have some," "yes," "spiritual," or "see the light." Note, though, that this is your space, so if you feel strongly about posting your religious and political views, you absolutely can. Now click Save Changes.

Here's the Basic Information page on Facebook.

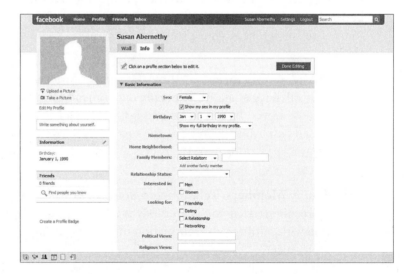

Personal Information

Next, open the Personal Information tab. You can take a look at this page in the next screen shot. This part might be uncomfortable for some, but you need to strategically brag here about what you do and how your business can help others. This is also where you need to think outside the box.

Just because it says Activities, you don't necessarily have to list things like aerobics, cycling, golf, and so on. For example, if you are a Realtor, you could write, "Enjoy helping families find their dream home." If you own a retail shop, you could write, "Passionate about bringing great products into customers' homes and providing a wonderful shopping experience." Maybe you are a life coach and you would write, "My days are spent helping others determine their goals and I guide them toward the realization of their dreams." The options are endless and you can be as creative as you like.

The secret here is to put "you" in the message and keep in mind that your ideal prospect may be reading this. Ask yourself, "What would make a possible customer want to further connect with me and get to know me and my business?" Note: at the end of the Activities portion, list a live link to your website. Now move on to the personal information.

- **Interests.** If you don't want to fill out the Interests section, you don't have to. However, here are some questions to ask yourself to help you determine what to write in this section: Where are you interested in going with your business? What are you passionate about? How do you help or serve people in your business? What product/service do you provide to them? Take those answers and put them in this section.

  For example: "Interested in becoming the best known organizer on the planet. Passionate about helping others organize their homes and offices to help them find clarity and peace in their lives. Serve people in the San Francisco area and throughout the state. Also interested in speaking opportunities and being a guest on radio shows."

- **Favorite Music, TV Shows, Movies, Books, and Quotations sections.** These can be filled out or kept blank. However, if you've written a book, put that in there. It's okay to let your personality shine through here.

- **About Me.** This is an important section when it comes to social media marketing on Facebook. In this section, you'll want to write two or three sentences inviting people to connect with you. Remind them how you can help them and invite them to call you or visit your website or blog. Use your personality and brand to attract people to you. The important thing is that what you write here should be about you. Here's a tip: end the About Me section with a live link to your website and your office phone number. A live link is created by using http://www. (in front of your website, blog, or internet TV show page).

Here's the Personal Information page on Facebook.

And now, click **Save.** Open the next tab, Contact Information.

Contact Information

You can see the Contact Information page in the next screen shot. Enter the e-mail address where you want prospects and clients to reach you. No need to type in your Instant Messaging (IM) screen name. Unless you are really into instant messaging, leave this blank. Give your office phone or cell phone number if that is where you want people to reach you. Put your office address if you like, but most importantly, enter your website address. If you have multiple websites, put them here. If you have a blog, put the blog address here. Also, add your Twitter name when you have one. Note: you will also see a prompt to create your Facebook badge. To learn all about Facebook pages and how they can play an instrumental role in your social media marketing, go to www.facebook.com/facebook-widgets/index.php.

Here's the Contact Information page on Facebook.

Education and Work

This part is pretty self-explanatory, but you can take a look at this Facebook page in the next screen shot. If you possess a special degree or learning certificate that would really separate you from the pack, include it here. Don't overlook the part about your current employer. As an entrepreneur or small business owner, obviously your employer is yourself. So put that down along with your title. The description portion again is your chance to brag or boast about what separates your business from others. Think about what makes you, your role, and/or your company unique. Write down your thoughts and summarize who you are in that space. Be as clear and concise as possible. Now, click **Save Changes.**

You will then see a section called Memorable Web Address. We will come back to this later in the book, too.

Here's the Education and Work page on Facebook.

That Box Below Your Photo

One of the most overlooked portions of the Facebook Profile page is this little box. It currently reads: Write something about yourself. To use this powerful marketing space on your profile, click on those words and begin writing. Remember, you want to stand out in the crowd of millions, so make this prime Internet "real estate" work for you. This little box stays visible when people are writing on your wall or visiting your profile. Stuck as to what to write? Here are some ideas for you:

◆ Write a welcome message.

◆ Use this spot to drive people to your blog and put the blog URL in this space. An example might be "For biweekly sales tips, subscribe to my award-winning blog at www.yourblogsitehere.com"

◆ Put your Twitter name here and invite people to follow you on Twitter.

◆ Use a sentence to describe again what you do and again list your website and your phone number.

◆ Get creative and change this box each month! Examples include tip of the month, quote of the day, success tip, share an industry statistic, insert a client testimonial, or put a weekly special.

◆ Feature a client of the month in this spot, share an article that you have written, or if you own a restaurant, put one of your specials in this box.

Adding Your Photo or Headshot

Adding a photo or headshot is easy to do. Here are the steps:

1. Click the **Profile** tab on the top. You see something that looks like a headshot shadow. This is where your headshot will go.

2. Click **Edit your profile picture.** Now, you have the choice to upload a picture, take a picture (with your computer), or choose a photo from an album that you have online (you probably do not have that yet). Click **Upload a Picture.** Now, you need to browse for the photo. Your photo must be in a .JPG, .GIF, or .PNG format. Select a photo and click **Upload Picture.**

3. Click on the **Verification Terms and Conditions,** verifying that it is you and you are not uploading someone else's copyrighted photo. Note that the photo must be 4 megabytes or less in size. Ideally, photos should remain current. If you change your hairstyle or if your overall look has changed dramatically from your existing photo, it's time to change.

Congratulations! You now have a great profile. Update it so that it reflects your current interests and your business. Now, you will need to add some friends to get the word out and begin networking. So let's get you going!

How to Add Friends and Stand Out in a Crowd

Facebook is all about connections. Seeing that face of a new friend, connecting with past friends, and finding new friends, prospects, and clients is a terrific platform for connecting with others. However, some people think they just don't know that many people, or they think the ones they do know most likely aren't on Facebook. Think again, because you might be surprised as to who you will find. Remember in the last chapter when we talked about mind-set and how that is your most important asset? Don't think you'll have problems finding friends, because most likely you won't.

Initially when you set up your profile, you might have added some of the suggested friends that were on that opening page. Now you will want to find some more. A Search box is in the upper right corner. Put your cursor on the Search box and enter a name of a friend. Now a list should display. It should be similar to the figure that shows a list of possible friends on Facebook. Do you see your friend? Now you see why a good photo is important.

Here's how it looks when your
Facebook photo is in place.

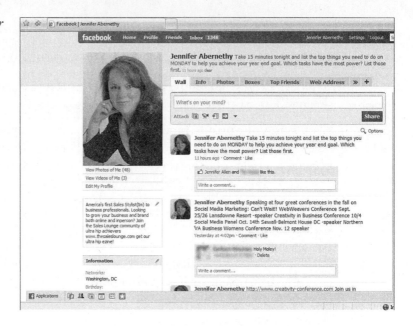

Many people might have the same name, so if you cannot see a photo, you might not be certain if that is the correct person. (Note: most experienced social media users do not like to connect to people without a photo.) Now that you have found your friend, click **Add a Friend.** A box displays asking if you want this person's comments in your daily news feed. You can see how this page looks in the next screen shot. For now, check yes. Note, if you are not certain that the photo (or lack thereof) is the person you are looking to connect with, send them a message by clicking on their name and asking if they are who you think they are.

A list of friendly faces on
Facebook.

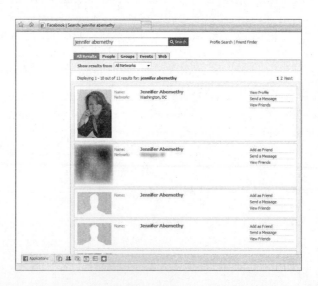

Add this person to a list. What does this mean? You can start organizing your friends by location, networking group, or type of client or prospect so that eventually when you have thousands of friends you can message them through Facebook according to group.

Adding a friend on Facebook.

Let's say you know Miss X from the XYZ networking group. Click **Add to List,** then click **Create List,** and populate the white area with the name of the networking group. Then press the **enter** key. You are not done. Remember, you want to stand out in a crowd of millions, so you should write a personal message. Click the bottom part of the box where it reads "Add a personal message," and write a short message, such as "Jane, so great to find you on Facebook. I look forward to connecting with you here online. Jennifer Abernethy, TheSalesLounge." On a personal note, you can also create a list for family members and personal friends. This comes in handy for photo sharing and so forth.

Online Cautions

When signing off using your name and website, do not end your sign off with ".com." If you do, after a short while Facebook will see this as spam and may discontinue access to your account. Additionally, only send out a small number of invites at a time, say 10 or so. If you start any higher than that, they may see you as a spammer.

Obviously, if it's your neighbor next door, you won't need to be so formal, but a savvy marketer will always sign with name and title, or name and website, or name and a tag line. Now, click the **Send** button. Just by adding a personal message you will begin to stand out in a crowd. Remember, people want to feel like they matter and they want to be connected.

Congratulations! You have now set up an amazing profile, you've added some friends, and you have uploaded your photo. As time goes on, you will find people who want to add you as a friend. When you go to your Home page and look in the upper right corner, you will see Requests. Look at this corner for friend requests. Click on **Friend Requests** and you will see a list of people who want to be your friend. Use your judgment about whom you want to connect with and whom you want to ignore.

For the most part, Facebook is today's equivalent of going to a convention and not knowing anyone in the room, and then after a bit of time passes, several people ask you for your business card and you give it to them. The difference now is that instead of a business card, they are asking to connect to your virtual business profile. Most people add just about everyone, but others are not comfortable with that. Go with what you are comfortable with. If you choose to "ignore" someone, they will not receive a notice telling them they have been ignored, but if they try to send you a message or look for you in their friend list they may figure it out.

Now let's get those friends feeling more connected to you and begin social media marketing.

What's on Your Mind?

The single most important task you can do on Facebook for effective social media marketing (aside from having a photo and good profile) is to update the "What's on your mind?" section at least once per day. Why? By doing this on a regular daily basis, people will get to know you and your expertise, it will also keep you in what experts call "top-of-mind awareness." They just won't be able to forget about you. They will grow to like you and then trust you. And people refer, recommend, and buy from people that they know, like, and trust.

How do you see the news feed? By clicking the word **Home,** you go to your Home page. You should now see the words, "What's on your mind?" You are about to enter your status update. As you begin connecting to friends, they will also enter their status update, which becomes part of the collective news feed. As a new Facebook user, you most likely don't have much appearing on that page just yet. However, as you get more friends, that page will become populated with the news feed of what's on everyone's mind. And remember, don't take this too literally.

The news feed is great for these things:

♦ Sharing tips and your expertise.

♦ Sharing websites and information with your target audience.

♦ Telling them what's new with your business.

♦ Sharing a testimonial.

♦ Telling them something exciting that is going to happen with your business.

♦ Networking and congratulating your friends, clients, and prospects when appropriate.

Okay, you're ready. Enter your first "What's on your mind?" status update found on the Home page. Before long, you will start getting comments about what you've written.

The Least You Need to Know

♦ Facebook has a wide range of demographics, which means, most likely, your target audience is participating.

♦ A great photo and a completed profile will attract more people who want to connect with you.

♦ Get creative and use all areas of your profile to promote your expertise and your business.

♦ Your status update is the single most important way to stay active and keep your friends engaged on Facebook.

♦ Keep your status update topics around 80 percent business and 20 percent personal.

Applications for Marketing on Facebook

In This Chapter

- How to add photos to your Facebook page

- Using video as a marketing tool

- Why the Notes application is effective

- Creating Facebook events

- Birthdays on Facebook

- Marketing your blog

Now that you have a great Facebook profile, you're probably enjoying updating your status every day. You've probably also been busy adding new friends. Now, how about adding some great applications to your Facebook site to make your Facebook presence even more intriguing?

In this chapter, you learn what you need to know about Facebook applications. There are a lot of them, but only a few that you need to start with. In fact, I think you'll find that it's fun to explore these applications and find out what they can do for you and your business.

What Are Applications?

Think of applications as great tools that you can install onto your Facebook site. They help you reach out and connect in more unique ways. Where do you find the Applications menu? Log in to Facebook, and click **Home.** Look near the bottom of your monitor's screen on the left side. See the Applications icon? It will appear on the bottom of every page on Facebook. If you don't see it, take a look at the following screen shot.

Here's where to find the Applications feature.

Applications tab

Click on the icon and an applications window will open up just above the icon. Your list is simple at this point, but over time it can get long as you expand on the applications you are using. Literally thousands of applications exist on Facebook. Let's begin by looking at what is already installed for you.

Photos

The Photo application is for uploading photos. As a social media marketer, you will want to upload photos so your friends and soon-to-be fans will be able to share your experiences. As of January 2010, Facebook reports more than 2.5 billion photos are uploaded each month. Facebook is hosting 20 billion photos at one time. The numbers are staggering, aren't they?

Okay, let's get started. Click **Photo.** Then click **+ Create a Photo Album.** Next, you'll see the following screen shot.

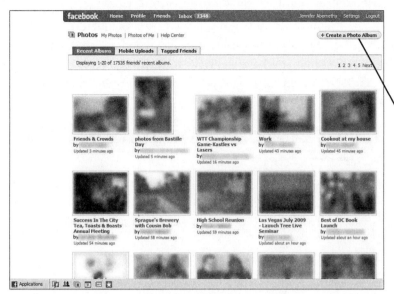

Here's where you create a new photo album.

Click here to create a photo album

Here's where you type in your photo album information.

You can then name your album of photos or photo, give the location, and describe the photos. Next, decide who you want to see your photos. You can choose everyone, your networks and friends, friends of your friends, or only friends. Or you can customize the distribution of it to share with specific people.

Did You Know?

It takes three seconds for someone to determine if they want to connect to you based on your photograph. Users without photographs are less likely to build up their network on Facebook.

Facebook will ask you to install Active X Control for faster installation, or you can use their Simple Uploader. Both options are on the page. When you use the Simple Uploader, you see this page. Next, you'll see the following screen shot.

Facebook then asks you to verify ownership. Read the Terms of Use. Take a look at the next screen and you'll see you're asked to Browse ... your computer to upload the photos. After you've certified that you have the right to distribute these photos (and they aren't the property of someone else) and you've found the photos through Browse ..., click **Upload Photos.**

From this screen, you can browse through your files and select photos. In addition, you're asked to verify that you own the photos.

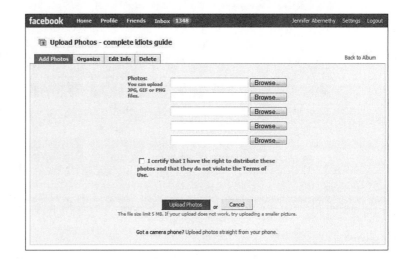

After you click the **Upload Photos** button, you can add a caption to the photo (or photos) and identify people in the photo by clicking on them and adding their names. Then, click **Save Changes.** In the following screen, note that you have the option to skip this step and click **Publish Now.** You then have the option to publish it on your profile page or save it in your profile under photos. This process is called "tagging" someone in a photo. When you are tagged in a photo, a copy will show up in your photos. When you tag someone else, they get a copy in their photos.

Your last option is to e-mail the photo to someone—even if they are not on Facebook. You can also add a message. Take a look at the next screen shot to see what I mean.

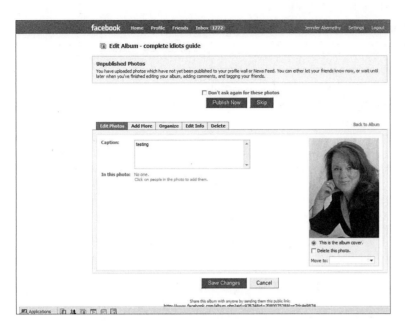

You can add captions on this screen.

You can share photos with Facebook friends, as well as those who aren't on Facebook.

Online Cautions

As of this writing, you can control the content and information you post on Facebook and you can control how it is shared through your Privacy and Application settings. However, for content that is covered by intellectual property rights, such as photos and videos ("IP content"), you specifically give Facebook the following permission:

"You grant us a non-exclusive, transferable, sub-licensable, royalty-free, worldwide license to use any IP content that you post on or in connection with Facebook ("IP License"). This IP License ends when you delete your IP content or your account unless your content has been shared with others, and they have not deleted it. When you delete IP content, it is deleted in a manner similar to emptying the recycle bin on a computer. However, you understand that removed content may persist in backup copies for a reasonable period of time (but will not be available to others)."

Note: Facebook privacy settings continue to evolve. Be sure to check privacy settings from time to time.

—Facebook's Statement of User Rights (August 2009)

Video

Video enables consumers to be entertained while also being informed. You might say this is "edutainment." Videos make your company's brand and services come alive. The video application is already installed for you on Facebook. Here, you can share your videos, record videos from your computer, and upload and publish videos from your mobile (phone). Go back to the Applications menu in the lower left of your screen and click **Video.** Here's what you'll see.

The Facebook Video application screen.

Upload and Record here

Many people spend time on Facebook, and as you get into video marketing, you will want to include Facebook as one of the major platforms for delivering your marketing message. You can either begin recording (you must have a computer with a webcam to do this) or you can upload a video. Recording from your computer is very easy. No, really! Click **Record** and then the following screen will display.

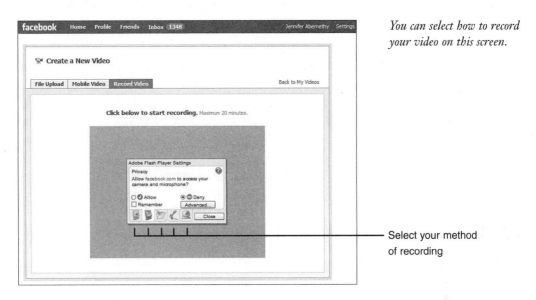

You can select how to record your video on this screen.

Select your method of recording

Click **Allow** option and then select your recording device (a mobile webcam, a computer webcam, or microphone for just recording audio). Then click **Close.** Your screen will show a video image of you. See yourself on the screen and click the **red button** to record. You will have a maximum of 20 minutes. Note, social media videos are most widely viewed when they are three minutes or less. Take a look at the next screen.

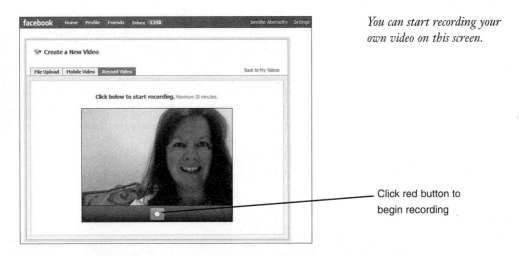

You can start recording your own video on this screen.

Click red button to begin recording

Just like with the photo application, Facebook asks who is in the video with you. This is so you can tag them (send it to them). You can title the video, put in a description, and decide who can see it. You will also notice Facebook asks you to Choose a Thumbnail. This is a photo icon that will appear next to your video when you e-mail it out or post it on Facebook. You can put anything here—a photo, logo, and so on.

Netiquette

Don't tag people with the video if they aren't in the video. You will be labeled as a spammer and lose respect by those who are taking the time to open it thinking that they are in it. This goes with other applications as well, such as Photos and Notes.

When you click **Choose a Thumbnail,** you can browse your computer or use a screenshot from your video as the thumbnail.

You can then share the video on your profile or share it with specific Facebook friends, by clicking the **Share** button. Or you can tag your video by sending it to certain people who are in the video with you. You can do some slight editing to the video, delete the video, or if you are technically savvy, embed the video to your other websites or social media platforms.

Here's how it looks when it's ready to edit or tag and share with friends.

Notes

The Notes application on Facebook is another underutilized tool. Facebook Notes can help you share your expertise, continue to cultivate your following, and virally get your information out to the masses. Go back to Applications and click **Notes.** Click **+ Write a New Note.** Here's what comes up on your screen.

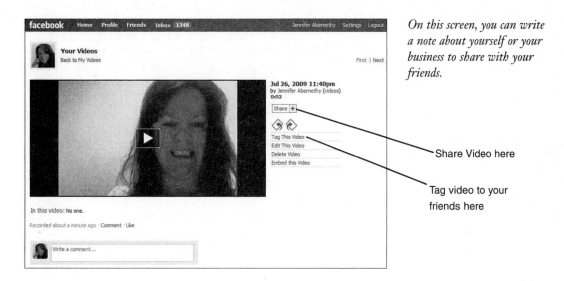

On this screen, you can write a note about yourself or your business to share with your friends.

Here is your chance to write about a new service you are providing or to share your thoughts on an issue or problem. (Remember to keep politics and religion out of it.) Most importantly, write as if your ideal clients are reading it. What would they want to hear? What would interest them? Again, you can tag people that you mention in your note, but only if you mention them. You can also upload a photo or logo to go within your note.

At the bottom of this screen, you are asked to save your note, if you want to send your note to your profile, who to make it visible to, and if you're ready to publish your note. Your friends, clients, and prospects can comment on your notes, and again, your name and voice is in front of them. You're really building relationships through your communication online.

Another very cool thing about the Notes application is that you can import your blog into Facebook. This is different from the Social RSS feed, which we will get into later in this chapter. After you learn how to do this, it is easy. Open up the Notes application again. On the right side, you will see Notes Settings. You can import your blog (no one else's, just yours) here. This will feed it into your notes each time you publish an entry.

If you begin importing notes from your blog, your Notes page will then include both notes typed on Facebook and posts from your blogs. Take a look at the following screen shot. Once here, you will click on **Edit Import Settings.**

From this screen, you can import your blog into your notes.

See Applications Menu

Click to add blog

You are then directed to the following screen shot. You will need to enter your blog's website address in the text box. Note, it doesn't need to be your RSS feed, because Facebook magically posts your content for you. You have to check the disclaimer underneath the URL and then click **Start Importing.** We will discuss blogs later in Chapter 16, but it's good for you to know this is here.

As a best practice, use the Notes application on a regular basis. Provide value, information, and entertainment, and your followers, friends, and fans will love it.

Use the Notes application to promote your business.

Events

Remember the days when a business owner had an event? It was typically an open house or a holiday gathering. Signs were posted at the office or store location, and a postcard or an invitation was sent through the mail. Perhaps the owner even made some phone calls. Today those rules still apply. And perhaps these gestures are even a bit refreshing because we don't get much in the mail anymore.

However, you can now post your event on Facebook. There are 2.5 million events created each month on Facebook. It's a great place to post the event because it is another publicity avenue for your event.

What types of events are on Facebook? All kinds; in fact, for social media marketers, the possibilities are endless. There are events for open houses, wine tastings, book signings, group meetings, recitals, teleseminars, webinars, lectures, book launches, seminar holiday parties, classes, conference calls—the list goes on and on. To create an event, go to Applications and scroll up to Events. You will see upcoming events posted by other Facebook users, your friends' events, past events, and birthdays.

This is the Events applications page on Facebook.

Create an Event here

View Friends' Events here

View Upcoming Events here

In the upper right side of the screen, click on **+ Create an Event.**

Use this screen to fill in the event's details.

You will fill out the following required information to post your event: event name, tagline, host, event type/category, the event's description, and the start and end time. If this is a one-day event, this is easy. However, if it runs, say, on consecutive Fridays, it's a bit tricky. In that case, just put the date when the event starts and describe the recurring times in the Description section. Also type in the event location (which is required) and the street address (if applicable). Then click **Create Event.**

Next, you can upload a picture or logo and certify that you have the right to distribute the photo/logo. Then, consider the various options offered as shown in the following figure.

Remember, you are creating community, so get creative with what you and your invitees can do with this invite, both pre- and post-event. You can also decide if you want the event open (to anyone), closed (to invitees only), or secret (only those that you've invited or are members of your group or fan page; we will get into fan pages in Chapter 6).

Then, you can publish the event to appear on the Home page and in the Events section. Lastly, you can invite friends who are on Facebook (or e-mail friends who are not) and include a personal message.

You can show a guest list or hide it; allow guests to upload photos, videos, and links; or you can pass on these options.

You can choose Facebook friends to invite to your event.

You can then publish your event, and you will see your Event page, which will be similar to the one that follows.

A published Facebook event.

From this screen, you can edit the guest list, cancel the event, message guests with event updates, print out your guest list, publish photos, add video, and include links. Ask your invitees to RSVP online. You can also add other information like parking details, bad weather plans, or other details that will make the event exciting. Try it for your next event. Note, don't depend on this as the only way to invite people, but do make it a part of your invite campaign.

Birthday Networking

Power Facebook users know that one of the best ways to network and market themselves is to be seen, heard, trusted, and liked. One of the networking techniques that many use is sending birthday wishes. On your Home page on the right side, you will see a list of upcoming birthdays. Look at that list and then click on the birthday person's name and write a birthday greeting on their wall. You can sign off with your company name, if you like. But most importantly, just take five minutes every day and see whose birthday it is. Go to their Facebook profile and write on their wall and say "Happy Birthday." It's a nice thing to do, and strategically, it's great PR for you and your company. Also, it feels good when you are on the recipient side, too.

Gifts and Links

There are two additional applications that are populated into your applications menu as a first-time user: Gifts and Links. Gifts are virtual gifts that you can post on your friends' profiles. You have to pay several dollars for some and others are free. Facebook is starting a virtual currency program at this writing. As a best practice, I would stay away from gifts. It's not a good use of time and most savvy networkers feel the same way.

The Links application is just what it says. Within your status update, you can post a link to a website, blog, or article. When you click the Links application, you can see all the links that your friends have posted.

Social RSS

This is the most popular *RSS* reader application in Facebook. As a Facebook user, you can use this to add your blogs and live Twitter updates to your Personal Profile. As of October 2009, there were just under 300,000 monthly active users utilizing Social RSS.

By adding this application, you can create a new box tab that appears at the top of your Facebook Profile page. Or later on, when you learn how to create a Facebook Fan page, you can have it appear there. Your articles will be posted automatically from your blog to your Facebook page by using this service.

> ## def•i•ni•tion
>
> **RSS** stands for Really Simple Syndication, but sometimes it also means Rich Site Summary. It helps create website feeds that allow you to publish frequently updated texts, such as from blogs.

The benefit of using this is that it keeps your content on your site fresh and updated and helps drive traffic to your website. To find this, go to the Application icon and click **Browse More Applications.** Then, in the Search bar, search for Social RSS. You'll see the following screen.

The main page for the Social RSS Facebook application.

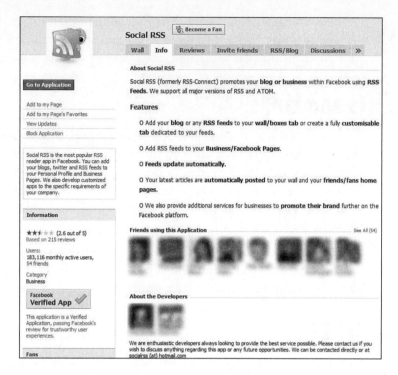

Click on Social RSS to add this application. Here's what you'll see.

You can read through this page to get more information on how you can best utilize this application for your business.

Networked Blogs

This is a fun application that promotes your blog and the blogs of your strategic partners, clients, and friends. Remember, social media is about promoting and marketing not only your own business, but those of others as well.

This application also does something else. It puts your blog onto a directory of blogs on Facebook. This enables your blog fans to promote your blog on their Facebook page as well as blogs they like to follow. To get this application, go to www. networkedblogs.com. Note, to add your blog, you need a Facebook account.

Here's the screen for the Networked Blogs application on Facebook.

Are you beginning to see how all your social media marketing is beginning to work together? Don't be overwhelmed. You can use some or all of these Facebook applications now, or wait until you are ready. The important thing is that you know they are there and available to you. This keeps you one step ahead of the competition and gives you multiple ways to network and market your business using social media.

As we go on throughout the book, and you learn more about the other social media sites like LinkedIn, Twitter, and YouTube, you will eventually want to incorporate them into your Facebook page. This is more advance marketing, but after you create your presence on those sites you will want to upload the YouTube Video Box application, Twitter application, and My LinkedIn Profile application on Facebook. So hang in there! You are on your way to learning more fabulous ways to use social media marketing.

The Least You Need to Know

♦ Although there are thousands of applications on Facebook, there are just a few that you really should know about and utilize for your business marketing on Facebook.

♦ Photos and videos are a great way to keep Facebook followers up-to-date and engaged with what you are doing with your business.

♦ Writing about your expertise using the Notes application on Facebook is a great way to keep your website content fresh and your readers connected to your business.

♦ Posting events and honoring your friends' birthdays are two good ways to keep your name and brand in front of your followers and those you network with on Facebook.

♦ Using the Social RSS application will help you promote your blog on Facebook.

♦ The Networked Blogs application places your blog in a directory, which allows Facebook users to promote your blog on their own Facebook pages.

Chapter 6

Facebook Fans and Group Pages

In This Chapter

- ◆ Should you join Fan pages and groups?
- ◆ Creating a Fan page
- ◆ Great examples of Fan pages
- ◆ Applications you can use on your Fan page
- ◆ Creating a Facebook group
- ◆ How to attract raving fans

In this new world of social media marketing, it seems everyone is becoming their own brand. And that's perfectly fine. You need to start thinking of yourself and your company as a brand.

And as with any good brand, you need to provide a place for your fans and followers to gather. With over 350 million people on one platform, Facebook Fan pages and groups are a great place to start. Guess how many users join a Facebook Fan page each day? Over ten million! That's a lot of fans. Don't you think that some of these fans might as well be yours?

Choosing Fan Pages and Groups to Join

Before we jump into creating your own Fan page or group, let's briefly discuss the strategy involved in joining other people's groups and Fan pages. One of the strategies of savvy social media marketers is to create Fan pages and groups on Facebook for their businesses. They also strategically join groups and become fans of their friends', prospects', and clients' businesses.

I was attending a social media conference a year or so ago and one of the presenters shared a story about how his girlfriend wanted to go to Harvard for her MBA. Well, one of her strategies was to join the Harvard Business School Fan page on both Facebook and LinkedIn (see Chapter 12) and begin networking with alumni. She ended up networking online and eventually talking with a member of the MBA candidate selection committee. The presenter ended the story by telling us that his girlfriend was now attending Harvard Business School. Obviously, she needed more than that connection to be accepted at Harvard, but oftentimes the people you know do make a difference.

Keep in mind that as people view your profile on Facebook, they will look at the groups you are in and the people or businesses you are fans of. It becomes a reflection of who you are, just as those networking groups and organizations that you join in your community and nationally do. This is the same thing; it's just printed on an Internet page and the group happens to be virtual. Think strategically about whom to follow and what groups to join.

You might follow someone simply because you admire the person and you are a true fan, and that's okay. But I caution those who become fans and join groups that might be fun from a personal viewpoint. Sometimes these casual alliances don't look good from a business viewpoint, so keep that in mind. Remember, you are marketing your business and brand. Be authentic in your approach and conscious of the groups you are joining. I call this "conscious social media marketing." Always be aware of what you join, write, say, and do online, and all will be fine.

There are several ways to choose Fan pages to join. First, you can look at the profile pages of your friends and see what Fan pages they've joined. When you see their list, you can click on the icon and it will take you to that Fan page where you can become a fan. Another way is to go to the Search bar on the upper right side of the page and type in the company name, a product, or a person's name, and see if their Fan page pops up. Or you can go to **www.facebook.com/pages/?browse** and see a list of all the Fan pages broken down by category. Here's an example of what you might see when you are on this site.

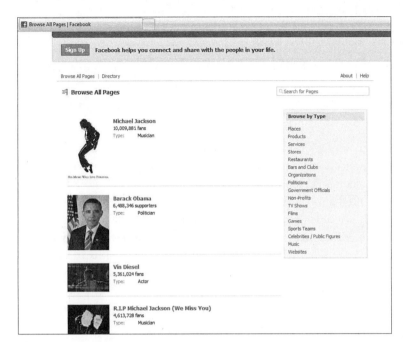

Popular fan pages are shown on the Home page, but you can also browse by type, such as products or organizations.

Do You Need a Fan Page or Group?

If you are not sure why you are creating a group or Fan page, perhaps you should hold off until you experience more clarity. Remember, this is your chance to interact with current and potential customers, but you need to keep your message and brand consistent.

If you know you want to move forward with a Fan page or group, take a few minutes to answer these questions before you create your page. It will help you focus on what your objectives are for your Fan page or group:

- ◆ Who will monitor the Fan page or group?

- ◆ Will your group be open, private, or secret?

- ◆ Will you post daily on the Fan page?

- ◆ Will you want your fans to post their links and videos?

- ◆ Where will you promote your Fan page or group? In your office, store, on your business cards, or in your e-mail signature?

- ◆ What will be your goal when starting the group? Do you ultimately want to educate, inform, or meet people in person or together in a group?

◆ Will you create multiple administrators for your group or Fan page? You have the ability to do that on Facebook.

◆ Will you begin discussion boards? Who will monitor the page and how often?

What's the bottom line? Think about your business strategy carefully. If it makes sense, go for it.

By creating a Fan page or group on Facebook, you create a place to have a stronger interaction with people and another community forum for them to engage with you. You can promote business specials, news, updates, and events, all on one site. Take advantage of all the preinstalled applications, such as the Video, Photo, and Events applications, that are already there waiting for your marketing touch. Fans and group members are looking to stay connected to you, so reach out in different ways online.

Creating Your Own Fan Page

Your focus is now clear, and you're ready to create a Fan page. For many of us, it might be uncomfortable to think of ourselves as so important that we need to create a Fan page. Who would have imagined that? After all, most of us don't have a lucrative recording or film contract, and we are not a household name (at least not yet, anyway). However, with social media marketing, you need to change your thinking. Remember what I said about mind-set? Your friends, best clients, and followers want a place to rally around you. Your business champions will be proud to wear a badge that reads, "Hey, I'm a fan of (you/your business)."

There are many benefits to setting up a Fan page for your business. Here are a few big ones:

◆ Everytime someone becomes a fan of yours on Facebook, your business logo or photo and Fan page name appears on your fan's Profile page. This is great viral marketing because now all of the fan's friends will see your information, too.

◆ By showing you have fans, this gives prospective clients confidence in you. It certainly won't hurt your business.

◆ The Fan page has room for an unlimited number of fans, whereas your personal/ professional profile page is currently limited to 5,000. (Note, this could change in the future.)

◆ Your Fan page enables you to have a Welcome page where you can poll your fans, post videos, have discussion boards, and have your blog feed into that page.

- ◆ The Fan page enables you to listen to your fans and have a dialogue with them.

- ◆ Your Fan page enables your fans to have star status by posting videos about your product and expressing their views.

- ◆ It's more free PR for your business and personal brand.

The Community Coffee Fan Page

Sometimes it helps to see an example, and we can all learn from those who've done it well. Look at this fun Community Coffee Fan page.

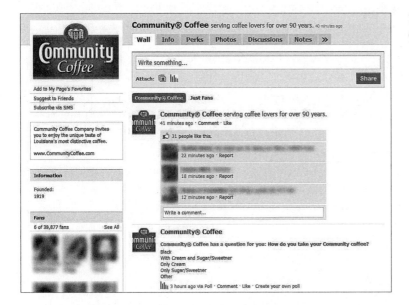

The Wall on the Community Coffee Fan page.

Community Coffee has done a great job creating an interactive and engaging Fan page. First, their bright logo occupies the photo space. Next, remember the box below the photo? They have used it to drive people to their website. Then, they have a line mentioning the year they were founded. Finally, they boast a fan base of over 40,000 fans. And growing daily!

When reviewing the Community Coffee Fan page, review all tabs across the top and just see how they market themselves. A fun one to look at is how they've incorporated polling. As of this writing, their page contains some right-facing arrows at the end of their tabs. Click on them and a drop-down menu will appear. Click on the word "poll." Look how Community Coffee uses the polling application by asking fans what is their favorite holiday coffee blend.

Their status updates or posts do many creative things to engage their fans. Take a look at their Fan page and see how they engage fans by asking questions and sharing thoughts. I also like the custom tab they created called "Perks." Click it and you will see this is where they collect fan information for direct mailings and discounts.

You can do the same with your Fan page. Let your fans experience what goes into operating your business. There is a reason why reality shows are so popular. People are intrigued by what is real. They want to know what happens behind the scenes. Take your fans with you on your journey. Remember, people want to feel part of something. It might as well be your community.

How to Set Up Your Fan Page

I'm not sure why they don't put this on the Home page, but for now the easiest way to create a Fan page is to go to **www.facebook.com/pages/create.php.** You should arrive at the following page.

This is where you start creating your Facebook Fan page.

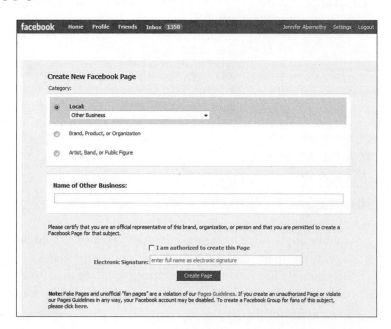

You will most likely use the first tab to describe your page (unless you are a national celebrity, product, or public figure), so click on that and select the type of business you own. If you don't see your type listed, click **Other.** Then at the bottom you will see Name of Other Business; you type the name of your business there.

Following are the other steps for creating a Fan page:

1. Check the **certification link** to confirm that it is indeed your business and that you're authorized to create the page.

2. Next, fill in your electronic signature, which is your name. This is necessary because many people falsely represent certain companies or celebrities. You do not want someone falsely representing your business, either.

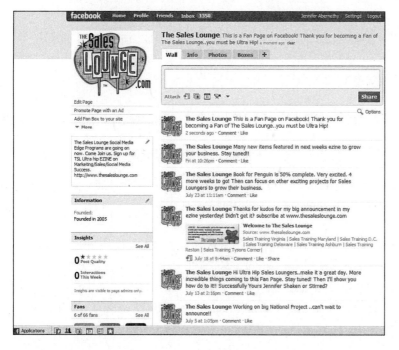

This is a newly created Fan page for The Sales Lounge.

3. Click **Create Page.** You should see the page like the one that follows.

4. Fill in the box below the photo that says, "Write something about (Your Company)."

5. Click **Edit Information** (around the middle, to the right; you'll see a little pencil icon). Here's what you'll see on the screen.

After your Fan page is created, fill in the details about your business.

6. Now, fill in the information that you deem appropriate, and then save it. Fill in the next box that asks for detailed information and save it.

7. At the top right, there is a question mark icon that displays Change Picture when you put your cursor over it; this is where you upload your logo or photo. Under the Photo and Edit Page, you'll see the phrase "Add Fan Box to your site."

   This might require some technical help, but basically, it enables your Fan page wall to be seen on your website. The goal of this is to attract people who come to your website to become a fan of your business on Facebook.

8. Click **Add Fan** Box to your site, and you will see some HTML code. This code will be given to you and can be put in the code that is behind your website. If the thought of HTML is giving you shivers, don't despair. You can hire someone to do this for you or, better yet, simply ask a tech-savvy friend who owes you a favor.

   You have an option to feed (automatically send) the updates you put on your Fan page, which is labeled Include stream. Another option is Include fans, which would show your fans. You can do both, either one, or neither. If you choose neither, you get a small Facebook Fan page link that shows your logo and name. Connecting to your website is something worth checking out.

9. After your fan page is ready, update your What's on your mind? status.

Alert your friends that your Fan page is up and ask them to write on your Fan page wall. Hint: this way they will also become a fan. Remember to become a fan of your own Fan page. This way your Fan page will appear on your individual profile page.

Try This _____

The more often you update, the more often your Fan page will appear in the Highlights section of the Home page on Facebook. To see the Highlights, click **Home** and look at the right side of your screen.

Your Fan Page Strategy

It's important to think about how you want to run your Fan page. Do you want to use it simply to communicate with fans? Do you want to have discussion boards? What types of photos will you upload? Do you want fans to review products and services for you? Will you place events on your Fan page? Who will monitor your Fan page?

Think about these questions so you can make strategic decisions about your Fan page. And remember, as you get more fans, you will need to monitor it daily.

Applications for Your Fan Page

You can use many applications on your Fan page. The ones I've listed in this section are just a few for you to consider. Just like your regular Profile page, you have a wall with the information tabs on your Fan page. With the Fan page, you can also easily list events and start discussion boards.

You can also add some of the other applications that were recommended for your profile in Chapter 5, such as Notes and Social RSS. The following are some additional fun applications that you can add when you are ready:

- **YouTube.** Have your favorite YouTube videos on your Fan page. In Chapter 15, you will learn how to create your own YouTube Channel.

- **My Google Calendar.** Have your Calendar of Events on your Profile or Fan page when using Google Calendar. This is great for entrepreneurs, speakers, and those who have lots of public events.

- **Poll.** Remember the polling feature that we saw on the Community Coffee Fan page? You can add that to your own page. Go to Applications and search for Poll. Click **Poll** and add the application. It will then ask you to Add to Page; it's asking what page you would like the poll to appear. When you upload the application, it will ask you, then "Add Poll." Create a poll by entering your questions, answers, and clicking **Submit.** To remove the poll from the page, you have to click **Delete** on the Polls Results page and click **X** on the page.

There are a lot of things you can do to further develop your Fan page. However, for our purposes here, we are working to get you started with the basics. When you're ready, you can move on to more advanced applications and marketing strategies.

Groups on Facebook

People join groups because they share a common interest or cause with the group. You'll see everything from groups about politics to groups for people who love garlic. Some are also centered on an individual or a business.

Just like the Fan pages, there are many reasons why you might want to join groups and perhaps even create your own group. The following are just a few reasons to give groups some thought:

♦ When people see your profile, they also see what groups you are in and support.

> **Did You Know?**
>
> One difference between a group and a Fan page is the way they are seen on individual profiles on the information tab. If someone joins your group, your group name appears only as a hyperlink on their Facebook page. If they join your Fan page, your logo or photo, along with a direct link, will appear.

♦ Join your friends' or clients' groups to show your support. It's good networking and good PR for your brand.

♦ When people join your group, your group name will appear on their profile with a link to your Facebook group. It's more viral marketing for your business.

♦ Creating a group enables you to further promote your business and brand presence on Facebook. You can create that community spirit within your group and share news, events, and discussions.

Creating Your Own Group

Before jumping in to create your own group on Facebook, think about the "why." Will this be a private group with weekly or monthly discussions? Will this just become a place to send messages out to a specific group of people? Do you want to only attract people you know or will it be open and allow anyone in the world to join in? These are good questions to ask yourself and to be ready to manage them because once you create a group, it is a reflection of your business and brand.

First, in the Search bar, type **groups.** You should see a page similar to the following pages.

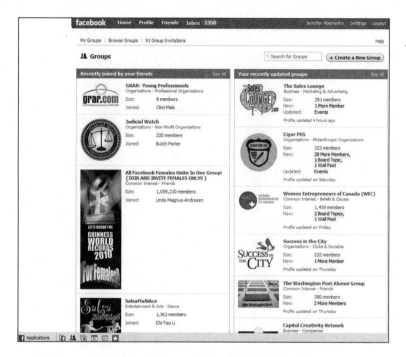

Do a search for groups and you'll get a list that looks similar to this.

If you don't have many friends yet, your left column might appear blank. If you are not in any groups, your right column will be blank. Look on the top right and click **+ Create a New Group.** Note, you can browse groups on this page as well. The following screen is what you'll see next.

Enter your group's name and description along with the type of group. Follow the online instructions, but note that the street and town can be kept blank if this is a virtual group. Some organizations that meet in person create their groups on Facebook as well. Click **Create Group.** The next screen will pop up for you to upload a picture or logo for the group.

Here's where you enter your group's information.

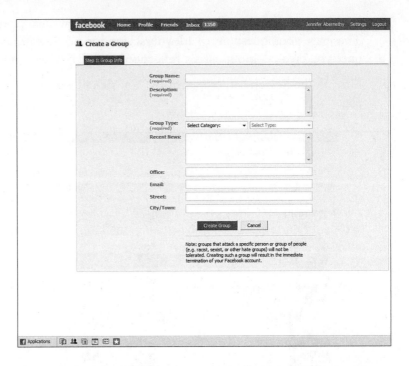

You upload a photo or logo after you've created your group.

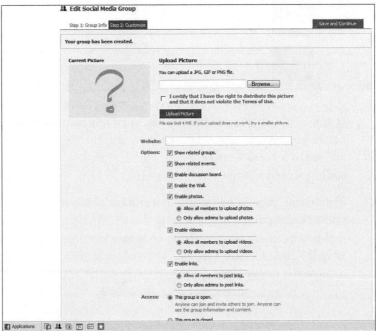

You'll need to certify that it is you. Type in the hyperlink to your website (www. yourwebsitename.com), and then check or uncheck the appropriate boxes. At the bottom of this page, you're asked if you want to make this an open group, which means that anyone can join. Or you can make it a closed group, which means that you, as the administrator, must approve members requesting to join, but the public can see that the group exists. You can even make it a secret group. A secret group will not appear in the search results or in the profiles of its members. Membership is by invitation only and only members can see content.

Think strategically about which group option is best for you. Savvy marketers might utilize all three. For example, say you have a VIP club in your business. You might want to make that group secret or closed. Let's say you are a speaker and/or blogger and you want everyone to know about your group. If you want them to learn about your expertise and share experiences, then you might want to create an open group. Again, there are no rules here, just do what works for you. Don't be afraid to experiment; you can always change what you are doing if you don't find it's working for you and your business. That's the great thing about social media marketing. It's constantly evolving, so experimenting is acceptable and encouraged.

Creating Raving Fans on Facebook

An interesting phenomenon has happened on Facebook and other social media sites. As mentioned earlier in the book, everyday people are creating loyal followers and *raving fans* who are helping to market their business and brand worldwide. How are they doing that? First, they are doing a great job of initially introducing themselves to you. Remember, this is a social platform, so instead of focusing only on selling, they are also introducing themselves and meeting others. They focus initially on adding friends and do so in an authentic, sincere way. Then, they make people feel good about connecting with them.

You might know the saying, "People won't remember what you say, but they will remember how you made them feel." The same is true when using social media. Whether you are writing a personal note when adding someone as a friend, writing on his wall, or responding to a note he sent to your inbox, try to keep a positive tone and keep the focus on your prospective customer. Again, you are building your

def•i•ni•tion

A **raving fan** online is someone who essentially is proud to give you a virtual thumbs up. They like what you do. They support you. They are an advocate of your business and/or brand and are proud to say they are a fan on their Profile page.

business. Eventually, you will want to begin taking it to the next level, which involves really engaging your friends and uncovering their wants and needs. You can do this with phone calls, polls, online questions about what they're looking for, and so on.

If you are adding many people locally, arrange to meet with a group of them. Get to know them, or invite them to lunch or breakfast. You are now starting to take the networking to a different level. Another activity you can do is call five new Facebook friends on the phone each week. Get to know them and tell them you are glad you both connected. You will learn a lot about the person, he or she will feel good that you called, and you never know where the relationship will lead. This is a powerful strategy, but it takes work. Most successful people are not afraid of work, and that is why they are successful.

The other activity that successful social media marketers do, which ultimately creates raving fans, is that they publicly (online) compliment others or they recommend others to their own network. Here's the point: don't simply make it about you. Help your friends grow their businesses. Share resources and publicly "shout out" online what great things your friends and colleagues are doing. This will go a long way with your friends. They will thank you and respect you for it.

Another strategy for creating raving fans is to feature perhaps a client or friend of the week on your Facebook Profile page or Fan page. People love to see their name in lights (whether they admit it or not).

Also as you venture into video, you will want to have your friends in some videos. That not only promotes your business, but theirs as well if you ask them to say their name and give their website. We will be talking a lot more about raving fans throughout the book as we introduce more social media sites and tools, so stay tuned.

The Least You Need to Know

- Think of yourself and your business as a brand and remember that everything your write, say, and do online reflects on your brand.

- Encourage your top clients and friends to support your Fan page.

- Use your Fan page as a marketing tool to further communicate and collaborate with fans and your business advocates.

- Creating a group on Facebook is another way to build a community around your business.

- Successful social media marketers create raving fans for their businesses because they are great at promoting others and they make people feel good about networking with them.

Chapter 7

More Facebook Marketing Strategies and Netiquette

In This Chapter

◆ Clever ways to keep your fans happy

◆ Using proper Netiquette

◆ Getting creative with video on Facebook

◆ The Marketplace on Facebook

◆ A Facebook marketing checklist

Now you have a multitude of fans, so your next challenge is to keep those fans happy. You don't want them to just join your Fan page or your group and then disappear.

In the pages ahead, you'll learn some unique tips to help you maintain an enthusiastic fan base. You've already learned some marketing strategies for Facebook and now that you're ready, we'll kick it up a notch.

Keeping Your Fans Engaged

As you've learned by now, there are many ways for you to attract friends and followers. Are you still uncomfortable with having fans? Well, if you are, let me put this as gently as I can—it's time to get over it!

Try This _____

For one or two weeks, type in a different status update in What's on your mind? every day. Try asking a question or providing a tip. See if you begin getting more friend requests and comments on your page.

When you go to watch a baseball game, you are a fan because you admire what the team stands for or maybe you admire the ability of a special player. You might not know them personally, but you are a fan. Now that you are on a worldwide platform, you are now on center stage, even if it is only your Profile page. You can attract and maintain fans that will be loyal to you, support you, and tell others about you and your business.

Here are some tips to keep your loyal fans happily engaged with you:

- Listen to your fans. What are they hungry for? What are they responding to? Run a poll. See if some of your posts get more responses than others.

- Create a great customer experience online. For instance, follow up, be energetic, and keep the customer in mind with everything you post.

- It's okay to grow slowly. It's not a race to get the most followers. Think quality over quantity.

- Post relevant links using the Links application.

- Include people on your journey. Changing your office? Share the journey. Writing a book? Share the journey. Heading to a great conference? Share the journey. As I mentioned previously, reality shows are a big hit because people want to see the "real you."

- Create events using Facebook, and choose settings to keep the event open. This allows friends to share the event with their own networks.

- Invite followers to get your newsletters or tell a bit about themselves on your Fan page. Give them reasons to come back.

- When people write on your Wall or when you add them as a friend, treat them like a VIP guest to your business.

- Engage people. This is your outlet to millions of people.

◆ Get creative. Think of new and unique ways you can inspire your followers to participate in online conversations with your business. Invite them to send in videos, offer free webinars, or invite them to post on your blog. Use Facebook to drive them to your other marketing outlets.

◆ Post photos while keeping those in the photos in mind. Don't post embarrassing or goofy photos, because people might not appreciate it. Ask for permission first.

◆ Regularly congratulate people or feature your clients and prospects on your page by commenting on their success or on their status updates. Remember, everyone wants to be recognized. Feature a fan of the week.

◆ Everything you write can be picked up on the search engines tomorrow. Remember my advice about conscious social media marketing? Keep that in mind when posting on the Internet.

◆ If you don't like what someone is posting on your site and you are getting a bad feeling, block them. Go to Settings, then Privacy Settings, then to BlockList. They will not be notified at the time you block them.

Here's another good strategy that a lot of power Facebook users utilize. Go to your Profile page and you will see your friends and their photos listed on the left side. It should look similar to the following screen.

Your Facebook Profile page with the edit box open.

If you click on the **pencil icon** on the right side, you can strategically place your friends' or prospects' photos in that honored spot on the left. You can choose six, nine, or twelve friends to remain there. Otherwise, Facebook will continuously rotate the photos among all of your Facebook friends. Some people choose to feature their top clients or followers in that area. Others simply choose people whom they admire.

What Not to Do

Have you enjoyed reading the Netiquette sidebars throughout this book? People who are successful in social media marketing are people who respect and follow the unwritten rules of what works and what doesn't on social media platforms. Netiquette describes not only what's proper, but also what's improper on the Internet.

So in the tradition of television's *What Not to Wear*, let's cover *what not to do* on social media platforms:

- Refrain from politics and religious rants. Let's expand that a bit: refrain from *all* rants.

- Do not write private messages to people on their Wall. Send them via private e-mail or into their Facebook Inbox. You can access their inbox right under their photo where it reads "Send _____ a message."

- Do not begin selling your products or services as soon as someone adds you as a friend. It's a big turnoff on Facebook when people post their products or services on your wall just as soon as they meet you.

- Don't write when you are angry or have had too much to drink. Ever.

- Do not use the Notes feature to "tag" people who are supposedly referred to in the note when they really aren't mentioned at all. Many people do this thinking it will get their notes read, when in fact it turns people off.

- Don't post photos from the crazy New Year's Eve party that you wouldn't want posted in front of prospective clients. Trust me. They will see it.

- Just as in e-mail, if you write in all caps, it appears as if you are yelling.

- Don't write negatively about the competition or about others in general. People surf around online and you never know who may come across your page or profile.

Video Ideas for Facebook

You can use the Flip Mino video camera by Pure Digital (recommended in Chapter 3) for wonderful videos on Facebook. It has built-in software that allows you to easily download the video and import it directly to Facebook. However, if you have another video camera and you know how to download videos from it, that is fine to use, too.

The great thing about putting videos on Facebook is that they give you the ability to ...

- Post them on your profile and/or Fan page.

- Share with others.

- Embed the video on your website or blog.

> **Did You Know?**
>
> Can you guess how many videos are uploaded each month on Facebook? Ten million videos a month! Isn't that an amazing number? Video is becoming huge on Facebook.

Facebook makes it easy to share your video and make it viral. We get more into videos for social media in future chapters, but while we are examining Facebook, here are some ideas for you to try:

- Are you an expert in your industry? If so, give a 30-second tip each week.

- Having an open house or a holiday celebration with clients? Have the video camera ready and ask people about their thoughts regarding your business.

- Speaking at an event? Get some audience testimonials after your speech.

- Record some of your top clients talking about why they enjoy what they do.

- Take a group of your top clients/prospects to dinner. Ask them to share what they are looking for in their business. Help promote them in your video.

- Are you a Realtor? When you hand clients the keys to their new home, ask them to record their thoughts on video and then share it on your profile page.

- Are you a recruiter? Share interview tips each week. Keep it short and succinct.

- Are you a writer? Share the top takeaways in an article you've published. Include a link where friends can read it online. If it's not online, tell them where they can find it in print.

- Have a new product? Give people a sneak peek when it arrives at your business. Smile as you take it out of the box. Remember, people want to see real situations.

- ◆ Are you a motivational coach? Share your tips of wisdom once a week with a motivational/inspirational message. This allows people to get a feel for who you are.

- ◆ Are you a florist/baker/artist? Share some of your dream creations on video each week or month. Bring the wow factor to your page. People love to "oooh" and "aaah" over great images.

- ◆ Are you an account rep/professional organizer/interior decorator? Share a tip or have a client give a testimonial and then show before and after images.

The list can go on and on. The good news is, again, it doesn't need to be a slick Hollywood production. The more real and relevant the material is to your prospects, the better. Experiment and don't be afraid to show it on Facebook.

Later, I will show you how to take that video and put it online on other sites to drive people to your website, blog, Facebook Fan page, and other social media sites. You just might be on your way to becoming the next social media celebrity.

The Marketplace Application on Facebook

The Marketplace application is a little gem of a find. It's not for everyone necessarily, but it's good for you to know what it can do in case you see a need for it in your marketing efforts.

The Marketplace application is what many are calling the "Craigslist" of Facebook. To find it, go to Applications and search for Marketplace. Then open the application and add it to your profile. Here's an example of what you'll see.

As of this writing, there are nearly three million active monthly users of the Marketplace application. If you are a Realtor, the marketplace application is a great place to post a listing of a home or townhouse for sale or rent. If you are an auto dealer, you can list your cars for sale here. Do you sell or make children's clothes or furniture? Put it on the Marketplace. It's another avenue for you that is free and could, potentially, reach just the right buyer.

It's also useful if you need to hire someone or find a job. Looking to hire an intern? Put your listing in the Facebook jobs on Marketplace. This is a good application for, in particular, Realtors or retail merchants who can sell individual products or solutions. You also might find something you need to buy here. Hint: it's a good place to find furniture for your office.

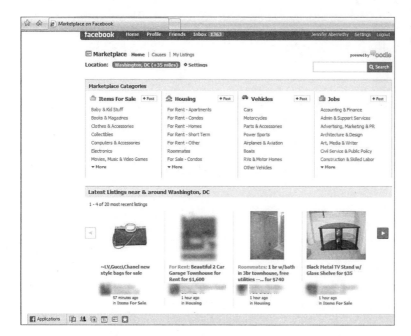

Facebook's Marketplace application.

Savor Chat

This is not a Facebook application that is found on the Application menu, but it integrates directly with the Facebook platform, so it is worth mentioning.

Savor Chat enables you to create and host your own chat room. You can make your chat room public or private, send direct messages to individuals or group members, and invite your Facebook friends. It is perfect for networking and for meetings with Facebook friends who are currently online and those you want to join together in a separate forum for additional discussion.

It also enables you to have live discussions about projects or upcoming events. So it's a tool worth checking out. You can create your own branded virtual chat room and host your own meetings and discussions. Go to www.savorchat.com. You should see this screen first.

You can sign in using Facebook or Twitter and then you can create your own room. You'll see the following screen.

You can name your room, list the times your room is open, place it in a category, and save the room. You can also browse rooms that are currently set up and join in if they are open.

The Home page for the Savor Chat: a Group Chat for Facebook and Twitter.

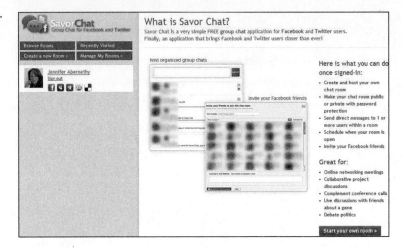

This is where you name your room on Savor Chat.

Get creative with your business on Savor Chat. Perhaps you can host an online monthly meetup, a business break, or a literary luncheon. What would your prospects or customers be interested in discussing? This is another online tool that merges your Facebook friends with a live text chat tool for engagement and interaction.

Facebook Marketing Checklist

You've learned a lot, haven't you? I don't want you to get overwhelmed, so let's take a breather and make up your official Facebook marketing checklist:

❏ Your dynamic headshot. Use one that reflects the best of you and your brand.

❏ Your amazing profile with your website, phone number(s), and a description about what your business can do for people. Make it uniquely your own and say what you need and want to say. This is an advertisement for your business.

❏ Text below your photo. Use this space to drive people to your blog or website, or just have a warm welcome message. Change it up every month or quarter.

❏ A daily status update (What's on your mind?) entry. This is key so that you will maintain energy around your page, you will appear in your friends' news feeds, and you are keeping top-of-mind awareness. Think of it as generating publicity for your brand every time you post. Status update ideas include listing or sharing a tip, letting friends know what you are working on, congratulating a client, announcing a new client partnership, posting a job or open house (if you are a recruiter or Realtor), letting people know about an upcoming event, announcing a new product, sharing news about your business or giving a general business tip, recommending someone to connect with on Facebook, and inviting people to join your group or Fan page.

❏ Add friends and include a personal message. Then put them on one of your lists.

❏ Think about creating a group on Facebook that would further bring together your clients and prospects.

❏ Log on daily for 20 minutes, add friends, and post a greeting on a friend's Wall.

❏ Check your inbox daily for messages. Respond with a note along with your name and website, name and business title, or phrase on what you can do for people.

Example: "Hi John, Thank you for the note. I look forward to your postings on Facebook. If I can do anything to assist you, please do not hesitate to call. Jennifer Abernethy, America's Sales Stylist to Business Professionals, www. thesaleslounge.com."

❏ Go to the Home page and look at upcoming birthdays. Send out a birthday greeting by clicking on the name, and it will take you to their Profile page. Write a greeting on the Wall and sign with your name and website.

❑ Invest in an Internet video camera or flip camera. Create a video marketing strategy on Facebook.

❑ Add the appropriate applications that will help your business.

❑ Use Events as a way to virally grow your brand, whether you host your own event or RSVP to others. Come up with a catchy name for your event. Click the **Share** button and post it to your profile with a quick message. When you RSVP for someone else's event—whether it's a yes, no, or maybe—write on the Wall with your name and website address with a short note. You never know who is going to stumble upon it and visit your site. Get creative and post a video on your Event page.

❑ Post a video RSVP to someone else's events. Go to Applications, search for events, find events that you want to RSVP for, open the page, look for the video section, and click **Upload Video.** It's that easy.

❑ Keep your mind-set positive. You never know where your social media marketing is going to take your business. Stay in it for the long haul.

So now you're practically a Facebook expert. The only thing left is to customize your settings and get everything just the way you want it. In the next chapter, you learn how to do just that.

The Least You Need to Know

◆ Treat your Facebook friends and followers as if they are the top VIPs in your business.

◆ The number-one activity you can do on Facebook to build momentum and keep your fans engaged is to update the What's on your mind? status every day.

◆ Always follow the unwritten netiquette rules when interacting online.

◆ The video revolution has begun, so incorporate it into your social media marketing.

◆ Try different strategies, such as the Marketplace or Savor Chat, to engage your friends and fans.

Part 3

Twitter

In this part, you learn why all the world is Tweeting. Are you scratching your head and wondering what the fuss is about? You don't need to wonder any longer. This part introduces you to Twitter with step-by-step instructions and screen shots.

Not only will you learn how to create an amazing Twitter profile, but you'll also learn why this is a powerful social media tool. You also learn about the do's and don'ts of the Twitter culture, how to write great tweets, and how to attract amazing followers. When you have completed this part, you will be astounded at the newfound power at your fingertips that the Twitter applications offer you. The marketing strategies and recommendations you'll read about will help you build momentum and incorporate new ideas in your social media marketing strategy.

The Networking Cocktail Party of Social Media

In This Chapter

- ◆ The evolving world of Twitter
- ◆ Why you should join Twitter
- ◆ Understanding the language of Twitterers
- ◆ How Twitter can help your business
- ◆ Choosing the right username

It's not surprising that *The New York Times* called Twitter "the fastest-growing phenomena on the Internet." Twitter has quickly become a part of our everyday media and social culture. So how did we get to this point? Twitter began in August 2006 as a micro-blogging site with the sole purpose of answering (in 140 characters or less) this question: What are you doing right now?

In 2006 and 2007, many people were posting items, called "tweets," such as "going to Starbucks," "watching television right now," or "looking forward to buying the new Mac laptop tomorrow." But initially, many users were turned off because there wasn't a clear explanation on the site about how to actually use it.

Since 2007, though, Twitter has become a valuable tool for entrepreneurs, artists, media personalities, reporters, and marketers. In this chapter, you'll learn why Twitter is a terrific way to market your business and services. You'll also learn about building strategic alliances, attracting raving and dedicated fans, the finer points of Twitter culture, and much more.

The Twitter Culture

What used to be a place where you shared what you are doing right now in 140 characters (or less) has turned into a place of sharing tips, tricks, information, motivation, inspiration, and a whole lot of communication. It is a content-rich platform where power Twitterers are wonderful about sharing your name, following you while you promote your business, and potentially, strategically partnering with you.

> **Did You Know?**
>
> By the end of 2010, it is estimated that there will be more than 100 million Twitter users, with an average age of 39.

What do I mean by power Twitterers? They are a very motivated, enthusiastic group who are eager to share, learn, and network. However, they also want to add income to their bottom lines.

You'll find many different types of people using Twitter—coaches, consultants, celebrities, corporate CEOs, artists, nutritionists, speakers, Realtors, recruiters, and entrepreneurs. You'll also find airline companies, restaurant chains, hotels, tourism destinations, and media outlets such as radio, TV, and print.

This is the Twitter.com Login screen.

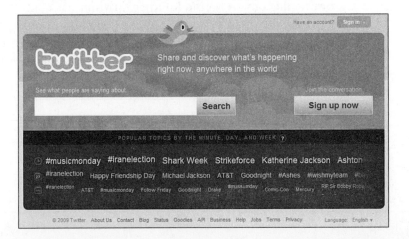

To be successful and keep a loyal following, you must abide by the "unwritten rules" of Twitter culture. I'll touch on these rules throughout the book because they're so important, but in a nutshell, keep these Twitter tips in mind to get loyal followers, network, and grow your business:

- Share information.
- Care about other users.
- Provide value.
- Share your expertise.
- Be welcoming and generous.
- Be authentic.
- Be likeable.
- Do not plagiarize or "Twagiarize".
- Do not spam.
- Have fun with it.

Keep these tips in mind and you'll be on your way to becoming a valuable member of the Twitter community.

Online Cautions

One of the things you do not want to do is to constantly be in "sell" mode. Be interested in others and share your expertise, but don't constantly sell your services, particularly when you first begin using Twitter.

Blocking People on Twitter

Unfortunately, there are spammers on Twitter who have a very disingenuous way of following and attracting folks. What's a spammer? Twitter recently released this list that describes who and what is considered spam:

- Following others to gain attention to your account or links.
- Creating several accounts to promote the same product or links.
- Sending large numbers of @reply messages that aren't really genuine replies. (@reply messages are personal replies to Twitter users; you'll learn more about @replies in the next few pages).
- Creating updates just so they show up in search results.

◆ Disguising links (similar to bait and switch; writing about one thing but linking to another).

◆ Developing a large number of users (relative to those following you) who have blocked you.

If you block someone, you're saying that you don't want them following or contacting you.

How do you block users? You'll find this by clicking on their photo, or *avatar*, in the Followers section on your own profile. On the left side of the page, you'll see an Actions heading. You can click **Block** to keep that person from following you.

def•i•ni•tion

Avatar refers to the "personality" or image connected with the username, or handle, of an Internet user on a social media site such as Twitter. It can also be a computer's representation of one's self or alter ego on 3-D sites like Second Life. An avatar can also be your professional "headshot."

You also have an option to block a user when you receive an e-mail notification that you have a new follower. You'll see a link—block Jane Doe—in the e-mail. If you already know this is a spammer, click the **Block** link and you're free of this pesky follower.

Why You Should Join Twitter

Although Twitter is a social networking site, it has also been called an information site. There is so much great content on Twitter that's being passed around from tweeter to tweeter. Think of it as a giant cocktail party where people share tips, resources, links, videos, and inspirational quotes. If every true "cocktail party" was like that, everyone would want to attend, right? And no one would want to leave. That is the appeal of Twitter.

More often than not, it's not just *what* you know, but *who* you know. Twitter is an amazing resource for all-around networking and getting to know people from all over the world. In one day, you could have a conversation on Twitter with someone from Scotland, California, and Australia. The more people that you know and who know you, the more empowered you become with information, new ways of looking at things, and new ideas. You'll eventually find new champions for your business and even new customers!

Imagine that your competitors are on Twitter and they're experiencing amazing conversations, sharing their expertise, and making a lot of new connections. Wouldn't that make you feel a bit behind? Well, even if they aren't on Twitter today, chances are they will be soon. Here's your chance to be a leader in your industry!

As of this writing, Twitter has already merged into the mainstream television media where reporters on CNN are saying, "Follow me on Twitter." Larry King has a live *Twitter feed* going across the bottom of the screen during the middle of his show. You almost can't go to a conference without finding someone Twittering away from their seat.

In fact, at a technology conference, you're more likely to have conversations on Twitter than you are in person—even if you're both attending the same conference. Does it now seem like the whole world is "a'tweeting"? If it isn't, it may soon be.

def•i•ni•tion

A **Twitter feed**, also referred to as a Twitter stream, is a stream of live Twitter updates scrolling horizontally or vertically on one's TV or computer screen.

Okay, so let's get down to the details. How can Twitter help your business?

Twitter is an amazing tool for the following:

- Using PR strategies for your business

- Marketing your business

- Networking for your business

- Driving traffic to your website

- Getting others to talk about your business

- Attracting and keeping loyal customers

- Asking your followers/customers questions

- Staying informed by reading what people are thinking

Twitter Terms You Need to Know

Twitter has an entirely new language, which has emerged as the short "sound-byte" chatter" within the Twitter culture. If you're new to Twitter, you might feel like you've entered *The Land of the Lost* when reading tweets like this: "Thanks for the RT on #followfriday see u at the Tweetup."

Here's the translation: Thank you for the retweet (sharing my tweet to your network and referencing me) on Follow Friday (the day that tweeters recommend people to follow). See you at the tweetup (also called a meetup—a location that was decided we were to meet through tweets on Twitter).

Netiquette

"Twaigiarizing" is the act of posting someone else's tweet and not giving the original tweeter credit, similar to plagiarizing. So if you do post something that was
written or originated by someone else, give them credit by incorporating their Twitter
username preceded by the @ symbol.

As Twitter folks merge their tweets into other social media sites such as Facebook,
the Facebook "language" is also shifting as people update their Facebook status via
Twitter.

This is the Twitter.com tweet stream.

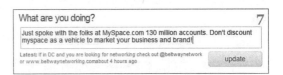

Don't worry; you'll be a savvy Twitterer in no time. To get you on your way, here are
some terms that every Twitterer simply must know:

- **Tweet.** Commonly referred to as a status update or what's on your mind. People
  use this to post links, share thoughts, and give information, all in 140 characters
  or less.

- **Retweet (RT).** An RT is the same as quoting someone on Twitter. Simply use
  RT@(person's username). Example: RT@SalesLounge (then repeat the tweet).
  Some Applications such as TweetDeck (which we discuss later in this chapter)
  allow you to automatically RT with a push of a button. Cool, huh? An RT is the
  forwarding of a message out to your followers, which helps it become more viral.
  The fun part is when people start RT-ing what you write.

Here's a tweet that contains a retweet (RT).

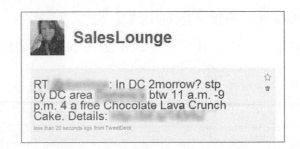

♦ **Hashtags.** This is simply a way to group or "tag" tweets together to be searched for later or followed by others interested in that topic or event. A Hashtag is preceded by the # symbol and is usually made up of an acronym of letters for an event or cause.

This is a tweet using a sample Hashtag.

♦ **Trending Topics.** This describes what the Twitter users are talking about most often. The Trending Topics are always changing depending on what is happening in the news, entertainment, or online worlds. When the news turned to #balloonboy in Colorado back in October 2009, #balloonboy was a trending topic for days.

> **Did You Know?**
>
> Hashtags help to create these Trending Topics. Getting your network to use your tag can help move it to a trending topic.

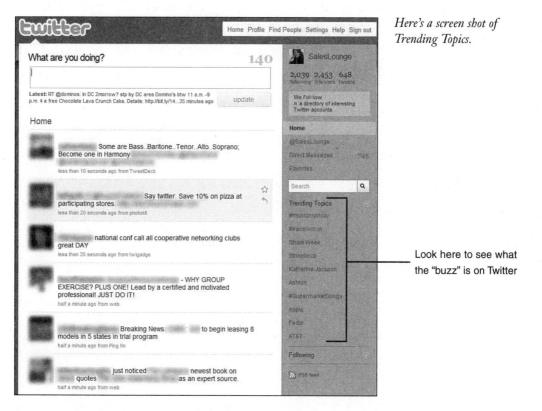

Here's a screen shot of Trending Topics.

Look here to see what the "buzz" is on Twitter

◆ **Followers.** These are the people who are "following" your tweets. These can be your potential friends, advocates, champions, business referrers, strategic partners, customers, and fans.

◆ **Peeps.** Another term in Twitter culture for your followers.

◆ **Updates.** Twitter keeps track of how many times you post a tweet. They are referred to as updates.

◆ **Direct Message(DM).** This is your inbox on Twitter. Someone might send you a Direct Message via Twitter, which is only seen by you and that person, if that person chooses to send it to you privately. A Direct Message can be automated or genuinely typed and sent to you by someone on Twitter. It is good to know, however, that if both parties are not following each other, you cannot DM that person privately. Any messaging would be public until both parties are following each other.

◆ **#FollowFriday.** Each Friday, power Twitterers recommend people to follow by putting the #FollowFriday in front of usernames of folks they want to recommend. #FF is also commonly used.

Example: "Great Peeps for #FollowFriday,@efame,@eddierents @ RuthSherman,@MeredithLiepelt, @BarbaraWayman."

By recommending people to follow, you'll quickly become likeable in the Twitter culture. When someone from another network, city, or even country recommends you on Follow Friday, you know you're doing something right on Twitter. One of your goals should be to eventually be on the #FollowFriday list.

This is an example of a Follow Friday tweet.

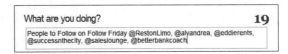

What are you doing?   **19**

People to Follow on Follow Friday @RestonLimo, @alyandrea, @eddierents, @successnthecity, @saleslounge, @betterbankcoach

◆ **Tweetup.** A term a Twitterer uses when she wants to meet in person.

◆ **Tweeting.** This is the act of posting a tweet.

◆ **Tweeps.** Another word for the people who follow you; same as peeps. It often refers, more generally, to the people (or tweeple) who participate on Twitter.

◆ **Twictionary.** An unofficial listing of Twitter terms. Find it at www.twictionary. com.

How Twitter Helps Your Business

When initially viewing the Twitter landscape, many entrepreneurs and business own-ers just cannot imagine how typing in 140 character comments on a site can help their businesses. So if that's how you feel, you're not alone. My best advice is to look at this as a free networking and PR avenue for your business.

If your ongoing tweets make use of the Twitter tips that we've already talked about, you'll begin attracting new followers and then some of their followers will start to fol-low you. There's a natural progression that occurs after you get those first followers.

Here's what usually happens next: after someone recommends you to his or her net-work, you will get even more followers. Your new followers simply tell their network how great your services or products are. Next, the tweeps in your new follower's net-work decide to check out your website. At that point, there's a good chance you'll land a new client or at least develop a solid prospect. All this takes time, of course.

Why don't you try this goal? Get five new people (tweeps) to follow you during your first week on Twitter. (Hey, that's five more than you had last week!) In the second week, you shoot for five more; then in the third week, you shoot for 10 more, then 20 more, and so on. All you need to focus on are a few tweeps at a time.

Okay, let's get into the nitty-gritty about how Twitter can help your business.

Creating a Tech-Savvy Image

In today's business world, you can't afford to look like a dinosaur. You want to be seen as an on-trend and in-the-know entrepreneur. In fact, some say if you aren't using Twitter, your business savvy might appear suspect to others. Conversely, after you're on Twitter, you'll look like a savvy techie (even if you aren't). You will be marketing yourself and your business while networking with the tech-savvy in crowd of tens of millions.

Communicating Information About Your Business

Twitter also helps you quickly send information out to your followers. Let's say you're speaking at an event, holding an open house, running a big special, or announcing a new client partnership. Or maybe you're closing your business early on Tuesday for some reason. Now you can send that message out with a few simple keystrokes and—voilà!—you're done.

Building Your List

Another Twitter benefit is that it can help you build your list. In the past years, the list referred to your mailing list. Today, it refers to your e-mail list, but you can also gather office and home addresses as well. To the small business owner or entrepreneur, your list is your gold mine. You want to build a list with which you can regularly communicate with folks outside of Twitter and other social media platforms.

How does Twitter help you do this? By driving people to your website, where you invite them to sign up for your e-zine or newsletter. You'll learn what you need to know about e-zines and newsletters in Chapter 20.

Networking with Colleagues, Clients, and Prospects

Twitter is also a great place to build rapport with folks you've been networking with. Let's say you meet someone at a networking event. Find out if he or she is on Twitter. If so, tell him or her you'll become a follower. More than likely, people will follow you back and you'll begin building a rapport. You'll share your expertise, tips, and information with each other. This approach also builds credibility and, hopefully, likeability, which certainly helps every business owner.

More Ways Twitter Helps Your Business

You're a busy professional who wants to ensure that your social media choices give you a lot of bang for your buck. To help you decide if Twitter is for you, here are a few more quick tips suggesting ways to use Twitter:

◆ Use Twitter as a PR tool to promote your business as a great place to work or to do business with. Tweet something good about your employees or clients. This will give you not only happy employees and clients, but it just makes you look (and feel) good!

◆ Share interesting links or information about your industry to position yourself as a subject matter expert. Let's say you run ABC Catering. Instead of only tweeting about ABC, tweet about an article you've read that covers new trends in wedding cakes. This approach also shows you're willing to be a "sharing resource," which will ultimately expand your business reach.

◆ Create a sense of community around your business. Commenting on fellow entrepreneurs, business owners, clients, and followers will make them feel more attached to you and your business. We've talked about how networking can bring you new business and help you retain your clients. But if your tweets show genuine interest in others, this engenders a neighborhood feel.

◆ Create top-of-mind awareness for your brand. By tweeting each day, you will keep your name and business in front of people. When genuinely used, a daily tweet or two can be an incredible source of PR, marketing, and branding for you and your services. Companies pay a lot of money for advertising. Remember, Twitter is a free way to get some advertising for your brand or company name.

◆ Learn what your community, customers, and market are looking for. When you read and have dialogue on Twitter, you'll know what your followers want and what they have to say. You'll learn things that will help you make decisions about the direction of your business.

◆ Invite your current clients and prospects to follow you on Twitter. They'll learn from you and you can follow them back, which will ultimately make you, your clients, and your prospects feel more connected.

> **Online Cautions**
>
> The Twitter culture does not like negativity. You can share your point of view, but refrain from name calling or pointing fingers.

What's in a Username?

Before creating your Twitter account, think about your Twitter username. Your username on Twitter is your handle or your call name. It's the word that will be placed directly below or next to your photo, or avatar. It can also be an instrumental part of your branding strategy.

In fact, a great Twitter username will be part of all of your marketing. It will go on your business cards, your e-mail signature, your Facebook and LinkedIn pages, and your blog. So think carefully about it. Oh, one more thing—you have only 15 characters for your username.

This requires thinking a little differently from what you're used to. When we all first got into computing, our usernames weren't made public. We wrote them down and filed them away. Well, with Twitter, it's very different. Your username on Twitter is very public.

So as you begin thinking about your strategy and why you want to use Twitter, carefully plan your Twitter username to attract your target audience. There are also many ways your chosen username can help you reach out to the people you want to follow you.

As you get more savvy on Twitter, which will happen faster than you can imagine, you'll learn that one way to find people is to type in an industry within the Find People tab on Twitter.com.

Here's an example: Say you want to find someone in sales or a sales expert. Well, if you type in the word "sales," using Find People, anyone with the word "sales" in their username will pop up. Most people who use "sales" in their username have something to do with sales. The same is true with the word "realtor" or "financial." So your username could include the name of your industry.

Another way to find people is to search by their business name or actual name. Many people use their business name for their username. When setting up your account, it's important to include your actual name so that people can find your Twitter profile.

Try This _____

A fun way to create a great Twitter username? Gather a group of friends and associates and brainstorm. Tell them you are creating your Twitter username to align with your profession or your passion. Share your ideas and ask for theirs. Then gauge your friends' reactions to the various suggestions. (Remember, the maximum number of characters you can use to create your handle is 15.)

After you get a good name that draws a good reaction, claim it! You'll be amazed at how effective this brainstorming approach is and at how quickly you'll discover a great name to use on Twitter.

You might want to brand your own name, such as @JohnDoe. That's fine, too. Or you may want to use the name of your business as your username. That's also fine.

In the next three chapters, you'll learn about applications that will help you manage Twitter. Applications such as TweetDeck and TweetLater make Twitter easy to keep up with. What's my handle? I invite you to follow me @SalesLounge.

The Least You Need to Know

◆ Even if you don't immediately understand how it will ultimately help your business, get on Twitter and become involved in the conversations.

◆ Don't be in constant sell mode, because the Twitter culture hates spammers.

◆ On Twitter, you need to relate to others, share information, help others, be yourself, and reflect a positive image of your business.

- Participate in #FollowFriday, which involves recommending people (or peeps) to follow.

- Retweet someone when you can to show that you're part of a community, that you don't always have to take credit for everything, and that you're willing to give the spotlight to someone else.

- Think about your overall Twitter marketing and branding strategy when you select your username and photo or avatar.

Chapter 9

Creating a Twitter Profile

In This Chapter

- ◆ Your Twitter profile
- ◆ How to find people and follow them
- ◆ What's a tweet?
- ◆ Direct Messages, @Replies, and Trending Topics
- ◆ To follow or not to follow everyone?
- ◆ Applications to help your Twitter mobile experience

Remember what I said about first impressions? Well, they count on Twitter as well. From your engaging photograph to a nice short bio with a website link, creating an amazing Twitter profile will only add to your marketability in the culture of Twitterers.

Let's get your profile ready and get you meeting and tweeting like a pro. By the end of this chapter, you'll love how easy it can be to be a savvy social media marketer on Twitter.

Setting Up Your Twitter Profile

Let's get you started on Twitter. First, go to www.twitter.com, and you will see a page that looks like the following screen.

*Click **Sign up now** to get started on Twitter.*

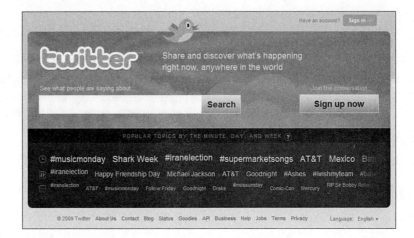

Welcome to Twitter. It looks pretty basic, but inside is a happening social experience that you'll be glad you're a part of. Click on the green box that reads **Sign up now.** The next page you come to looks like the following figure and is important.

Here's where you sign up to participate on Twitter.

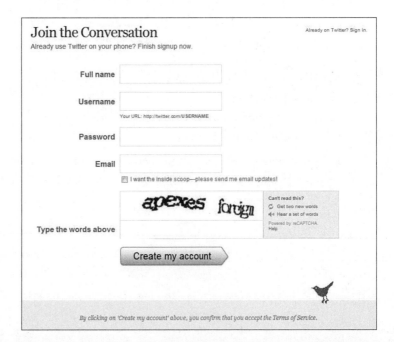

1. First, enter your business name or personal name for Full Name. Ensure you spell it correctly.

2. Tab to the next section that reads Username. Remember a good username is important because it will be your call name or handle. The Twitter world will come to know you by this name. Enter your username, using up to 15 letter characters with no spaces.

3. Now, enter your password and e-mail address. You'll be referring to this password and e-mail address in the future when we merge Twitter with Facebook, so be sure you write it down.

4. Go ahead and check that you want e-mail updates. They don't seem to send them that often, which is a good thing.

5. Type in the security words that you see on the page (using capital letters and spacing as appropriate). If you cannot read the security words, click **Get two new words** or **Hear a set of words.**

6. When finished, click **Create my account.** You should see the following figure.

Online Cautions

If there is a username that really carries your brand, then grab it quickly. With so many joining Twitter each month, the most common surnames are going quickly. While you can always change your username, it's good to think about long-term identity and branding when you are initially creating your username.

You can skip this step and find your friends after you finish your profile.

Find people. Follow them.

You can invite folks by sending them an email. See what you'll send them.

Enter some email addresses:

Separate multiple email addresses with commas, ex: joe@twitter.com,jane@twitter.com

Invite

Skip this step

7. As a new user, I suggest you click **Skip this step** (at the bottom). You can always go back and add your friends. For now, we want to get your account set up. Next, you should see the following figure.

If you want to follow celebrities, figureheads, and popular publications, here's where you can find them.

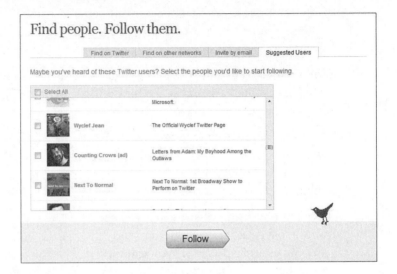

8. Twitter gives you a varied list of celebrities, figureheads, and popular publications to follow initially. Go ahead and pick a few (or all of them), just to get you started with a few folks to follow. You can always, however, skip this step or stop following them later if you don't like what they are tweeting or simply don't want to follow them any longer.

9. Click **Follow** and you land on the following page.

10. For fun, type in something that is less than 140 characters (characters are letters, numbers, symbols, and spaces). Now click **Update.** You just sent your first tweet. That was easy, but there is a lot left to do so let's keep moving.

11. Now click **Settings** (at the top right). Next, you arrive at the Settings page, which looks like the following figure.

This page is also important because you want your Twitter Information page to look professional to attract and maintain followers.

1. First, select your time zone.

2. Next, put in your URL (or business website). Note: make sure you put "http://" in front of the "www" so it will be a live link to your website.

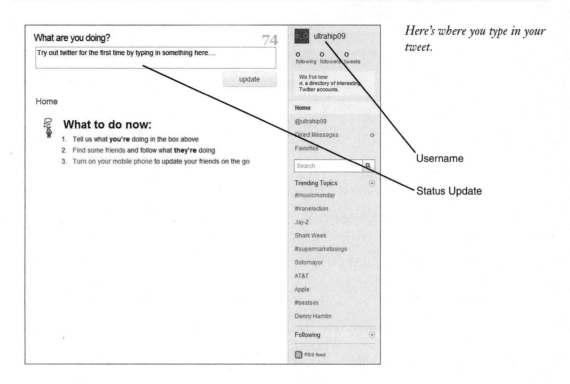

Here's where you type in your tweet.

Username

Status Update

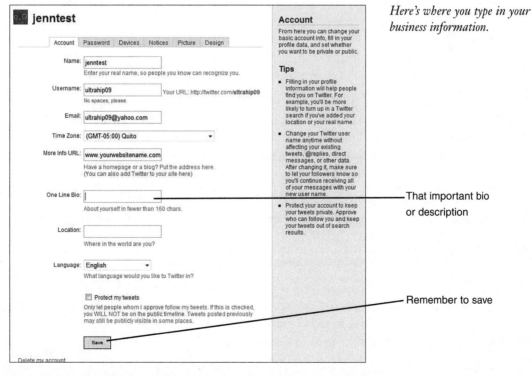

Here's where you type in your business information.

That important bio
or description

Remember to save

3. Next is an important step—enter a one-line description of you, the business, or the group that is being represented. You can use a series of one-word adjectives in this area as well.

Here are some examples of what others have put in this line:

◆ America's First Sales Stylist to Entrepreneurs & Business Owners. Helping Them Grow Their Biz!

◆ Human Servant, Promoter, Personal Brand Evangelist, Speaker, Author, Serial Optimist, TrueBeliever, and HopeDealer!

◆ Technology Speaker, Geeky Girl host of http://GettinGeeky.com Chief Hooligan @Synapse3Di_

◆ CEO of largest limo/bus company in DC with lots of interesting back seat stories

◆ The Coolest Motivational Speakers Ever. Identical Twins, Unique Perspective.

Next, you enter your location. You can put your town and state, state only, or just your country. Some people put their cell phone number here or something interesting like "wherever you would like me to be."

At the bottom of this page, you are asked to check a box to protect your updates. This means you don't want just anyone seeing your tweets. As a marketer, though, this is PR for your business, so my recommendation is not to check that box (for now anyway). Once you enter your information, click **Save.** Congratulations! You are beginning to look like a real pro! After you click **Save,** on the Settings tab, click **Picture.** You should see the following.

You need to have a photo or logo in this box versus the blue bird avatar that is automatically provided. This way you will appear as a legitimate Twitterer. Browse through your computer to upload your photograph or logo. Then click **Save** and follow these steps:

1. Go to the Settings tab and click on **Design.** You can change the colors of your background for your Twitter profile. (We will get into custom Twitter backgrounds later.) Next, click **Save.**

2. Now click **Profile** and take a look at the right corner.

3. Congratulations! You now have a great-looking Twitter profile. For fun, click **Home** and type in another tweet. Say, perhaps, "I'm just learning how to Twitter … any advice?" Note: by now Twitter has most likely sent you a confirmation e-mail, so check your e-mail inbox.

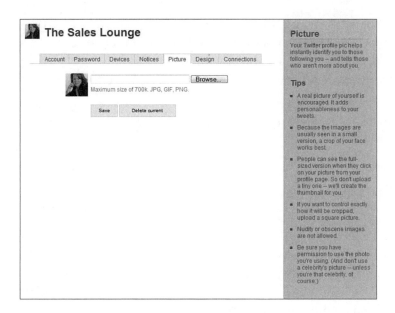

Here's where you upload your photo or your business logo.

Finding People on Twitter

You already have a few people you are following from the initial list that Twitter provided to you when you created your account. How do you find and follow other people? The easiest way initially is to sign in to your Twitter account and click **Find People.** Here's what you'll see:

Here's where you start looking for people on Twitter.

Now click **Find on Twitter.** Do you see where it asks who you are looking for? Type someone's name. If that person has a username that's different from their real name, their name will pop up as long as they have listed their real name when they created their account. Here are several additional ways to search for people using this Search page:

◆ Type in their last name with no spaces in between first and last name, or try the last name only.

◆ Type in their industry, such as dental, sales, or real estate.

◆ Type in their company name.

◆ To follow major publications or TV networks, type in New York Times, USA Today, CNN, BBC, or whatever you're looking for.

When the search results pop up, click the avatar or person's photo to check them out, read their bio, and then decide to follow or not. The system isn't perfect, so don't be discouraged if you can't find the person you are seeking. There are still other ways.

Another way to search for a topic or person is to go to www.search.twitter.com and type in the person, place, or subject you are looking for. For example, want to find out if someone is tweeting about the Hamptons? Type "The Hamptons." This search will find the keyword you are looking for within the tweet itself. Try typing in "PT Cruiser." All tweets will pop up that mention the words PT and/or Cruiser.

Check your industry. You can then decide whether or not to follow those people whose tweets pop up on screen. Remember the #followfriday that was mentioned in the previous chapter? Stay on www.search.twitter.com and type in #followfriday and see the names that populate the screen. Here's a fun one: stay on www.search.twitter.com and click **Advanced Search.** The Advanced Search page will appear.

If you are interested in locating people who are tweeting near your location or another worldwide location, you can do a search on that. Or type in "Airline Deals" in the first line and you will see tweets based on that subject (and most likely either find some great deals or find companies to follow that regularly publish great deals). I hope you can now see why they call Twitter a great informational tool, because there is so much information at your fingertips. We will get into more ways to find people as you continue to learn about more advanced applications.

Did You Know?

You can find the most popular tweeters at http://twitterholic.com.

What's a Tweet?

Now that you have the basics set up on your Twitter Profile page, let's review the types of tweets you should be thinking about. At first, you should just get a conversation going. Ask a question, offer a tip, and share your expertise while you are gaining followers. As you get more comfortable typing in the 140 character format and having your tweets become the your company's voice on Twitter, you'll need to start taking your tweets to the next level.

First, you want to think about strategic tweets that people would love to retweet (RT) to their network. What would people like to share? Again, it doesn't matter if you're an interior decorator, recruiter, coach, plumber, tailor, writer, speaker, consultant, or accountant; anyone can write a tweet that is helpful to others. The goal here is to be retweeted around the Twitter network. When someone retweets you, it gives you credibility and tells you that you are writing something that is valuable. It might take several months before you are retweeted, but when you get your first one by someone somewhere else in the world, it can be rather exciting.

As mentioned in the previous chapter, another type of tweet you can do is to retweet someone else, particularly early on but also as you become more experienced. This does two things: it helps you fit into the Twitter culture and it spreads goodwill. You are sharing that person's Twitter handle and thoughts with your network, which is a good thing. Tweets you will see often are motivational or inspirational quotes. These are fine and well meaning, but these types of tweets are starting to lose popularity with the power Twitter crowd as of this writing. An occasional quote is fine, but as a best practice don't consistently tweet motivational, historical, or inspirational quotes. People want to read your thoughts, your insight, and your expertise, and by doing these types of tweets, your popularity will increase rapidly.

Another type of tweet that's common involves providing links. Again, these are good, but think strategically if this is all you want to provide. Ideally, it's nice to mix it up a bit with links, personal commentary, tips, advice, retweets, and, of course, recommendations for #followfriday. The most popular mainstream tweeters combine information and entertainment. Therefore, they're providing infotainment to their followers.

Deciding When to Tweet

There is no correct answer to this, but because you're a beginner, it's good practice to Tweet once first thing in the morning before 9 A.M. Tweet again around noon, and then again in the evening. Now, of course, if you are hosting an event or attending an event and want to tweet throughout the day to report what's happening at the event, that is an acceptable practice. Some people seem to tweet literally all the time. Some do this by automating the tweets, others just love to tweet. There is no right or wrong, just try not to overtweet. Many find this annoying, particularly if you are in constant selling mode and not relating to others. Do what works best for you. However, at the very least, tweet one time per day or, if you can, once in the morning and once at the day's end. And always remember to respond to others.

An interesting project to do after you have been tweeting for a little while is to go into your web hosting site and look at the AWSTATS. Look at where people are coming from to get to your site. Look at the days of the week and the times. See if there is a correlation with your tweets. If you do not know how to do this, ask your web master. If you do not have a web master, ask the hosting company that is hosting your website if they have a dashboard or panel you have access to, in order to see how folks are finding your website.

Try This _____

For several weeks, try tweeting at different times of the day. See if you notice a difference in direct messages, retweets, or visits to your website. Ask a question and see if you get answers or if the participation is higher at certain times of the day. Wait until you get at least a hundred followers, however, to test this out. The more followers you have, the easier it is to measure your results.

Direct Messages, @Replies, and Trending Topics

As you become more engaged with the Twitter community, you will begin to get Direct Messages from your followers. It is important to note that if someone is following you and you are *not* following them, they cannot send you a Direct Message. On your Twitter profile, go to the Home page, and then click on the right sidebar to see Direct Messages. Click on **Direct Messages** to see your messages.

In the next chapter, you learn about TweetDeck.com—a platform that makes it even easier to see your Direct Messages. However, for now you need to know where this information is on Twitter. You also want to check it daily. Put your cursor on the right side of the Direct Message and an arrow and a trash container will appear. The arrow is to send that person a direct reply and the trash container is to delete the message. You can also go to the top of the screen where it reads "Send _____ a direct message." When you click on the drop-down box, a list of your followers' usernames will appear so you can choose who to send a private Direct Message.

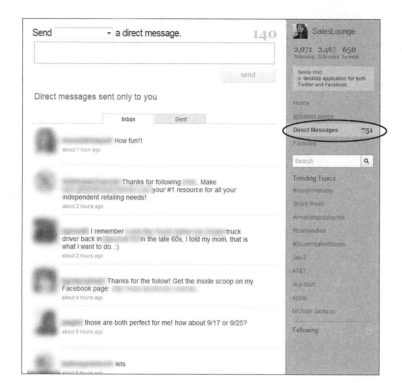

Here's the Direct Messages page in Twitter.

On this same page, you will see Trending Topics. These are the topics that are most commonly discussed at that moment on Twitter. For some companies, conferences, or marketing directors, they regularly will try to get their "topic" to be a Trending Topic on Twitter. That simply means a lot of people are talking about their particular topic, which is giving them a lot of PR and marketing for their brand.

Inviting People to Follow You

Now that you're becoming a savvy social media marketer, one of the ways to grow your following is to put your Twitter handle or username everywhere you communicate. Put it on your business card, your e-mail signature, your website ("follow me/us on Twitter"), your letterhead, and your other social media platforms, such as Facebook and LinkedIn.

As you get into video, mention your Twitter name there, too. When you do a PowerPoint presentation or speech, open and end your talk with, "Follow me on Twitter." If you write an article, always end your byline with "Follow me on Twitter @_____." By marketing your Twitter name, tweeting some great stuff (remember infotainment), getting recommended on #followfriday, and by people retweeting you, you will get many new followers.

To Follow or Not to Follow?

One of the debates among tweeters is: should I follow everyone who follows me? Or should I only follow people I want to follow? This debate still goes on, but here are some thoughts that might help you with your decision. If you follow everyone that follows you, the benefits are ...

- ◆ You can send each other private Direct Messages.

- ◆ The person whom you are following feels good that you are following them and this generates goodwill.

- ◆ You never know when/if this person could become a strategic alliance in your business, a client, and/or a referral source.

Some tweeters feel that if someone is taking time to follow them, then they could at least give them the same courtesy and follow that person back. People who fall on this side of the debate usually have close to the same number of followers as they are following.

On the other side of the debate are those who do not want to follow everyone who's following them. This rings true for many celebrities or high-profile individuals or businesses. You'll see many that have tens of thousands of followers, yet are only following 10 people. Then you have the non–high-profile people but active Twitterers who have a lot of followers, but their ratio of followers to those they follow is lower. For example, they may have 5,400 followers and are only following 900. These are people who either don't have time to go in and follow everyone (there are auto-follow tools that we will discuss later) or they have decided to follow only those they want to follow.

I fall somewhere in the middle. However, I quickly unfollow people who are spammers (always selling) and I don't follow people who appear to be (I'll be polite) less than professional. I mention this now because there are tools that allow you to highlight your favorite tweeters and group them by category. This makes it easier to follow larger numbers of people. You'll learn about that in Chapter 10. What's the bottom line? Do what is most comfortable for you. This is your business and you are marketing it, and you might want as many people to know about you and your services as possible. A best practice, however, is not to automatically follow everyone, but check out their profile first. There are many spammers and porn industry sites on Twitter and you don't want to follow them and appear on their Twitter page as one of their followers. If this happens accidentally, remember you can always block them, too.

Twittering via Mobile Service or BlackBerry

When you sign up for Twitter, you will get an initial e-mail that asks you if you want to activate your phone. If you want to tweet via your phone, go ahead and do this. You'll then see the following.

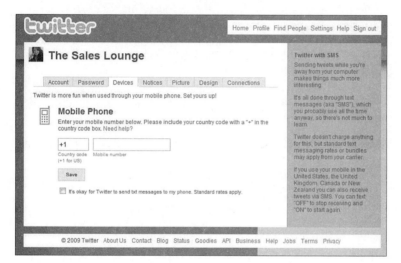

Here's where you enter your mobile phone information in Twitter.

Enter your mobile number and click **Save.** Note that Twitter doesn't charge for this, but your carrier's standard text messaging rates usually apply. Then select the box that reads, "It's okay for Twitter to send text messages to my phone." Then click **Save,** and Twitter will supply you with a code to enter via your mobile device. They will then send you a verified message. After your mobile phone account is verified, your Devices tab contents will look a tad different.

While the focus in this book is on social media marketing and not necessarily everything mobile, it is understood that this is an important way to communicate for many people. At this writing, one of the best third-party applications you can get to support your Twitter experience from your mobile phone device, such as a BlackBerry, is to get the TwitterBerry application www.orangatame.com/ota/twitterberry/.

> **Did You Know?**
>
> Facebook is currently more popular with mobile users than MySpace, Twitter, and Bebo combined, according to the company's findings. (Source: CCS Insight, Press Release, 7/2009)

It allows you to view your tweets and Direct Messages in a better format for your phone viewer screen. There is another good program called www.tinytwitter.com, especially good for small screens. If you use an iPhone, there are many applications I can recommend here. Google Twitter for the iPhone and you can find a list. One of the original applications, however, can be found at http://www.stone.com/Twittelator.

There are many other applications and devices to make your mobile Twitter experience better. You can Google mobile twitter devices and see the many websites and discussion boards. Also, ask your friends or new Twitter friends what they use. Coming up, we discuss all types of Twitter applications that will enhance your Twitter social media marketing from your PC or laptop.

The Least You Need to Know

◆ When creating a Twitter profile, your username and your bio box description are important parts of your marketing efforts on Twitter.

◆ Finding a specific person on Twitter can be a challenge, but there are options for advanced searches.

◆ Think strategically about your tweets and make them easy to retweet, engaging, and a good mix of information and entertaining commentary.

◆ Deciding whom to follow back is a personal decision.

◆ Twitter works with mobile phones, so you can tweet via your iPhone, BlackBerry, or other mobile device.

Chapter 10

Great Marketing Applications for Twitter

In This Chapter

- Ways to manage and leverage your Twitter experience
- The Basics of TweetDeck
- Learn how to upload photos and video on Twitter
- Automating tweets and followers by using SocialOomph

Your Twitter experience can be made exponentially better by utilizing some terrific applications. These applications can help you network more effectively, organize tweets, and get creative with your Twitter social media marketing strategy.

In this chapter, you'll also learn about applications that make using photos and videos a snap. Okay, so let's get started. First, we talk about how to manage all those followers you have.

Managing Your Twitter Experience

When one begins using the www.twitter.com platform, the entire universe and power of the Twitter experience isn't fully exposed. Yes, you get streaming updates from all the participants you are following, you have the ability to see direct messages, and you can see trending topics. However, this is just a small fraction of what is going on in the Twitter landscape. Some questions you might consider are:

♦ Who else is using Twitter?

♦ Where can I find more people to follow in various industries?

♦ Where can I find people in my industry?

♦ What are consumers talking about as they relate to my industry?

♦ There are certain industry leaders I want to follow, but I can't seem to find them. Is there an easier way?

Let me pull back the Twitter curtain and show you what Twitter has to offer you and your business.

The Basics of TweetDeck

TweetDeck is a fabulous tool to add to your social media marketing business arsenal. TweetDeck is constantly upgrading their site, so your version may look slightly different from the one featured here. However, this should give you an idea of how the site works. There are many great things about TweetDeck, but let me try to narrow it down to five:

♦ It's a time saver. You can view and manage all your inbound tweets and easily read all your favorite "peeps" and Direct Messages in one place. It pulls these specific tweets out of the fast-moving river and places them into a column for you to read when you are ready.

♦ You can categorize your incoming tweets as well as tweets of those you aren't following by industry, subject matter, or any keyword.

♦ You can easily send a Direct Message to someone or retweet someone's update from the TweetDeck platform with a press of a button.

♦ You can easily arrange it so that if anyone tweets about you or your company, the tweet is automatically sent to you (it is pulled into your Mentions column), whether you are following the writer or not.

◆ You will feel informed and a part of the discussion, and you can learn by what and how others are tweeting.

So let's get you set up on TweetDeck. Go to www.tweetdeck.com and download the application. The software is free. You'll be asked for your Twitter username and password. When you get in, you will see four columns: All Friends, Mentions, Direct Messages, and TweetDeck Recommends.

This is what you see on TweetDeck.

Following is a description of what you should see.

◆ **All Friends.** You will see tweets from your friends who you are following.

◆ **Mentions.** If anyone mentions your twitter handle in a tweet, such as replying to a tweet you send out or just referring to you in a tweet, it will show up in this column.

◆ **Direct Messages.** If someone sends you a private Direct Message, it will show up here. Additionally, each time you send a Direct Message, it is listed here. Note, if you choose to set up an automated or auto message to any new follower, that message will show up in this column.

◆ **TweetDeck Recommends.** This column lists people TweetDeck suggests you follow.

Pretty cool, huh? Now you can see all your friends' tweets. Remember, anyone you are following is a "friend."

Symbols on TweetDeck

At the bottom of each column are some symbols or icons. *Again, be aware that new ones show up often because the TweetDeck staff is continuously adding new symbols and functionality.*

Look at the row of symbols at the bottom of each column.

There is an arrow symbol on each column. By pressing this, you can change the order and move your columns from left to right and put them in the order you prefer. You can always change it as you add more columns to TweetDeck (we will look at that shortly). The next symbol at the bottom of most columns is a *cloud* icon. This shows you the most popular topic or username in each column.

def•i•ni•tion

A Twitter **cloud** is a cluster of single words or a (visual) written description of words that you have tweeted most often.

To generate a Twitter or word cloud for your website or your blog, take a look at www.wordle.net. Here is an example of a word cloud.

The next symbol, which has a downward arrow in the middle of it, is used to filter out a column. Say you have a column on a specific topic (you learn how to create a custom column in a minute). You want to click the filter icon. And now let's say you just want to see recent tweets on Twitter. Take a look at the following screen.

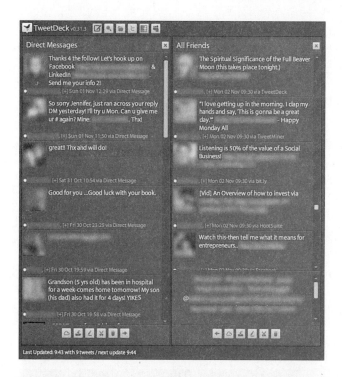

This is an example of a tag or word cloud.

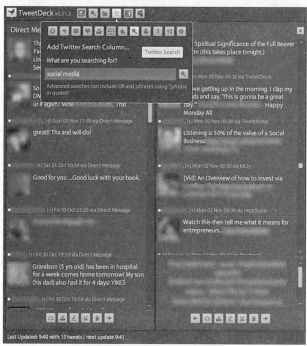

TweetDeck with a social media column.

The second column is social media. Now look at the bottom where the column is filtered with the word "Twitter." You can also include or exclude words via your search by clicking on the **+** sign next to the Search box in your filter search. As your Twitter presence expands, this is a great feature on TweetDeck to know about. You can use this as an industry research tool to help your business.

Okay, now the next symbol, which looks like a pen, is used to mark your tweets. This is a bit hard to see, but just before the list of all the usernames in your column (just below the photo), there is a white dot. When you hover your cursor over it, you'll see "Mark tweet as seen." Click it and the white dot will disappear.

Try This _____

You can delete any column by clicking on the **X** in the upper right corner of the column. Try it, then click on the search magnifying glass and create your own custom column.

The next symbol is a pair of scissors, which will clear your "seen" tweets from the column. The next symbol is the trash can, which allows you to delete all the tweets in that column.

Now let's go over the symbols across the top of your TweetDeck application. Again, please know TweetDeck is always evolving and your version may be different from what is here.

Take a look at the symbols at the top of TweetDeck.

The following list looks at each one so you are knowledgeable about where to find them:

  ◆ **The first symbol looks like a dialogue bubble.** This is where you type your tweet directly into TweetDeck. It is like typing directly on Twitter, so click on it and it will take you to "What are you doing?" You can enter in your 140-character-or-less tweet. To send, simply hit Enter on your keyboard.

- **The next symbol is a magnifying glass.** Click on it. This is where you can type in names, industries, and keywords, then you can create columns based on that. Type in "newspaper" for example. Hit Enter. Watch a column pop up with every tweet in the world that mentions the word "newspaper" within it.

- **The next symbol looks like a file folder.** This launches the TweetDeck directory where you can search for people and tweets by subject.

- **The next symbol opens up the Twitter column that leads you to 12 sub-directories.** While they all aren't covered here, there are a few that I think you should know about. The previously mentioned magnifying glass is a great search tool. The next symbol I like in the twitter column is 12. That's 12seconds.tv. You can create a 12-second video tweet and upload it to Twitter. Just click on **12** and follow the simple directions. The last one is the envelope. You can send Direct Messages to people by clicking on it. Go through each of the symbols under the Twitter column. Most are self explanatory. Have fun … you can't make a mistake.

- **The next symbol is the Facebook icon.** Click on this symbol to enable your tweets to go to Facebook at the same time. They will be incorporated into your Facebook status update.

- **The next symbol is the MySpace icon.** Click on this symbol to enable your tweets to go to your MySpace page.

Refresh, Single Column, Tools, and Settings

In the upper right corner of TweetDeck, you'll see more symbols. The first are two arrows. This refreshes your Twitter screen. Sometimes you may not be sure if your TweetDeck page is updated. If not, just click on **refresh**. The next symbol, which looks like a "1," allows you to have a single-column view of TweetDeck open on your screen.

Online Cautions

Did you know that TweetDeck enables 150 actions per hour on its site? If you go above that, you will not be able to use TweetDeck for a certain period of time. Twitter did this to try to deter spammers. So consider yourself forewarned: Don't overutilize it in one sitting. Look in the upper-right corner of TweetDeck for the number of actions you have left. It reads: Remaining API.

The wrench symbol is important to your Twitter experience. It is where you can further customize your TweetDeck settings. By now, if you are new to TweetDeck, you've probably been hearing a sound, which is supposed to be a loud chirp—but many say it sounds like a submarine! When you open the Settings, you can turn off that sound by unchecking the box next to "Play notification sound."

Now go through and customize your TweetDeck experience further by clicking on the other tabs across the top. You can change the colors of your text and the font, you can adjust the times that your columns are updating within the Twitter API tab, and you can add other Twitter accounts if you like in the Account section. Go through each of these and set up what works best for you.

Here, you can change your
TweetDeck settings.

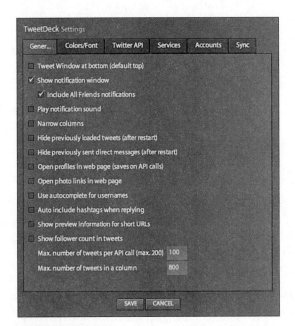

Customizing Your TweetDeck

Now that you know where the basics are on TweetDeck, you can make your TweetDeck platform work for your business. Here are some questions to ask yourself:

- ◆ Who do you want to follow? Search for and follow them. When you have the folks you want to follow, create a group for them (or a special column) and their tweets will be grouped together. You can always add more people to the group.

◆ Based on your industry, what types of people do you need to follow? Create a column or columns around your industry. Are you a motivational coach? Type in "motivation coaches" by using the Search tab. Are you a nutritionist? Type in "nutrition." An IT recruiter? Start a column for those tweets. Narrow down the industries until you get the types of tweets that you want to see in one column. You will want to have multiple columns to make this work best for you.

◆ Perhaps you want to create a column just for news or media, such as *The New York Times, USA Today*, and so on.

Okay, so that is TweetDeck 101. Now you are beginning to take your Twitter experience to the next level.

Third-Party Applications That Work with Twitter

There are other applications from TweetDeck that can help your experience, and one is called Seesmic (www.seesmic.com). Here's what it looks like.

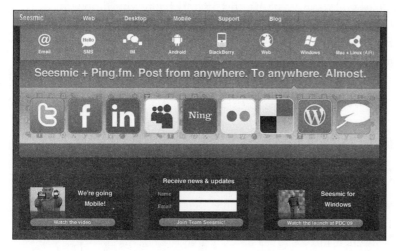

What Seesmic looks like.

Seesmic is similar to TweetDeck in that it organizes your tweets in columns or in single rows by tweets. Some people prefer Seesmic, but others have said it's a little trickier to use than TweetDeck. As of this writing, Seesmic just launched a web-based platform (www.seesmic.com/web). Again, it's similar to TweetDeck, although it does allow you to display single-line tweets. Video posts are popular with Seesmic. Figuring it out can be a bit confusing initially, but there are many loyal followers.

Another popular program is Twhirl (www.twhirl.org). Twhirl runs on Windows 2000, Windows XP and Vista, and Mac OSX. It also shortens URLs and displays your new messages—the screen is just smaller. You can post images, search tweets, and use spell check. It automatically finds posts that are mentioning your name or business name. Twhirl is also a popular application for viewing and managing tweets.

Photos and Videos on Twitter

What started out as a place to do a quick microblog or a 140-character tweet has now found new and innovative ways to keep readers engaged. One way is by posting photos and video. Remember infotainment? People like pictures because seeing is believing. And the new audience on social media is loving video. What better way to marry the two than by utilizing all three methods together on Twitter?

Photos: TwitPic and Yfrog

There are several ways to get photos on Twitter, and one is by using TwitPic (www.twitpic.com), which enables you to share photos on Twitter from your mobile device or computer. It's free and easy to use. Yfrog (www.yfrog.com) is also easy to use. Just go to these sites, give them your Twitter username and password, upload your photos from your computer, add your tweet, and click **Send.** It is also good to include an interesting sentence to encourage your followers to click on the picture link you are tweeting about.

Video: Twiddeo and TweeTube

Video is everywhere, and with our cell phones and pocket-held video cams, anyone can produce or star in his or her own video. Keep in mind that just as with all the other social media platforms and methods, the videos that you post are a reflection of your personal and professional brand. Ask yourself: How will my prospects, customers, and advocates like this? Is it informative? Does it give them a fun glance of my personal side? Is it providing infotainment, just information, or just plain fun?

Twiddeo (beta.twiddeo.com) is a powerful but simple service that lets you do one thing and one thing only: it helps you post your video updates on Twitter. You can upload from the web, upload from your camera phone, and record from your webcam. You can also easily use Twiddeo to upload videos to Facebook, your website, and multiple other social media platforms. Twiddeo is easy to use!

TweeTube (www.tweetube.com) allows you to share your photos, videos, and website URLs. It's a great tool to merge e-mail, Twitter, your desktop, YouTube, your mobile device, and your website together to send information. It's also a great way to disseminate information from any of your media platforms. Warning: do not post videos or photos of anyone else without getting written permission. You don't want to end up with a lawsuit on your hands or upset someone who may not like that photo of themselves.

SocialOomph

You might be wondering how people with a thousand, ten thousand, or even a million followers are managing it all. Well, there are two ways. They might have teams of people who manage their Twitter social media. Or they could be automating some of their tweets.

Everyday entrepreneurs and business owners can use an application called SocialOomph (www.socialOomph.com). This enables you to automate some of the process so you can get back to business. SocialOomph enables you to schedule tweets, send welcome messages to your new followers, and unfollow those who unfollow you. It's all done automatically. The jury is still out as to whether some of this functionality will win you more friends or followers (or less). However, it is good to know it is there. As you begin tweeting and following people, look at their welcome messaging, which should trigger ideas.

> ### Did You Know?
>
> SocialOomph assists over 150,000 customers. It also enables you to "vet" someone for several days while you decide if you want to follow, ignore, or block the person.

Autofollowing

Let's talk about autofollowing. You can set it up so that Twitter automatically follows all the people who follow you. There are two schools of thought on this. Some people feel if someone is following them, then they should return the courtesy and follow them back. Others feel that they want to be selective and not follow everyone. There is no right or wrong here. However, if you're not a public personality, and you have, for example, 4,000 people following you and you are following only two, you will appear as an elitist in the Twitter culture.

The opposite is also true. If you are following 4,000 and only have two followers, you will look like a spammer, so it's a fine line. The rules are still evolving, so again, the choice is yours.

To Autotweet or Not to Autotweet?

We talked a bit earlier about automatically sending tweets, or autotweets, through an application like SocialOomph.com. Many people do it, but a lot of folks within the Twitter community feel automated tweets take away from "social" conversations, sharing information, and networking. After all, if everyone automated their tweets, essentially no one would be reading the tweets (now that's kind of a funny thought). So think long and hard about automating your tweets. After a while, the powerful Twitter user can tell which tweets are automated and which are live from a person. Many also block autotweeters since it can become a nuisance because they aren't participating. They're just sending automessages, which can be a bore. However, check out TweetLater and see if there is some functionality that will work for you and your business as your Twitter following expands.

The Least You Need to Know

- ◆ How you manage your Twitter experience depends on your personal preferences.

- ◆ TweetDeck, Seesmic, and Twhirl are application tools that help you manage your Twitter experience.

- ◆ Learning how to upload video and photos on Twitter is easy because applications such as TwitPic, Twiddeo, and TweeTube and Yfrog are user-friendly.

- ◆ SocialOomph.com is a tool that helps you automate functions, such as scheduling tweets or automatically following someone back.

- ◆ Be cautious not to overly automate, because people want to hear from real people, in real time with real responses.

Additional Tools and Applications to Use with Twitter

In This Chapter

♦ Twitter applications for businesses with employees

♦ How to track tweets that mention your company

♦ Discover fun and creative Twitter applications

♦ How to analyze your Twitter account

♦ Twitter marketing checklist and sample Twitter pages

Just when you thought you knew everything about Twitter, you find out there are great applications to use with it. In this chapter, we talk about creative sites that you should explore. You'll find that some of these really do make sense for your business.

It is important to note that new Twitter applications appear daily, so keep an eye out for new options. In this chapter, I've highlighted the current popular applications that can help you with your company branding and strategy. These can help you manage the time you spend on Twitter.

Managing Multiple Twitter Users or Accounts

If you have a company that has several employees who are on Twitter for business reasons, a few of the applications discussed in the following sections might be helpful. Maybe you're in a situation where your company uses multiple Twitter IDs? Check out the following tools that can make your life easier.

CoTweet

CoTweet (cotweet.com) is an application that helps companies that have multiple users on their Twitter profile. Each Twitterer from the company is identified by his or her initials at the end of each tweet. This works well because each writer can maintain his or her own identity, and businesses have the option of assigning different tweet types to different employees.

The Home page of CoTweet.

GroupTweet

Do you have a team in your business that likes to communicate via Twitter? GroupTweet (www.grouptweet.com) enables the team members to be "grouped together," and they can tweet each other "privately within your company" without it going out to the public. The tweets are privately viewed only by employees within your company. This fosters collaboration and employee communication. Trust me, your employees will like this.

This is the Home page of GroupTweet.

HootSuite

This tool calls itself "the professional twitter client." Big companies such as Disney, Fox Network, Dell, and *National Geographic* use this tool, and this has added to its popularity among business owners. If you create multiple Twitter profiles, HootSuite (hoosuite.com) enables you to easily manage them, preschedule tweets, and measure your progress. You can even add multiple Twitterers within your company to your business profile and monitor their tweets and track statistics.

Here's the Home page of HootSuite.

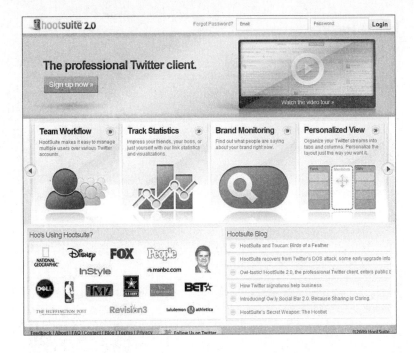

Splitweet

This site is recommended for heavy Twitter users who have multiple accounts, or for big corporations with multiple Twitterers or Twitter accounts. With Splitweet (splitweet.com), you can update and manage multiple Twitter accounts easily from one screen.

> **Netiquette**
>
> When selecting the Twitter team that will represent your company, make sure the team members are aware their tweets will be in the search engines for days, months, and possibly years to come. They need to be aware that what they tweet is PR and that they are the face of the company on Twitter.

You can also choose to send updates to one or all accounts in one step. There is also a feature that will notify you when your company is mentioned on Twitter.

Monitoring Your Name or Keywords

Do you want to know when someone mentions your name in a tweet? Maybe you'd like to know if someone sends a tweet that mentions the name of your product? Or maybe you're interested in everything that's said about one specific topic or a few keywords? Here are the applications that can help you track all of that.

Monitter

Monitter (monitter.com) enables users to get a live stream or real-time view of what Twitterers tweet within 10 to 100 miles of a specific zip code. You can also find out what a specific town is saying about you, your business, or specific keywords that you type in. Simply insert the keywords that you want to track on Monitter.

Here's the Home page of Monitter.

Tweetbeep Alerts

Savvy business owners need to keep up with what is being said or written about them online. Tweetbeep (tweetbeep.com) does just that. It tracks Twitter tweets that mention your name, your business's name, or affiliated products or services. The Tweetbeep alerts are conveniently sent to you via e-mail. It's Twitter's answer to Google Alerts.

Here's the Home page of Tweetbeep.

TwitHawk

TwitHawk (twithawk.com) is another monitoring tool. This marketing application helps you connect with Twitterers in your area who are tweeting about specific keywords or topics that you've chosen. For example, when someone tweets about those specific keywords within a certain demographic area (or globally), TwitHawk sends those people your prewritten custom response. For example, if you own an ice cream store and your keyword is IceCream, and someone tweets about IceCream, TwitHawk will send them a tweet and say something like "You like Ice Cream, so do we … visit us 24/7!" Take a long look at the site. There is a lot of strategy that must go into using it, but it might be worth a look.

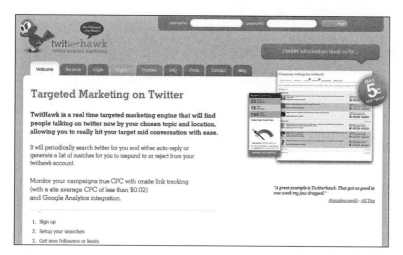

Here's the Home page of TwitHawk.

Getting Information About Followers and Other Twitterers

Are you getting a little overwhelmed trying to check out the people who are following you? You might want to use some of the tools in this section to help you evaluate the peeps you want to follow back—or ignore!

Checking out new followers may not seem like a big deal when you first get started, but if you start getting a hundred followers a week, you'll be glad you've got some of these applications to help you control your time and the quality of your connections.

Twimailer

Twimailer (twimailer.com) helps you maintain a well-matched list of people you have decided to follow. Instead of getting a basic e-mail or a notification that you have a new follower, Twimailer lets you see immediately how many followers they have, as well as their last few tweets. You can get a feel for their style while viewing other additional stats on each person, then you can choose to follow the person (or not) without ever having to sign on to Twitter.

Here's the Home page of Twimailer.

Tweepler and Twitoria

Tweepler (www.tweepler.com) simplifies the way you manage your Twitter followers. You can easily sort through new followers and accept or ignore them on one screen. Tweepler makes evaluating followers easy by giving you the new follower's stats and the three most recent tweets in one screen view. You then have some information that can help you decide whether or not to follow this person. Tweepler users claim it helps keep their lists clean from spammers.

One of the new trends on Twitter is quality versus quantity when it comes to having followers. Twitoria (Twitoria.com) allows you to easily find out which of your followers has not been regularly tweeting. You can then decide if you want to keep following them or not.

ExecTweets: Following Executives

To get in touch with your inner CEO, you can follow well-known business executives on a site called ExecTweets (exectweets.com). It's a resource site to help you find and follow some of the nation's top business executives on Twitter. To get on the list as an "exectweeter," it appears you need to be nominated.

Tweets can be viewed by industry, which is good for deeper navigation, and the site lists hot topics or a topic cloud of popular keywords that are being discussed that day. Popular executive links are also displayed on the Home page. This site seems to skew more heavily male than female executives, but hopefully it's because the word just hasn't gotten out yet. To their credit, ExecTweets does provide a prominent post asking users for suggestions to make their site better.

Twellow

Twellow (www.twellow.com) is the self-proclaimed Twitter Yellow Pages. Get your profile listed in the Twellow directory. It can't hurt—you never know where your next customer will come from.

Tweet Management

You're at a conference and you're tweeting every hour with a summary of events. Wouldn't it be nice to have the luxury of more than 140 characters? Or maybe you want to make it simple for a reader to tweet your blog? Here are some applications to help you do that and more.

TwitThis

TwitThis (www.twitthis.com) allows visitors to your blog or website to easily post Twitter messages about you or your business. It also makes it easy for visitors to your website or blog to tweet about what you say. Post the TwitThis button to your website or blog pages by following the instructions and coding provided on their site. This is a great viral marketing tool.

Here's the Home page of Twitthis.

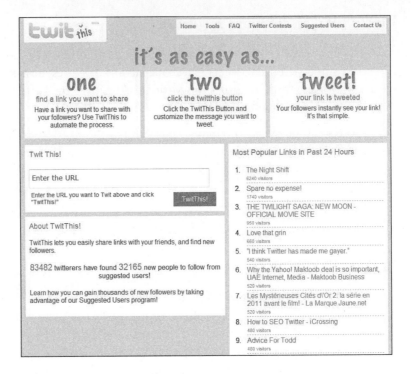

FutureTweets and Twtlong

FutureTweets (futuretweets.com) helps you schedule tweets to send in the future. Perhaps you have a big event or launch, or you will just be out of town and don't want to forget to tweet. With FutureTweets, you can schedule your tweet ahead of time for a specific date and time. Users can even schedule recurring tweets to post daily, monthly, or even yearly. However, remember that you don't want to automate too much—this *is* a social network.

As you start to use Twitter, at first you may say "How can I say enough within 140 characters?" Quickly, however, most get used to it and find creative ways to stay within the 140-character limit and still get their points across. But as you grow more comfortable with Twitter and as your following expands, there will be times you will need to post a longer tweet. Twtlong (twtlong.com) can help that with!

You can type a longer tweet and add photos, video, and maps. Simply go to the site, enter in your tweet (and photos, video, etc.) then click on **Add a Long Tweet.** You may be asked to allow the application to "speak" to your Facebook and Twitter sites. Once that is done, you can review it and click **Okay** and it shortens your info into a tiny link. The neat thing, too, is that you can send it to Twitter, Facebook, or share it with a multitude of other social media sites. It's a great tool!

Other Fun and Useful Applications

Are you tired of your plain Profile page and want to add a little pizzazz to it? Well, there are applications to satisfy your need for a little creativity, too. In this section, you'll find some fun and inventive ways to enhance your Twitter experience.

TweetMeme

TweetMeme (tweetmeme.com) can take a few minutes to understand, but there is a lot of information on this site that can be of value to you. TweetMeme aggregates all of the links on Twitter and determines which links are most popular. Then, TweetMeme is able to gather these links into categories and subcategories, making it easy for users to find the types of informational links they might be interested in.

The Twitter Toolbar and useTrackThis

Want instant access to Twitter? Then consider downloading this The Twitter Toolbar (thetwittertoolbar.com). You can use the toolbar to access online Twitter tools, check your Twitter stats, post your updates, and more. Versions are available for both Firefox and Internet Explorer.

Does your company track a lot of shipping of merchandise? useTrackThis (useTrackThis.com) enables you to track any UPS, FedEx, DHL, or USPS shipment. You can receive direct messages to your Twitter account as your shipment makes its way to a location.

BubbleTweet

BubbleTweet (bubbletweet.com) is a really unique and fun application, and I think we will see more like this in the future. BubbleTweet lets you post a short video message (up to 30 seconds at this writing) that bubbles up and magically appears on your Twitter page as a circular video burst when visitors land on your Twitter profile. It doesn't automatically play each time— visitors go to your twitter profile; it creates

Try This _____

Go to www.bubbletweet.com and enter your Twitter name. Pick the webcam or upload a short video from your handheld camera. Welcome people to your profile. Limit your video to no more than 30 seconds— really, the shorter the better. Give it a try!

a unique URL with the words bubbletweet in it. Your original Twitter profile, however, always stays in place. This is fun. Try it!

You can also change your BubbleTweet daily. Participants get creative with this short video by introducing themselves or welcoming visitors to their profile.

Twitter Gallery and Twtpoll

Twitter Gallery (twittergallery.com) is a site that provides free themed backgrounds for you to have on your Twitter Profile page. While ideally a custom background is best, prefabs from the Twitter Gallery are great to use to add personality and energy to your profile.

As of this writing, the company that created Twtpoll (www.twtpoll.com) says this tool ranks as its most popular Twitter application. Many businesses use Twtpoll to engage their customers, and then use the data to report back to their customers in their newsletters, marketing materials, or blogs. You can even brand your poll site to have the look and feel of your company or business.

Amy is an on-air anchor in Florida and here's her Twitter Profile page, @TVAmy, with a BubbleTweet.

Talking video bubble

Twtvite

Over time, you are going to meet many new people on Twitter, and some of these people are in your business district or located in towns you are traveling to. As you become more connected on Twitter, you will begin to see the term "tweetup." A tweetup is a meetup or a meeting of a group of folks from Twitter. Typically, a group of people on Twitter will schedule a get-together at a specific location. Through Twtvite (www.twtvite.com), you can create your own tweetup and invite folks.

You can also search by location to find tweetups in towns to which you are traveling, and ask if you can join in. Twtvite allows you to organize and manage your tweetups, and assists you in making further strong connections. Your event can be made public so anyone can join, or you can make it private so only your list will see the event. There is even an event manager component to this site where you can track RSVPs, and provide a map and other information about your tweetup. Tweetups using Twtvite go on all over the world.

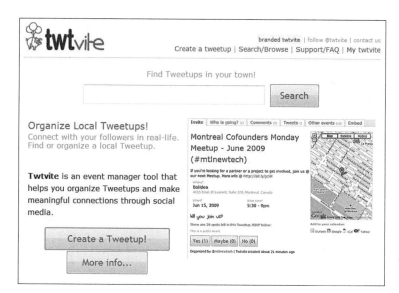

Here's the Home page of Twtvite.

TwtQpon and TwtBizCard

You can get really creative with TwtQpon (twtqpon.com). TwtQpon allows you to create coupons for your business services or products and share them exclusively with your Twitter followers. Many large national brands that use Twitter regularly offer discounts to their followers, and now small businesses and entrepreneurs can offer a Twitter Qpon to their followers as an incentive to do more business. It could be a good way to market test your loyal following on Twitter.

It's starting to look like the day of the paper business card is over. Take a look at TwtBizCard (twtbizcard.com) for your Twitter business card. A one-time donation (of your choice) is all that is required. You can get and share Twitter business cards with your friends. You simply log in, enter your business information, name, phone, e-mail, website address, and so on. Click **Create a Twitter Business Card** and you have a nice business card with your photo. Twtbizcard then gives you choices as to which social media networks you can send it to.

Analyzing Your Twitter Account

Alright, so now you know more than you ever thought possible about Twitter. And you've just read about the many amazing Twitter applications and sites that can support and expand upon your Twitter experience. However, how do you measure your return on investment (ROI) when it comes to the time you're spending on Twitter? How do you know if your marketing efforts are working? In this section, we'll review some sites that help you analyze your Twitter presence.

Twitter Grader

So you thought your grading days were over? Not so fast! The Twitter Grader (twitter.com/grader) will give your Twitter account, website, and Facebook pages a grade or ranking. It analyzes the number of followers, how many you are following, the number of tweets, and the quality of your followers. Then it gives you a grade from 1 to 100, with 100 being the best, of course. It will also show you how you rank among the Twitter Elite in your state or town.

You simply need to register and then enter your username and get your grade. Under the blog section on Twitter Grader, they do a great job of explaining what types of algorithms go into obtaining your grade, so be sure to read that. Twitter Grader also has some neat tools to check out under the Tools tab on the Home page.

One is called TwitSnip, which is a simple tool for posting to Twitter. It lets you "quote" text on any web page. Here's what it does: when you are on a web page and there's something that you want to quote, it will look for the Twitter name or @user for the website and link it back to the source. It even shortens the URL for you. You will find those under the Tools tab on the Home page.

The tool also has "graders" for your website, press releases, and Facebook page. They will rank and measure its effectiveness based on a number of factors. Go see how your sites measure up.

> **Did You Know?**
>
> As of summer 2009, Twitter Grader notes they had graded over 900,000 individual Twitter accounts and Twitter Grader was used over 20,000 times per day. Whew! That's a lot of grading going on.

Twitter Grader asks you for your website URL and for the URLs of your competitors. Then it provides you with a report. The team behind Twitter Grader seems to have fun because they also posted a new grader on April Fool's Day that was called the personality grader. They asked for your first and last name and then they "graded" your personality. In fact, many people thought it was for real and it caused quite a bit of commotion!

Twitter Grader can at least give you a feel for how you are doing compared to others and perhaps nudge you a bit to help you boost your online grade. Be sure to share your grade with your followers after you use Twitter Grader.

Here's the Home page of Twitter Grader.

TwitterCounter

I believe you will really like TwitterCounter (twittercounter.com). Enter your Twitter username on the right side where it reads "Show twitter statistics for @" and then click **Show.** A graph and stats bar will appear showing your Twitter following growth. On the right side of the graph, you will find the TwitterCounter Stats Details box, which is useful for analyzing current trends and forecasting future predictions for your Twitter account.

Another interesting feature is that you can also type in your competitors' or friends' Twitter usernames and see how they are doing compared to you, which is always interesting. You might also enjoy seeing the featured users on the right side of the screen. TwitterCounter finds some really good Twitter users to feature, and you can follow them directly from this site. This site is also a good one to put into your weekly or monthly social media reporting tool box.

Online Cautions

When analyzing the number of followers compared to your competition, don't get too caught up in the numbers. Remember: it's better to have quality followers than it is to have a huge quantity of followers. This does not need to be a race. In fact, if you focus on the race, you might not win. Focus on quality tweets and followers and engage them.

Here's the followers' graph for my Twitter name, @SalesLounge, on TwitterCounter.

Twinfluence

Twinfluence (twinfluence.com) provides some interesting analysis and shows the power and reach of your quality following. Want to measure the type of influence your network of connections has? Try this tool.

Here is an example: Back in August 2009, I ran a Twinfluence report on my Twitter name, @saleslounge. At that time, I had 2,118 friends that I was following and 2,505 people that were following me. The combined total of my followers and their network is a whopping 13,092,001 people. Are you beginning to see the power of being retweeted or recommended? Your sphere of influence can be huge!

On the Twinfluence website, the terms and the algorithm used to obtain this data is described in great detail.

Tweetburner and Qwitter

Want to know how many people are clicking on the links you share? Tweetburner (tweetburner.com) is designed to help you track your tweets that include links. With Tweetburner, you can shorten URLs and track the clicks your tweets accumulate.

Here's the Home page for Twinfluence.

We all want to know when we get more followers, but do you want to know when someone stops following you? If so, Qwitter (useqwitter.com) will tell you. This site sends you an e-mail when someone stops following you on Twitter. It's good, though, to be aware that the opposite situation also exists. When you stop following someone, they might also have this application installed and will be notified when you stop following them.

But guess what? That's perfectly okay. There is nothing wrong with no longer following certain people or companies. If used intelligently, the data you gain from this tool can be useful. Entrepreneurs and companies can analyze the data when they lose followers. For example, you can see if you've lost followers after certain types of tweets.

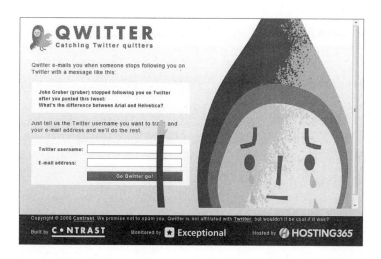

Here's the Home page for Qwitter.

Twitter Marketing Checklist

Are you enjoying Twitter and surprised by what it can do? Or are you feeling a bit overwhelmed? Don't worry; here is a Twitter marketing checklist to help you keep all this straight. Discuss these questions with your team and consider which tools you will start with as you begin to network, market your business, and build your following on Twitter.

- Should you use a headshot or a business logo? Twitterers love to see headshots, but if you have a company or brand that is really strongly marketed based on its name or logo, use the logo. There is no right or wrong here. Go with what feels best. You can always change your mind, you know.

- Who in your business will do the tweeting?

- Will you commit to tweeting at least daily?

- Do you have a strong bio line in your Twitter profile?

- Did you include a website or URL in your profile?

- Will you have multiple Twitterers within your business to represent your company?

- Will there be an automated welcome message to new followers?

- How will you engage followers—with polls, video, sharing tips, expertise, or TwtQpons?

- Will you host your own tweetup?

- Will you follow everyone that follows you, or only certain people?

- What Twitter applications will you use?

- Will you have a custom background? Who will do that for you?

- Are you willing to have fun, get creative, and regularly review your Twitter stats?

The Least You Need to Know

- There are Twitter applications, such as CoTweet and GroupTweet, that are useful for the small business owner or mid- or large-size company that has more than one employee on Twitter.

- Twitter applications, such as Monitter, Tweetbeep, and TwitterHawk, help you monitor when people are referencing you, your company, or products on Twitter. TweetDeck, Seesmic, and other tools do this as well.

- For the power Twitterer with multiple accounts and thousands of followers, using Splitweet or HootSuite is helpful.

- There are fun Twitter applications, such as TrackThis, BubbleTweet, Twitoria, Twtpoll, Twtvite, and TwtQpon, that let you get a little creative.

- You can analyze your Twitter experience and keep track of your stats with tools such as Twitter Grader, TwitterCounter, Twinfluence, Tweetburner, and Qwitter.

Part 4

LinkedIn and Other Social Network Options

This part takes you to another level by introducing other key platforms to market your business. You'll go from the white-collar platform on LinkedIn to the funky and fun platform of MySpace. You will easily see the differences and the opportunities to get more creative with these different sites.

Then, get your camera ready as you are introduced to the world of Internet video and Internet TV. You explore how to use video and learn which sites can host your videos. Don't worry about it being too technical. This is all delivered in an easy-to-read style. When you finish this part, you should understand how to build your presence effectively on these new platforms. Who knows? When you're done with Part 4, you might be the next Internet TV star!

12

LinkedIn: The Cable Channel of Social Media

In This Chapter

- Find out who is using LinkedIn
- Why you should join LinkedIn
- How to create an amazing profile
- Finding and connecting with people
- Discovering the power of the company search feature
- How to give and get testimonials and recommendations

Founded in 2003, many credit LinkedIn (linkedin.com) for getting the 35- to 65-year-old demographic of professionals comfortable with networking and sharing information online. After all, those age groups didn't grow up with MySpace and Facebook. And they certainly didn't get to use computers in elementary school.

LinkedIn is not the new social media kid on the block, but it is a widely respected networking platform for millions of professionals. Headquartered in California, LinkedIn operates an "online professional network," according to its website. I call this site the "Cable Channel of Social Media" because it has traditionally been vertical in its audience. What are the demographics? White-collar professional, more male then female, average age of 49, and an average income of $104,000.

Who Is Using LinkedIn?

With more than 53 million professionals representing 150 industries around the world, LinkedIn is a wonderful networking site. Here, you'll find, connect, and meet professionals of all kinds.

Who exactly is using LinkedIn? There are corporate CEOs, small businesses, and specific industry groups from around the globe. You will find CEOs of large corporations, directors of associations, corporate vice presidents, entrepreneurs, and small business owners. Furthermore, the types of industries represented are quite varied. There are 150 industries on LinkedIn and just about every university has an alumni chapter. In 2008, there were more than 90,000 groups on LinkedIn, so one can only imagine how high that number will eventually go.

And you, as an entrepreneur or business owner, now have the ability to search for and find these people. The fact that this is all free and available from the convenience of your keyboard is a bonus. In a world where it's all about having connections, LinkedIn is a great community in which to participate.

Degrees of Separation on LinkedIn

You've heard of six degrees of separation, right? It's the theory that we can connect to anyone on the planet by connecting through no more than five other people. On LinkedIn, your network is a group of LinkedIn users who can contact you through connections of up to three degrees away.

Here's how it works: you are at the center of your network. Notice those little number icons next to the name on someone's profile? These represent degrees of separation. As you begin searching, finding, and ultimately connecting to people on LinkedIn, you will notice this number next to names. This number refers to how many people, or degrees, you are away from knowing that person directly.

Let's say you see a "1st" next to John's name. That means that you are directly connected to John. So if you click on John's profile and you scroll down a little and look on the right side of the screen, you'll see a box that reads "How you're connected to John." For a first-degree connection, you'll see "You" and an arrow that points directly to John's name.

Those who are connected to your direct connections are your second-degree network. Let's say John is connected to Mary, but you are not. On Mary's profile, look in the "How you're connected to Mary," box, and you'll see "You" with an arrow pointing to John (and all other first-degree connections who are connected to Mary). Then you'll see an arrow that points to Mary, who is part of your second-degree network.

It's like this: you → John → Mary. And Mary's connections make up your third-degree network.

At the end of the day, as you build and build your network, you will find that we really are one to five people away from connecting to most of the people we want to meet. It truly is a small world after all—even if Walt Disney said it first.

Why You Should Use LinkedIn

By participating on the LinkedIn platform, you have the ability to market yourself, your services, and your brand. And yes, it gives you the chance to make amazing connections. In its early incarnation in 2003 and 2004, many used LinkedIn as an electronic rolodex. You would find someone you knew (or wanted to know), ask to join their network, and make a connection. Then after you connected, that person's name would get listed in your profile. And, if you so desired, you would then pick up the phone and call that person to reconnect and network.

Today, LinkedIn is so much more than that. It has become a much more "sticky" site where you can post PowerPoint presentations, incorporate your blog, let people know what you are reading, and tell others where you are traveling. They now even offer a place for users to put their status updates. This lets your network connections know what you are working on. Just that in itself is another example of viral marketing and the power of a 40-million-person network. Now, will all 40 million see your update? No, but that is not the point. Your status goes out to your network and it reminds them of what you are working on, and keeps you on the top of their minds. In the pages ahead, we'll get into all the logistics of status updates, and you'll see why this can be effective.

Another reason to join LinkedIn is that it's a great place to give and get testimonials and recommendations. You can find contractors, vendors, and strategic partners, and interact with those who may not be on the other social media networks, such as Twitter or Facebook. Think of this as another networking portal to market yourself or your business as the go-to expert. You can post questions to groups, you can answer questions in the various group forums, you can share links, and you can even start your own group. If nothing else, think of LinkedIn as an advertisement for you and your business. Remember, you never know where your next big customer or connection will come from.

Here are even more creative reasons why you should use LinkedIn:

♦ It's a place where your happy clients and customers can post testimonials on your behalf. And you can place a link on your regular website under "Client References" that links over to your LinkedIn testimonial page.

♦ You can share useful information to your contacts, such as posting links to your articles or to industry resources.

♦ You can combine LinkedIn status updates with your other accounts and further complete your social media presence.

♦ You can answer questions within groups or on the Q&A section to showcase your expertise without coming across as a shameless self-promoter.

♦ You can post your amazing PowerPoint presentations that highlight your expertise.

♦ You can research potential clients and prospects before you meet them.

♦ You can post job listings to grow your team.

♦ You can write and receive valuable and authentic testimonials and recommendations that will be read by your network.

♦ You can import your blog and share survey and poll results with your connections.

♦ You can create and market your events or business promotions.

Honestly, this list could go on and on! But I think I've given enough information for you to see that LinkedIn has become much more than just an electronic rolodex.

Creating an Amazing LinkedIn Profile

Let's begin by setting up your account. Go to www.linkedin.com and type in your information. Remember to use the name that you go by professionally. Whether it's Jeff or Jeffery, put the one most people know you by.

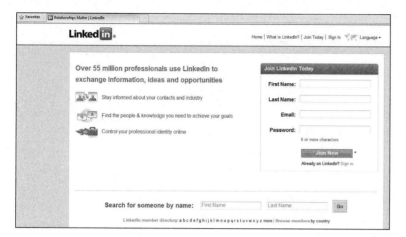

Here's the signup screen for LinkedIn.

Click on **Join Now,** and you will arrive at a page that looks like the following.

Here's where you create your professional profile on LinkedIn.

Fill out all the information and click on **Enter LinkedIn.** You will then get directed to the following page.

Here's the page you see after you create your account on LinkedIn.

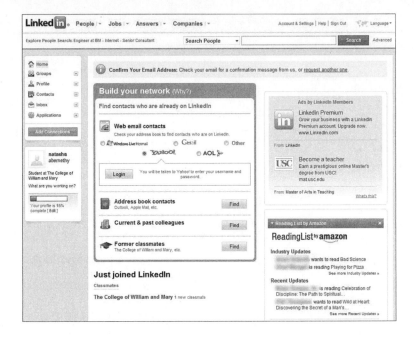

Do you see across the top where it reads, "Confirm Your Email Address"? You will now need to check your e-mail to confirm that you have set up an account. Then, we can go to the next step.

Just like the other sites, it's not recommended that you start building your network right away. Let's get your site built first, and then we can always go back and add connections from your current web and e-mail contacts. Next, you will go to a page called Account & Settings.

You have an option to upgrade your account for a monthly fee. There are three tiers; you can click on Upgrade to look at them. For our purposes here, we are going to go straight into the settings area without upgrading. You can start using LinkedIn without paying the monthly fee and just decide later if you need all the extras that come with the fee.

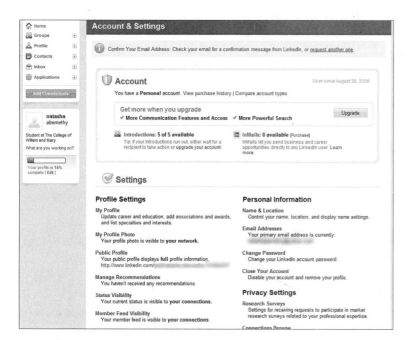

Here's the Account & Settings page on LinkedIn.

Your Profile Settings

Directly under Profile Settings, click on My Profile. You will now see a page that looks like this:

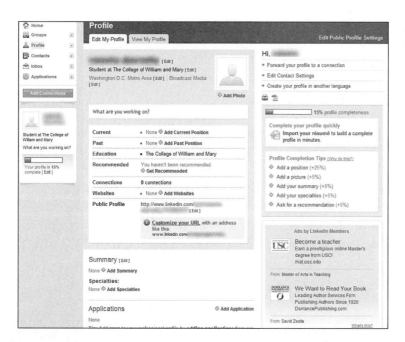

Here's the page where you edit your profile.

This is your basic Profile page. You can edit any of the portions in light blue by clicking on the **Edit** link. Remember, you are marketing yourself and your business, so list your title—if you don't have a title, come up with something creative to put there. I've seen people use things from World's Best Life Coach to Extraordinary Executive. Now add your photo by clicking on the **Add Photo** icon.

Just below that, you will see "What are you working on?" This is your status update on LinkedIn, so go ahead and fill that in. Next, fill in your current position. If past positions are important to your business, please fill those in, but also know you do not need to. Education is a good one to fill in, particularly if you want to network with alumni. Later in this chapter, we will get back to recommendations and connections.

Now, your website is very important, so click on **Add Website(s).** When you enter your website, be sure to type it as "http://www.yourwebsite.com" so you are creating a live link. When you click on the website link, you will arrive at the following page.

Here's where you can add more information to your LinkedIn profile.

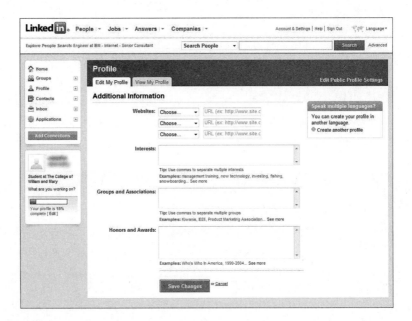

Don't be shy! Put all of your sites here, including your website, blog, and so on. LinkedIn only allows three sites to be listed on a profile. If you don't have three sites to list, be sure to link to your Twitter page or a Facebook Fan Page! Again, remember to use the "http://" to make it a live link so readers can just click and go to your site.

Next, fill in your interests, and again, get creative. Just like on Facebook and Twitter, you don't have to list interests like water-skiing and golf, but you should put down some of your business skills or how your company helps clients. You can also share why you are interested in helping people or why people can work easily with you. Share your business and/or expertise and what you can do for others in this spot. Your Groups and Associations are listed next, and if you have your own group or plans to create a group on LinkedIn, put that here as well. In Honors and Awards, list any that you have won. This is your place to shine, so go for it. Now click on **Save Changes.**

Your Profile Summary

Next, you arrive back on that page with portions filled in. Scroll down to the Summary section and click on **Add Summary.**

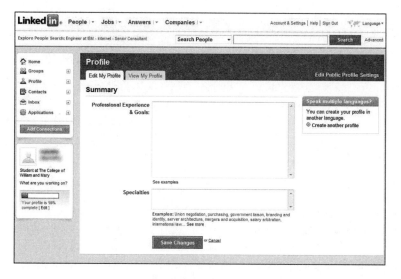

Here's where you can add or edit information in your Profile summary.

This is your opportunity to boast about what you do. LinkedIn describes this as "the place to give your elevator pitch" about you and your business. Realize that while we would like to think everyone is going to read our entire Profile page word for word, typically they don't. However, they might read the summary because it is placed in a prominent place on the screen. So take some time to think about what you want to say. If you had 15 seconds to say something to millions, what would you say? That is paragraph No. 1. Then, what would you say if you had another 15 seconds to close? That is paragraph No. 2. Finally, summarize in a short paragraph how you or your company helps people.

Try This _____

If you put your website, your Twitter user name, and your phone number in the Summary section, it will make it really easy for people to follow and find you. This is also a good spot to ask people to add you as a friend on Facebook or become a Fan on Facebook. LinkedIn has recently added a spot for you to add your Twitter username in your profile.

In the Specialties section, list what you specialize in or what your business does to help people. Continue to go through this page, updating, and adding what you like.

At the bottom of your Profile page, there is a Personal Information section. You can fill in this portion if you like, but it's not vital. You might want to put your business phone number. Just be careful not to give out too much personal information. This site is for business. LinkedIn is a bit more formal than the other sites. Readers here don't need to know about your relationship status, birthday, or how to contact you via instant messaging, unless you want them to.

Did You Know?

Just below your status update on LinkedIn (on the left side of your profile) there is a status bar. LinkedIn provides a chart on the right side of your Profile page highlighting the percentage points you gain as you complete your profile. As you give recommendations and testimonials and complete your profile, this status bar will continue to move right until you get to 100 percent.

The next section is Contact Settings. While they could offer more choices in this section, go ahead and see if any resonate with you. Let people know why you would like to be contacted.

Now click on **View My Profile** and look at what you've created. How does it look? Are there any typos? Does it convey what you want it to convey? Does it represent the true you? Remember, authenticity and transparency are the key buzzwords these days.

When you're satisfied with your profile, you can begin adding friends to your network. Click **Home.** On the right side of your screen, you will see a section that reads "People you may know." Just click the **Invite** button.

You then arrive at a page that asks you to give a bit more information. On LinkedIn, you can't just connect with anyone. You need to have something in common, such as an employer, an alumni group, or a current or past business relationship.

Because the LinkedIn system suggests you might know each other, it's likely you have some sort of connection. Fill out the form, and just like on the other platforms, write a short personal note. After you write the note, hit send and the recipient will most likely connect with you soon.

Another way to find people on LinkedIn is by using the Search bar at the top right side of the page. Type in a name of a friend or associate and see if they pop up. You might get several thousand results for that person, particularly if their name is popular. Don't panic. Modify your search. Look on the right side of your screen (see the following screenshot) to see where you can narrow your search by company, school, and location to find that specific person you are looking for. Keep searching and adding some friends to begin building your LinkedIn network.

Try This _____

When asking someone to connect, don't just use the standard text that LinkedIn provides. Stand out in the crowd by taking an additional 30 seconds and make the note personal. Sign with your name and your website and title. You will wow them!

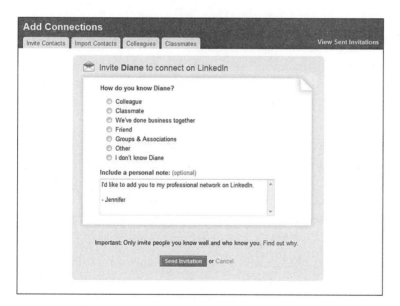

Here's where you can invite people to connect with you on LinkedIn.

Here's where you can start searching for people you know.

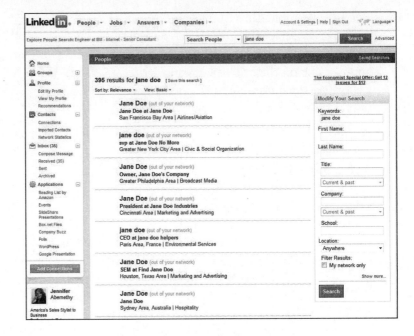

Powerful Corporate Searches and Connections

Part of the beauty of LinkedIn is that you can connect with current associates and past friends and business peers. But another great benefit is that you can find and connect with new people who can help you take your business both personally and professionally to higher levels.

The access on LinkedIn is often overlooked. Let's say you would really like to connect with someone who runs a large transportation company. Let's use Reston Limousine Service as an example. In the past, you would have to do a lot of Internet searching or even purchase a database service to get access to the names of their employees. Now, they are at your fingertips on LinkedIn.

With LinkedIn, it's right here. Type in "Reston Limousine Service" in the search bar, and instead of searching for people, change it to a search for companies. Literally, within 2 seconds, up pops information on the Reston Limousine Service, including their website, a brief bio, and all of their affiliate companies.

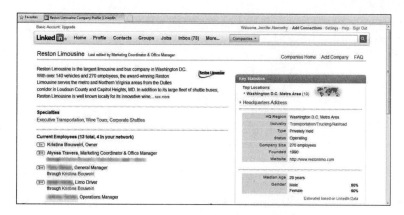

Here are the search results for the Reston Limousine Service.

Now, look at all the results you get when you click on the company profile. There are many ways you or your business can benefit from this information. Let's say you are a small business that makes a product or delivers a service that you feel Reston Limousine Service could benefit from. Or, say you work for a small nonprofit and are looking for a sponsor. What if you were looking for a speaker? Or again, going back to our original scenario, what if we wanted to consult with the CEO of Reston Limousine Service? Well, you should be able to find your connection here, or at least find the person who can recommend the best point of contact for you.

In the middle of the page, there are several lists of their employees with job titles and a See more link to view more employees.

If you continue to scroll down on that page, you can see new hires, former employees, and more company statistical information. Click on a name and you will see the e-mail application open.

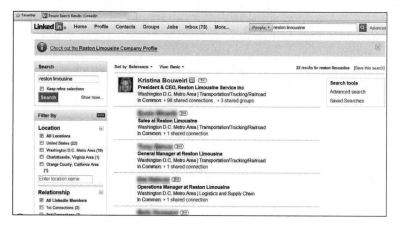

The search results for the Reston Limousine Service employees.

Here, you can use your connections to contact this employee from the Reston Limousine Service.

This is where you might send that person a personal note asking to be connected and giving the reason why. Lastly, you should take it to the next level and ask for a phone meeting. All that information at your fingertips in a matter of seconds! Pretty amazing, right? You seriously are just a few clicks away from some important connections. These contacts are no longer just for an exclusive few.

Recommendations and Testimonials

Everyone likes a good pat on the back and acknowledgment for a job well done. In fact, studies show that one of the most meaningful gestures we can do is to give public accolades to people. Earlier in the book I wrote, "In a world where we are so connected with technology, people are feeling more disconnected than ever before." If you give a LinkedIn recommendation, it will make others feel good about themselves and about you. A public acknowledgment is, to quote Martha Stewart, "a good thing."

You should know that the best way to get a recommendation is to give one. On the left side of the navigation bar, click the **+** sign next to "Profile," and you will see the word "Recommendations." Click on it and you will arrive at a screen with tabs for Received, Sent, and Requested Recommendations. This is where you can keep track of your recommendations "history." You even have the option to display it to your connections, to everyone that looks at your profile, or to no one. Now continue down that screen and you will see where you "Make a recommendation."

You can either recommend someone from your network of connections or put in the person's first and last name and e-mail address.

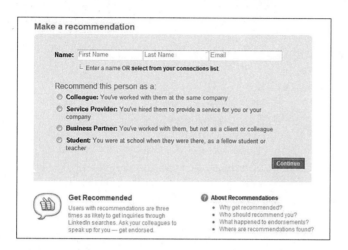

Here's where you can make recommendations on LinkedIn.

Netiquette

Definitely do not begin asking for recommendations the day you log on to LinkedIn. Get your profile set up, build some connections, add some of your peers and colleagues to your network, and give some recommendations—it's important to give before you receive.

Create your recommendation and a message is sent to the individual notifying him or her of your recommendation. That person will be prompted to see if he or she would like to return the favor.

Note: while they call this the Recommendation section, you should also use it to give and get testimonials. If clients mention to you a great experience that they've had with your business, ask them if they can write that testimonial on LinkedIn. If a colleague gives a great presentation, give him or her a testimonial on LinkedIn.

Here's where you write a recommendation.

The Least You Need to Know

 ◆ LinkedIn is a highly respected professional network with more than 40 million users.

 ◆ LinkedIn is a great way to reconnect with old and current connections, while at the same time finding new ones.

 ◆ LinkedIn has become a sophisticated "sticky" site that allows you to give updates, show PowerPoint presentations, join groups, incorporate your blog, and merge your social media presence with other platforms.

 ◆ Consider your profile to be your 30-second elevator pitch that explains why people should do business with you.

 ◆ Use the company search feature, and within seconds you will learn the names of the company's employees along with titles and detailed company statistics.

 ◆ The best way to get recommendations and testimonials is to give them.

13

Marketing Applications and Strategies for LinkedIn

In This Chapter

◆ Learn how to further personalize your LinkedIn Settings

◆ The power of joining and creating groups on LinkedIn

◆ Using the Company Search feature on LinkedIn

◆ The marketing capabilities of LinkedIn applications

◆ How to analyze and understand your LinkedIn network

After creating your stellar profile on LinkedIn, connecting to some friends and colleagues, and updating your status, you might be asking, "How do I do all that other stuff?" Many LinkedIn users are just now discovering the many wonderful applications on LinkedIn and how to incorporate those into their overall social media marketing strategy, so there's no need to feel left behind. This chapter gives you plenty of ideas and shows you how to find the many applications you can use to continue to grow your connections through the LinkedIn social media network.

Personalize Your LinkedIn Account Settings

Let's get your account setting set up first and then we will get into some of the marketing applications and strategies.

Log in to LinkedIn and at the top right side of the page look for Account & Settings. This is the page where you can personalize your settings and make your LinkedIn experience a bit more to your liking. Go through each of these areas and adjust your settings. Don't worry—if you are not sure about something, you can always go back and change it. I've highlighted a few here for you to examine.

Here's where you can really personalize your LinkedIn settings.

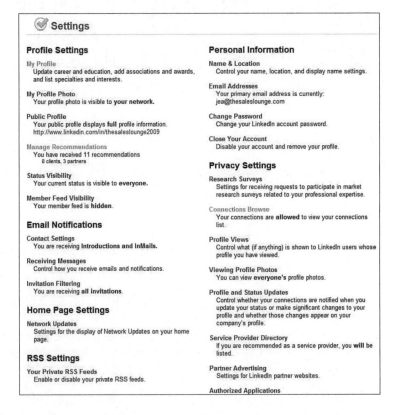

✅ Settings

Profile Settings

My Profile
Update career and education, add associations and awards, and list specialties and interests.

My Profile Photo
Your profile photo is visible to **your network.**

Public Profile
Your public profile displays **full** profile information.
http://www.linkedin.com/in/thesaleslounge2009

Manage Recommendations
You have received 11 recommendations
8 clients, 3 partners

Status Visibility
Your current status is visible to **everyone.**

Member Feed Visibility
Your member feed is **hidden.**

Email Notifications

Contact Settings
You are receiving **Introductions and InMails.**

Receiving Messages
Control how you receive emails and notifications.

Invitation Filtering
You are receiving **all invitations.**

Home Page Settings

Network Updates
Settings for the display of Network Updates on your home page.

RSS Settings

Your Private RSS Feeds
Enable or disable your private RSS feeds.

Personal Information

Name & Location
Control your name, location, and display name settings.

Email Addresses
Your primary email address is currently:
jea@thesaleslounge.com

Change Password
Change your LinkedIn account password.

Close Your Account
Disable your account and remove your profile.

Privacy Settings

Research Surveys
Settings for receiving requests to participate in market research surveys related to your professional expertise.

Connections Browse
Your connections are **allowed** to view your connections list.

Profile Views
Control what (if anything) is shown to LinkedIn users whose profile you have viewed.

Viewing Profile Photos
You can view **everyone's** profile photos.

Profile and Status Updates
Control whether your connections are notified when you update your status or make significant changes to your profile and whether those changes appear on your company's profile.

Service Provider Directory
If you are recommended as a service provider, you **will** be listed.

Partner Advertising
Settings for LinkedIn partner websites.

Authorized Applications

Some key settings to review are located in Status Visibility. You want to stay visible so that when you update your status, your network sees it. Click **Status Visibility,** and options are displayed to show your status to your connections only, your network, or anyone on LinkedIn. You decide, but just remember that the more people you get in front of, the wider you cast your net.

Here's where you choose who gets to see your status updates.

Under Email Notifications, click **Contact Settings,** and if you are willing to accept e-mail (or "InMail," as they refer to it on LinkedIn) from anyone, check the first box which reads "I'll accept introductions and InMail." Otherwise, if you want people to connect with you only through more formal introductions through someone in your network, check the second box.

Did You Know?

You can export your contacts on LinkedIn. Click **Contacts,** scroll down to the bottom of that page, and you'll see an Export Connections link. You can export your contacts as either a .csv file or a .vcf file, which you can easily load into most address book applications. (LinkedIn provides instructions on how to load your contacts for commonly used apps.) You can also save your profile as a PDF by clicking the PDF icon on your Profile page. This is great to do if you are worried about losing your contact information.

Then look at Opportunity Preferences and check those boxes that apply to you. LinkedIn has also added a box that you can fill in with any additional information about the desired projects or types of people you are looking to connect with. They do warn, however, not to put too much personal information here because this information goes to the entire network. Click **Save Changes.**

The next area below Contact Settings to review is the Receiving Messages section. Go back to Email Notifications and click **Receiving Messages.** You will find a screen that allows you to determine if you want messages to go directly to your individual e-mail account or to the LinkedIn InMail account. It also allows you to determine how often you are notified of information, such as daily or weekly. In the next section, we will discuss groups on LinkedIn, but just note that this is where you can also organize your incoming group messages.

Here's where you determine your Contact Settings.

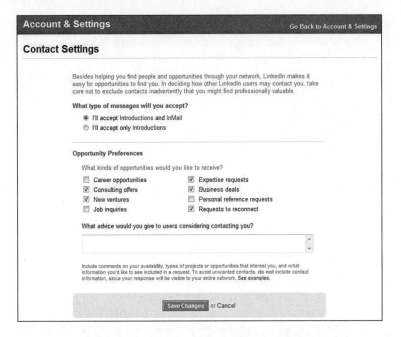

You can decide here how you want to receive messages and how often.

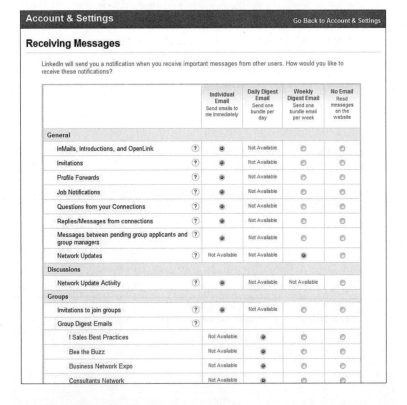

Want to know how to hide the connections on your profile so no one can see them? Many people do, and it's a personal decision. Go back to Account & Settings and under Privacy Settings, look for Connections Browse. This enables you to display or hide your connections to everyone in your network. Some people like lawyers, financial planners, and doctors might choose to hide their connections for legal reasons, but more so than not, most keep them open as that is one of the strengths of the LinkedIn network. Doing so enables you to see who is connected to whom, so you can ask for an introduction.

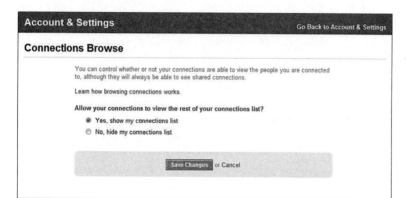

Here's where you decide if you want your connections to see your Connections list.

When you view other LinkedIn profiles or if other people view your profile, the system will tell you who has viewed your profile in the last seven days. Under Privacy Settings, click **Profile Views** and here you can decide if you want this information shown. If you do not want your name to appear on profiles you have viewed as someone who has visited their profile, then check "Don't show users that I've viewed their profile." If you only want your company and title to appear, check that. If it doesn't matter to you, click on **Show my name and headline.** Remember to save your settings.

Here you can decide if you want LinkedIn users to know if you've viewed their profiles.

Another setting for you to look at within the Privacy Settings area is Profile and Status Updates. This gives you the option of alerting your network when you've made a change to your profile and/or updated your status. Check the box that you are most comfortable with and click **Save Changes.**

Here's where you decide if you want your connections notified when you make changes to your status or profile.

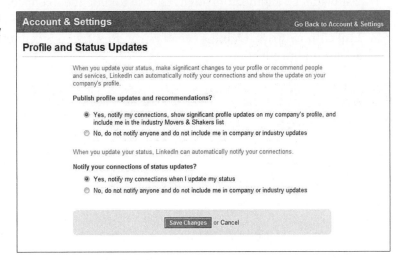

The Power of Groups on LinkedIn

There are more than 90,000 groups on LinkedIn, including alumni groups, corporate groups, industry groups, and professional groups. In fact, you name a topic, and there is most likely a group for it. Power LinkedIn users strategically join groups that will help their business by expanding their connections and reach. So think first about what types of groups you want to belong to, whether it's an alumni group or a professional networking group (that also happens to have a group on LinkedIn). However, also keep in mind what other types of groups could benefit from having you as a member. Who needs your services? See if they have a group. In 2008, LinkedIn added a great group directory search feature that makes it so easy to find groups. Let's give it a try.

You can find groups in many ways, but the easiest way is to go to your Profile page and in that left-hand navigation menu, you will see Groups right under Home. Click **Groups.** Note as a new user you will not see 47 groups, but you will see the light-blue Groups Directory on the left. Go there and click **Find a Group.**

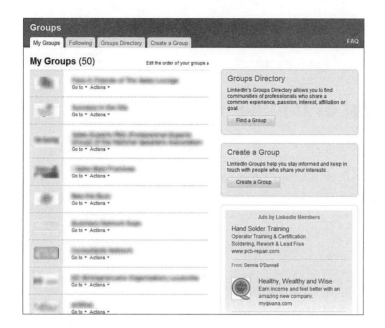

You can see your LinkedIn groups and search for new groups from this page.

Now look on the right side and click **All Categories.** You will see alumni, corporate, conference, networking, nonprofit, and professional groups. There are so many groups! Go through and find some that appeal to you and your business. I suggest that you look at the types of people that are members and view some of the discussion headers to see if they appeal to you. Then, join them!

You can search for groups by category from this page.

To join a group, pick a category and open it. Now find a group and click **Join this group.** The group manager will get back to you in either a few hours or a few days and let you know if are accepted into the group.

Making the Most Out of Joining Groups

For many LinkedIn users, after they join a group, they aren't quite sure what to do next ... so they do nothing. Yes, it's neat that the group name now appears on their profiles, but really they aren't getting any value out of it. Consider that there is a lot of power in groups, so we first want to ensure you get your best value out of being a part of one.

Member List

After you join a group, the first thing to do is look at the member list. How do you do this? LinkedIn moves it around from time to time, but at this writing it is found under the More tab. Click that tab and you will see Members. Click **Members** and all the names and titles appear. Welcome to another new network that you have just created for yourself. If you see someone you know or want to know, click on their name, look at their profile, and invite them to connect. That is one way to begin utilizing the group for your business.

Here's how you get to the group member list.

Participating in Group Discussions

Now we want to take it to the next level. In your group forum, there usually are some discussions taking place. Click the **Discussions** tab. You should see an array of discussions. Do you see something that you can comment on? If so, go ahead and click **Add comment** and a box will appear, allowing you to make a comment. Your name, photo, and title will automatically appear to the left of your answer. By participating in discussions, your name gets out there, your expertise is on display, and you might just make a new connection.

You can start your own discussions, too. Click the **Discussions** tab and on the right side, you see "Start a Discussion." Click that and you see a page similar to the following.

Here's where you can start your own discussion.

Think strategically here. If you are within a group that could use your services, what types of questions can you ask or what type of discussion should you start? Look at the types of questions others are posting and get some ideas. Another idea is that you can share an article or link with the group. A great place to do that is within the News tab within each group. By sharing articles and resources, you're seen as a strong contributor to the group. You will also be seen as an expert, so keep contributing when it makes sense. This gives you great viral visibility because not only does your name and website get posted within the Discussion or News section, but the information that you posted something will also go in your news feed to everyone in your network!

Creating Your Own Group

LinkedIn is another great place to have your own group. Remember, not everyone uses Facebook. Creating your own group is another way to build credibility and market your brand to people who may not be on Facebook.

When considering creating a group on LinkedIn, think about why you are doing it. Is it to make more connections? Is it to share information? Is it because eventually you want to invite them to a conference or a tweetup? Talk to your staff or mentors and strategically think about why you are doing it. Who will manage the group? Who will you not allow in the group? Sleep on it first and then make a decision.

There are several benefits to creating your own group, with control being one of them. Just think of the contacts you will make and the creativity you can apply. You can make this group into anything you want it to be. It is easy to create a group. Simply click the **Groups** icon in the left navigation bar. Click **Create a Group.** You will then go through all the steps to create your group. You'll upload your logo, give the group name and type, write a summary, give a description, and list your website.

Here you can create your own group on LinkedIn.

You can then decide if you want it to be an open group where anyone can join without approval, or you can make it so people need to "request to join" by answering the Access section on this page. If you decide that incoming members need to be approved, you will need to designate someone (or yourself) to approve them and allow them access to the group. Also don't forget to check the boxes to have your group in the display directory and to have all members display your group logo on their Profile pages. Doing this will create more great visibility and viral marketing for your business.

After you create a group on LinkedIn, market it everywhere. Have it on your website, talk about it on Twitter, and put it on your Facebook page. And don't forget to mention it in places such as your business cards and your e-mail signature.

Applications for Marketing on LinkedIn

Now that you have a great profile, know how to add friends, and have joined a few groups, let's get you to look like a real social marketing pro by taking you to the next level on LinkedIn. You do this by adding some applications to your LinkedIn profile. As of this writing, there are many valuable applications on LinkedIn and LinkedIn Mobile. Some of these are discussed in the next few sections.

Reading List by Amazon

This is a fun and interesting application. To find it, click Applications on the left navigation bar and find "Reading List" by Amazon. Open that and you will arrive at this page.

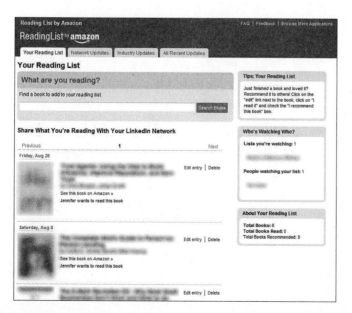

Here's where you can list the books that you're reading.

You can type in a book that you are reading or one you want to read and it will appear on your list. You can also see what your network is reading or recommending. You can look at your industry and see what people are reading and look at all recent updates using this application.

You can also scroll down and see your network's books; to the right of their name, you will see a gold box that reads "Watch (name) list." You can be alerted when that person adds a new book to their list. Likewise, people might begin following you if you regularly recommend books. There's a wonderful potential for great viral marketing here, particularly if you are an author, in a speaker bureau, a retail merchant with books, a book club member, a business consultant, or a coach. Actually, the opportunities are endless!

The Events Application

This is a wonderful tool to use not only to promote your own events, but also to find great networking and professional development programs. Go to the left navigation bar, find Applications, and then click **Events.**

Here's what you can do using this application:

- ◆ Browse Events within your connections.

- ◆ Find specific events by name or subject.

- ◆ Find the most popular events.

- ◆ See what events your network is attending.

- ◆ Add and create your own event by clicking the **Add an Event** tab.

Try This

If you are traveling to another location, look under events on LinkedIn and do an advanced search. Type in the location you are traveling to and see if there is an event you would like to attend for networking. This is a great opportunity to network!

The Add an Event page looks like this and is easy to use. You just give it a title, put in the date, and add the venue name, the location, and the time.

Add your website address or the website for the event. Check that you are attending and organizing. Add more details if you like. Preview the event online and then publish the event. And you did it!

Here's where you can browse and look for events.

On this screen, you can add the details of your event.

SlideShare Presentations

This application lets you upload and share your PowerPoint presentations and Word documents. And if you add audio, it's essentially a webinar. There are additional benefits, but first you must create a SlideShare account at www.slideshare.net and sync it to the LinkedIn SlideShare page.

SlideShare is the world's largest community for sharing presentations. Its website lists some of the things you can do with this application. If you sync it with LinkedIn, you should be able to do all of this as well, so make sure you click the **+ Sync Your SlideShare Account** bar to merge the two. You will see this tab on the top right side of the page just below the search bar.

Here are a few things you can do with SlideShare:

- ◆ Embed slideshows into your own blog or website (or now on your LinkedIn page).

- ◆ Share slideshows publicly or privately.

- ◆ Market your own event using SlideShare.

- ◆ From the slideshare.net site, you can upload your presentation and distribute it to Facebook, Twitter, and other platforms.

As I mentioned, you will see a + Sync button on the top right side of the page, and after you open the SlideShare application, you can click the **Explore** tab to see what others have done. This is yet another way to market yourself, your business, and your brand.

Here you can explore the slideshows that others have done.

LinkedIn Polls

Everyone likes a good poll. So how about creating one for your business? Want to try something new? Test it out with your connections on LinkedIn. Get their responses to your idea. Click the **Applications** icon and find LinkedIn Polls. What a great place to gauge what the business community is looking for or responding to.

Learn about LinkedIn polls and then create your own.

The cool thing about this is you can literally create and distribute the poll in five minutes. Just click **Create Poll,** and it will easily walk you through the process. You can target the poll to your network or to specific professionals, for example, sales professionals or coaches, or people in specific regions of the country. And, yes, it's free. After you get the results back, you can analyze the data and share it with your network. Are you seeing now that this is more than just an electronic Rolodex? LinkedIn has a lot of power inside it.

Company Buzz, Box.net, and My Travel

Wonder what people are saying or what the buzz is about your company? The Company Buzz application on LinkedIn shows you what the Twittersphere or Twitter users are saying about your company. You can view keywords, trends, and tweets. But, of course, you can do this only if you have your Twitter account set up. The Box.net application enables you to sort of "box" a document or documents into a file that others (whom you select) can see. You can also use this application for sharing videos and photos among colleagues, clients, or even friends. It's a great site and it's free!

My Travel is a fun application on LinkedIn. The My Travel application is for your business and personal travelers out there. See where your network is traveling to and let them know where you are heading. The thought here is if you are in the same city, you might be able to connect in person. Add the My Travel application, particularly if you travel a lot. You can display your current world location, upcoming trips, and share with your network. Bon voyage!

WordPress Application and Blog Link

Do you have a blog that you've created using WordPress? Now you can have that blog feed into your LinkedIn profile. Simply go to the Applications tab again on the left navigation bar. Click it and look for WordPress. Open it and enter your blog's URL. Then, you simply choose to display either all your blog posts or those that you mark or tag with the word LinkedIn. It will go directly to LinkedIn. The good news is that the system will prompt you on how to do this. Press **Save** and you are ready to go! Now your network will be notified when you post something new to your blog on WordPress.com or self-hosted WordPress.org.

The Blog Link application is similar to the WordPress application. However, you can use this one if you have created your blog using a blog service provider other than WordPress. If you're using a service such as TypePad, Vox, Blogger, and Live Journal, and even WordPress, you can use this application. As you enter a blog post, your connections will see your latest entry as soon as you update it. This service is powered by TypePad technology, which is a well-respected blogging service.

Google Presentation

Are you a fan of Google? Do you use Google Docs? If so, this application is yet another way to introduce your work and your expertise to your LinkedIn connections. You can upload a PowerPoint presentation or a file to your LinkedIn profile through Google Presentations. If you are not familiar with Google Docs, simply add the Google Docs application (docs.google.com) and you'll see the free templates, documents, and presentation templates. Create a three-page slide presentation sharing what you do on LinkedIn.

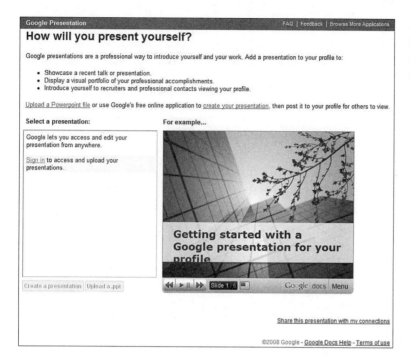

Here's the Google Presentation application that you can use to showcase your work.

Analyzing Your Connections on LinkedIn

As you continue to use LinkedIn, add connections, and join groups, your network is going to quickly grow. Wouldn't it be neat if you could take a demographic snapshot of your network? For example, learn where your network connections are located or what their industries are. Well, you can! Go to the left navigation bar and click on **Contacts** and then click **Network Statistics.**

You will see how many users you could potentially contact through an introduction. The number may astound you. Review the top locations of your network and the most popular industries of your connections. This is good information to know, and if it doesn't quite match where you are heading, you can adjust accordingly. It's another strategic way to analyze your social media sphere of influence.

Here's where you review your LinkedIn network statistics.

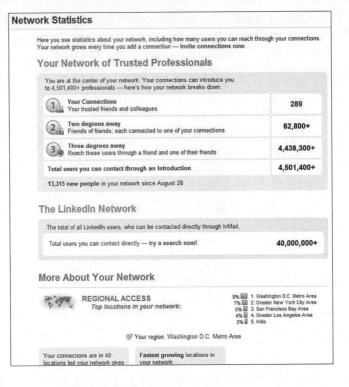

Here's where you review the top locations in your regional and industry access.

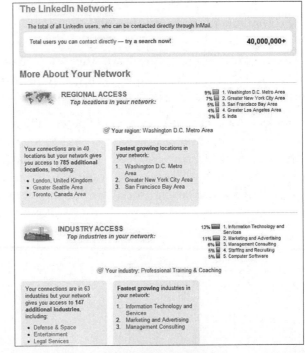

LinkedIn Mobile

Always on the go? Want to tap into LinkedIn from your mobile device? There's good news, because you can! Go to www.linkedin.com and click on **Home**. Scroll down to the bottom of the page and see the line that reads Tools. Find Mobile to the right and click it. You will see LinkedIn Mobile. Use your iPhone, Palm Pre, Blackberry, or any *WAP*-enabled phone.

Step-by-step instructions are on the site. You can download the application for an iPhone, access the application catalogue for the Palm Pre, or go to m.linkedin.com for your Blackberry.

def•i•ni•tion

WAP stands for "wireless application protocol," which allows users to access information via handheld wireless devices, such as cell phones.

The Least You Need to Know

♦ LinkedIn is much more than an electronic Rolodex.

♦ You will make many new connections if you seek them out and strategically connect.

♦ Joining and participating in discussions within LinkedIn groups is a great way to gain additional visibility.

♦ Events are a great way to gain viral visibility for your business, whether it's your own event or someone else's that you are attending.

♦ There are many LinkedIn applications you can use to help with your marketing.

♦ You can analyze your network by viewing the Network Statistics section on your LinkedIn profile.

MySpace, Streaming Social Media, and Internet Radio

In This Chapter

- ◆ MySpace and its powerful reach and features
- ◆ Profiles, site navigation, and applications for MySpace
- ◆ Exploring Justin.tv, Lifecasting, and Lifestreaming
- ◆ Get introduced to combining and streaming your content
- ◆ How to create your own Internet radio show

When reading the chapter's title, you may have thought you'd been transported to the year 2050. And if you haven't been involved with social media marketing, you may be scratching your head wondering about this futuristic language that is emerging with these social networking platforms.

In this chapter, we explore several popular sites and discuss marketing methods. Ready to be a part of the future? Okay, let's review MySpace, Lifecasting, and Internet Radio.

What's Happening on MySpace?

Launched in January 2004 and headquartered in Beverly Hills, California, MySpace is a social media platform you should not ignore. They call themselves a "technology company connecting people through expression, content, and culture." Today, MySpace remains one of the largest social media platforms with over 130 million member profiles internationally and over 70 million in the United States (as of July 2009, according to comScore, Inc).

This self-described "place for friends" underwent a redo in 2008 with newly designed pages that included status updates and applications. You can add your blog, videos, messaging, join groups, add a calendar of dates, and more! Like the other platforms, MySpace does have its own unique look and feel. So if you haven't seen it in a while, it's time to go back and take a look.

MySpace is the world's largest music community. It has been a very successful platform for those in the entertainment industry and also for those who *want* to be in the entertainment industry. When browsing through the site, you will see a lot of the top music artists, but also many "garage bands" hoping to make it big. Many bands credit MySpace for helping them to develop quite a following.

MySpace isn't bland; it's a colorful display of video. There's also sound, and all this seems to draw a younger viewing audience who eagerly participate. However, when looking through the site, you will also find business professionals, sales trainers, consultants, speakers, real estate agents, authors, and more who are branding and marketing themselves. What is encouraging for many folks who advertise or market themselves on MySpace is the amount of time that viewers spend on the site.

The average user spends nearly 3.5 hours on the site per day. And according to July 2009 comScore figures, MySpace users viewed a total of 33.4 billion total pages and spent 16.4 billion total minutes on the site, so this audience is really engaged. Still, consider it a part of your social media marketing and get your profile on there because, again, you never know where your next big customer or business partner is going to come from.

> **Did You Know?**
>
> Even though it's hard to tell the exact demographics on MySpace, there are ways to get around that. For example, do you want to reach the Latino market? There's the MySpace Latino site at latino.myspace.com. It's the same website, but written in Spanish!

Creating a Profile

Go to www.myspace.com. You will see a colorful page that most likely has a "flash style" ad on the top third of the page with video movement and a lot of information. Above that, you should see the search bar and the Sign Up! button on the far right side. Before you sign up, surf around to get a feel for the site. When you are ready, click **Sign Up!**

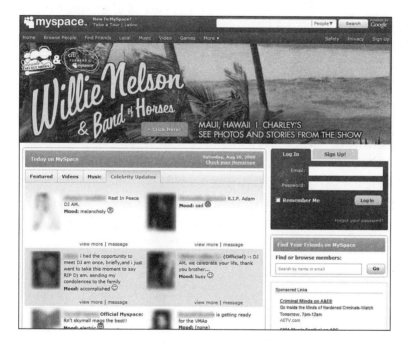

Here's the Home page for MySpace.

You arrive at the Sign Up page. Fill out the information, then click **Sign Up** and enter the given security code. If you are a musician, comedian, or filmmaker, see the separate Profile types on the right side of the Sign Up screen on this page and use those.

After you sign up and confirm your registration via e-mail, you can log in. You will get directed to a Profile page. Click on **Profile** and open the drop-down menu and click on **Edit Profile.**

Here's the Sign Up page for MySpace.

Here's where you create your profile on MySpace.

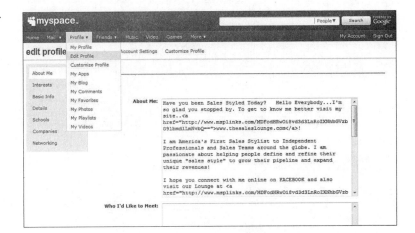

Next, fill out your profile. Come up with a great headline for yourself. Remember, you want to attract people to your business. Fill out the About Me portion. Share your expertise and how you can help people. There is a line that reads "Who would you like to meet?" Cleverly mention the types of clients you want to work with or people you would like to be introduced to.

Next, under Interests, you will see the General section. Here, you can invite people to follow you on the other social media platforms, such as Twitter, Facebook, and YouTube. Mention your blog here along with your website. Remember to keep your links live with the "http://" in front of the website pages.

Continue down the page and fill in your favorite books, music, heroes, and so on. Click **Preview,** then click **Save.**

Next, you're ready to move on to Basic Info, which is on the left navigation bar. Fill in information here as you complete your profile.

You should go through each of those and determine which ones to fill in to market your business. But here are a few that you should pay attention to:

◆ About Me

◆ Interests

◆ Basic Info (this is where you also upload your photo)

◆ Companies (at a minimum, list your current company)

Be sure you click **Save Changes** when you're done.

Next, you need to go back to Profile and the drop-down menu to Customize Profile.

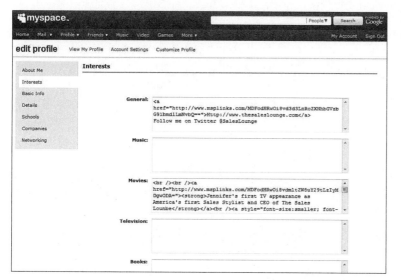

Here's where you can list your likes and dislikes on MySpace.

Here you can choose themes, change your page layout, and move or hide boxes (or "profile modules," as MySpace calls them). You can preview them by clicking on the Preview button on the top left. Then, when you're done, click **Publish** and then click **Exit.**

Here's where you can customize your profile on MySpace.

Next, you can add a few friends. But first, please note you may see a welcome note from "Tom." Don't let that surprise you, Tom is the co-founder of MySpace. (Note, as of this writing, it's rumored that the "default friend" of Tom may not continue. So if you don't see Tom, do not worry.) Just like the other platforms, you can search for people using the search bar. On MySpace, however, you can also search by e-mail address. There is also a place on the page to select your e-mail address carrier and search for friends you are already connected to via e-mail and invite them to connect to you on MySpace.

Here's where you find friends on MySpace.

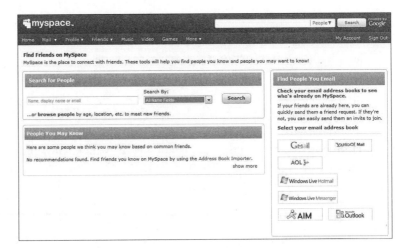

Account Settings

The Account Display settings are a bit hard to find. Go to My Account on the top right navigation bar and then click on **Miscellaneous.** A Profile page will pop up and this will allow you to determine what you want to be visible on your page. For example, do you want to display your groups, photos, and profile comments from others? Do you want music playing when people arrive on your page? You can set this up using the music player and the songs from your profile playlist.

Here's where you edit your Account settings on MySpace.

Account Privacy Settings

The privacy settings are also hard to find, but like the others, it lets you customize what others can view on your page. To find Privacy Settings, go to **My Account.** Then click **Privacy.** The General Privacy page displays. You can show people you are online or not, hide your birthday, determine who can make comments on your page, decide who can view photos, and you can block certain people from viewing your profile as well. Note, if you have younger teens on MySpace, it would be good to go through this with them.

Here's where you edit your Account Privacy settings on MySpace.

Eliminating Security CAPTCHAs

Tired of those squiggly letter codes popping up on your screen? They're called CAPTCHAs. To eliminate them, simply go to My Account, then go to No More CAPTCHAs and enter your cell phone number. MySpace will, in turn, send you a code to enter on this screen to eliminate the security CAPTCHAs.

Here's where you eliminate those squiggly lined security codes, called CAPTCHAs on MySpace.

Applications for Marketing on MySpace

There are many applications on MySpace. Many of them are for fun and for socializing, but there are also some that may be helpful to you from a business marketing perspective. To find the applications, click **Home,** scroll over to More, and then, on the drop-down menu, look for the Apps Gallery. These following sections discuss the applications you can use.

Video on MySpace

Certainly, MySpace is a site where you want to try to include video in your profile. Once you've decided what video to upload, MySpace makes getting your video onto the site very easy. Log on to MySpace and click **Videos** in the upper part of the navigation bar. Click **Upload** and then use the Browse feature to search for videos that are on your computer. Click **Upload** again to confirm. Because the MySpace culture is visual, try to upload one of your videos that best describes your business or maybe even client testimonials. Get creative! Sing a song, rap, have music playing in video, interview people, or do a skit. Just have fun!

Groups on MySpace

MySpace has many groups, so you can network and even create your own group. To find the groups, go to your Home page, scroll across the top navigation bar to More, and then use the drop-down menu to find Groups.

Here's where you find Groups on MySpace.

There are business and entrepreneurial groups (over 30,000 of them), fitness and wellness groups, schools and alumni, fashion, neighborhood groups, and many more. Search the group categories and see if you can find one that's of interest to you. On the same page to the left, you will also see the Create a Group button where in just a few easy steps you can be on your way to creating your own group on MySpace.

Forums on MySpace

Another way to network and strategically get your information and expertise is by participating in the MySpace forums. To do this, go to Home, scroll over to More on the navigation bar, and use the drop-down menu to Forums. Forums are great for discussions and further networking and to "listen" to what people are talking about.

> ### Did You Know?
>
> MySpace has added an IM, or Instant Messaging, feature. To enable it, simply go to My Account on the top navigation bar. Then click on the IM letters in blue on the top of the page.

There are many to choose from, with many of them having tens of thousands of members. You can find a Computers & Technology forum and others ranging from General Discussion to Fashion to Food & Drink. There are conversations happening, so join on in!

Here's where you find the list of forums on MySpace.

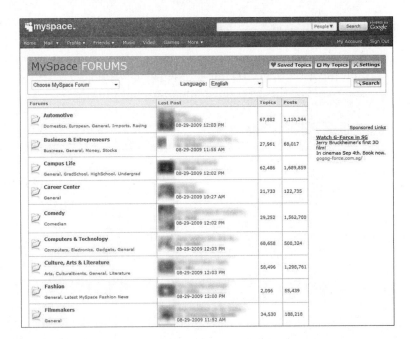

Your MySpace Blog

MySpace has an area where you can create your own MySpace blog and link it to a category on the site. Fair warning: you will see blog entries for just about every type, but focus on your own area and industry. There are people out there who want to hear from you, so keep it true to your style and vision. Blogging on MySpace is yet another way to share your expertise and your brand with the world. Not sure about blogs and what they are? You will learn more about Blogs in Chapter 16.

To create a MySpace Blog, go to Home and scroll over to More. Then use the drop-down menu to select **Top Blogs.** On the Top Blogs page, scroll way down to My Controls, which are on the bottom-left side of your screen. Tab down to Post New Blog and you will arrive at the Blog Control Center, where you begin posting your blog.

Simply enter the date, time, subject, and category of your blog. Then begin blogging. When you are done, you can add photos and links to your blog (and even a symbol for your mood) and then post them. Preview, then post it. You can post publicly or privately to friends and fans.

Here's the Blog Control Center on MySpace.

Recording Video

Have something to say today and want to get it on MySpace? MySpace allows you to upload and immediately record video from your desktop webcam. If you have a video in your arsenal that you want to upload onto MySpace, they make that easy as well. Click on the **Video** tab on the upper navigation bar.

You will see on the right side in red font Upload and Record. Simply click on those and MySpace makes it easy to upload and/or record.

Here's where you can upload or record videos on MySpace.

Streaming Social Media

Some are saying that "streaming" (or "lifestreaming" or "streaming social") is the next big favorite on social media. But what is it exactly? It is basically a record of a person's current online and offline activities. This record can be shared via video or blog posts or just with photos. Lifestreaming permits you to take any or all of the social media technology and give readers or viewers a snapshot of what is happening in your life.

The following sections discuss some great sites to get you started with Streaming or Lifecasting.

Lifecasting and Justin.tv

Keeping with the video and entertainment theme, a relatively new form of social media marketing is called lifecasting. Lifecasting is a video blog of sorts where a person does a continual broadcast of events or of a situation through video or digital media.

For example, a songwriter may have a camera running as he is composing. An artist may have the camera running as she is sketching. A retail owner may have the camera in his store window or at the cash register. Perhaps you are a radio broadcaster; you could have a camera running during a typical morning while you are broadcasting your radio show. Some use it just to talk and have people observe their life as they are just living it. It's an interesting concept, so keep an open mind about how you could use lifecasting in your business.

Justin.tv is a popular lifecasting website and live video website. As of January 2010, their website boasts over 500,000 channels broadcasting live video, including the Producers channel, which has Xbox Lifecasting. Other channels include Educational, Animals, News & Events, Sports, and More. For lifecasting from your office or place of business, this may be the solution you are looking for.

Netiquette

With lifecasting, you want to be yourself. Be real, authentic, and transparent. You didn't put on makeup? Don't worry. Didn't brush your hair? That's okay, too. Make it what you want to make it. It's okay to start a new trend, even if that involves not prepping yourself before going live. Just remember what you put online stays online, even if it's sitting on a server somewhere.

Here's where you can find lifecasting plus many other channels on Justin.tv.

Create account

Lifestreaming

Another term you may soon hear more about is lifestreaming. This is similar to lifecasting, but with a twist. Lifestreaming is an online record, if you will, of a person's activities. That record can be made via live blog entries, tweets, Facebook status updates, or with a stream of live chronological photographs. You then "stream" or send this information in chronological order out to your social media sites. There are many sites that can help you stream, and some of them are listed in the following sections.

FriendFeed

FriendFeed (friendfeed.com) is one of the sites that can help you feed and stream your information. Known as an aggregator of social media sites, FriendFeed (which was acquired by Facebook in 2009) is a website that enables you to feed all of your collected social networking services at once. It does this by providing a singular stream of updates from you to many of your social media sources. For example: you create an account on FriendFeed, and it will let your friends know when you share an update, video photo, and so on. It also works across many of the blogging services, so your blog updates can feed to wherever you direct them to among your social networks.

Tumblr

Tumblr (tumblr.com) is also another site that lets you "effortlessly share" or stream just about anything. Tumblr gets literally hundreds of thousands of posts through its blogging tool each day. It can do many things, but let's say you have videos on YouTube and photos on another site. Tumblr will combine them and put them in one easy place to view or stream it for you. It does this by combining the information and sending it to your friends from one place.

Tumblr is another site that makes it easy to share just about anything with your friends.

Internet Radio

You've heard of the days when our relatives and ancestors gathered around the big radio to be entertained and informed by the outside world. Now, we can do the entertaining and inform the world with our very own radio show. And we can do it all from the convenience of our home.

This would have been unimaginable 30 years ago, but now it is a reality. Creating your own Internet radio program as part of your social networking strategy will set you apart as the go-to expert in your industry, not to mention that it will give you and your business more national and international exposure. After recording, you can advertise and promote your program on all of your social media sites and even stream it to some of your sites live.

Did You Know?

Internet listeners are largely adults who can access the Internet at work with high-speed connections.

- Sixty-one percent of the entire Internet listening audience is adults between the ages of 25 and 44.
- Nineteen percent is between 45 and 54 years old.
- Fourteen percent is between 18 and 24 years old.

Source: The Arbitron Internet Listening Study, August 2009.

Live365.com

Live365 (Live365.com) reaches millions of people worldwide and features over 260 genres of music. As of August 2009, there were over 5,000 broadcasters from a combined 150 countries. Live365.com is self-described as music programming by "real people with a deep passion for music." If your business wants to start a radio program, Live365 attracts four million-plus listeners each month. According to its website, it provides broadcasting software, tracking and reporting, licensing support, and more.

BlogTalkRadio

Do you love to talk on the phone or with your customers? Ready to host your own radio show and partake in live interactive discussions? Now you can. All you need is a telephone and a computer and you are live—on the air—with an Internet radio show on BlogTalkRadio (blogtalkradio.com).

If you want to have your own Internet radio show, you should try BlogTalkRadio.

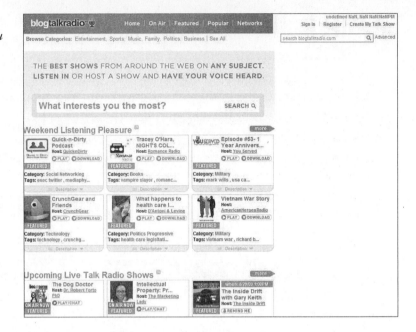

Online Cautions

You may think you only have one listener when recording your live radio show. Well, think again. You never know who may be listening to an archived version of your show. You don't know who they are or where they will be listening from. It's best to always be diligent about what you say and who you mention on the air.

Not sure how you would make it work? Perhaps you are a life or business coach who wants to talk with other subject matter experts that your audience will find value in hearing from? Perhaps you are a recruiter who wants to talk about the job market and interviewing skills? Maybe you are a tax accountant and want to host a show on tax practices or have a call-in show for answers to tax questions? Just about anyone can have a radio show.

People want to hear from you. With 5.7 million listeners each month, BlogTalkRadio is an amazing tool for Internet radio marketing of your expertise and viral marketing for your business. Once you complete the online host form, two dedicated telephone numbers will be assigned to you. One is for the callers so they can call in to participate and the other is for the show host. For the Free service, up to five callers can call in at a time. However if you upgrade, up to 100 can call in at one time and hundreds if not thousands can listen. You can broadcast up to two shows a day and have an optional text chat for each program so that you can have even more interaction with your callers. You can also send out links of the show's recording to your social media audience.

The site does a lot to help its host create a successful program, but one cool thing is that you can archive your show or stream it live. BlogTalkRadio also has a service that provides a simple cut, copy, and paste coding so that the hosts or the guests can place promotional "badges" (a new word for ads) on their own social media sites like Facebook, MySpace, Twitter, and their own blogs. Move over, Larry King and Ryan Seacrest, because here comes the next amazing radio host. Could it be you?

The Least You Need to Know

◆ MySpace is still a key player in the social media world, particularly for the music and entertainment industry.

◆ The average MySpace user spends nearly 3.5 hours on the site per day.

◆ Justin.tv has over 500,000 channels for video and/or lifecasting, where you will find people broadcasting and connecting 24/7.

◆ Lifecasting is on the rise and growing in popularity with the younger teen and 20-something generation, but entrepreneurs of all ages are beginning to discover creative ways to incorporate it into their social media marketing.

◆ Internet radio is booming and millions are listening online each month.

◆ It can take as little as 15 minutes to set up a radio show on certain sites, and you can begin broadcasting to the world.

Chapter 15

Lights! Camera! Sell!

In This Chapter

♦ Understanding the new and popular video marketing

♦ What you need to get started in online video

♦ Using big sites like YouTube as well as the up-and-coming smaller sites for your Internet video presence

♦ How to create your own Internet TV show

♦ Integrating video with the other major social media platforms and blogs

We all know the old saying "a picture is worth a thousand words." Well, today a good marketing video can be worth thousands of dollars—to your business, that is.

With faster-running laptops, wireless technology, and amazing recording devices, video nowadays looks and sounds better online than ever before. In this chapter, you learn why video marketing needs to be considered an essential part of your social media marketing identity. How are people finding video online? Through the many social media marketing sites. Start thinking video and wherever you go, bring your digital video camera. Ready to continue your journey toward becoming a social media superstar? Let's get started.

The New Video Marketing

The new video marketing is fun, authentic, and real. You no longer need big lights, studios,and production teams to get your video produced. Today, it's as simple as getting a handheld video camera like the Flip Mino by Pure Digital or a DV camcorder. Take some time to practice pointing and aiming, and you're ready to go live!

Today, anyone can potentially become the next Internet video TV star. The playing field is leveling out, and this is great news for the entrepreneur or small business owner. Today's entrepreneur can create an unlimited array of videos that will help with marketing and branding their businesses to the world.

Some popular examples include welcome messages to new customers when they arrive on websites and "how can we help you?" videos aimed at new prospects. Also, many people are using video to record testimonials of happy customers. Gone are the days of only having a written testimonial. Today, seeing and hearing testimonials is what audiences are responding to. How great would it be to have your prospects hear from your happy customers via video versus hearing it directly from you, the owner? It's much more powerful for an audience to hear about how great your services/products are from other people aside from the business owner. Video brings these testimonials to life.

Netiquette

Always get written permission from people to broadcast their image in your online videos. Usually, they will agree when they agree to do the video, but a best practice is to get a video release form signed. For ideas on wording, search online for video release form samples or contact your business attorney for assistance.

Television was designed as one medium to many viewers. Online video is crafted as one to one. Today, corporations, small businesses, and entrepreneurs are using online video and mobile products to seemingly speak one to one to their customers, prospects, and Internet audience through video.

By appearing onscreen within your customers' and prospects' computers, an interesting psychological transition begins to take place. Viewers begin to feel that they "know" you. They grow (hopefully!) to like you. And if you provide good information, they grow to respect what you do. Then when they meet you in person, the connection has already been made and people feel more comfortable with you.

Here are some examples of how entrepreneurs and small business owners are using online video:

♦ A tip of the day or tip of the week.

♦ Starting an Internet TV show.

♦ Auto dealers showing a maintenance tip of the week.

♦ Success coaches giving a motivational thought.

♦ Real estate agents sharing neighborhood reports via video.

♦ Sales experts sharing an online sales tip.

♦ Entrepreneurs recording from their home office or other creative locations, such as from a local café, park, restaurant, or museum.

♦ Marketing an upcoming workshop, product, or book.

> **Did You Know?**
>
> The .tv domain is becoming a popular website extension. Savvy professionals are thinking ahead and buying this domain for their business. Get yours today, even before you get into online video.

And the list goes on and on. But the difference today is that these videos are conversational and authentic. That's what people are responding to on social media sites.

Who Is Watching Online Video?

In July 2009, Pew Internet released an online video report that showed that people of all ages are watching more online video each year. The study went on to explain that the largest growing demographic was 30- to 49-year-olds, with 67 percent of that age group using video-sharing sites. But 50- to 64-year-olds are viewing as well. Only 34 percent watched online videos in the 2008 report, but in 2009 that number grew to 41 percent. This Pew Internet report shows that watching videos on the Internet is on the rise for all age groups.

The point is that these numbers are forecasted to continue to increase. Video is hot, hot, hot! So let's get your business "camera ready" and part of the online video revolution.

What You Need to Get Started

You need a good camera. Very popular today are the Flip video cameras from Pure Digital. They can be found easily and they are not expensive. The high-definition version is recommended so you get the crisp, clear image on the screen. However, there are many other video cameras that will work. You can also get a Digital Video (DV) camcorder. These are a bit larger than the handheld Flip, but they produce very good quality with better microphones and good image quality. Again, get the high-definition versions.

Cell phones with video can work, but the quality (as of this writing) isn't as good as a digital video camera. Cell phones are good, though, to catch something on the fly. However, if you are serious about making video an integral part of your social media marketing, invest in a camera. There are plenty of cameras on the market that aren't expensive.

In addition, many computers come with built-in web cameras (webcams), and that is a fine place to begin getting used to video. If you use a webcam, you will also want to invest in a good headset and microphone because you can also use this for webinars. The EYEBALL, by Blue Microphone, is a combination webcam and microphone. Order it online or find at select stores. (We will get into webinars in Chapter 17.) You should also get a tripod for your small handheld or DV camcorder.

What else do you need? Just like we said earlier in the book, you need a great mindset. Talk to your audience. Pretend your ideal client is on the other side of that camera. What would you say to him or her? Lastly, come up with a plan. What would your audience like to see? Bring them into your business by letting them get to know you, your products, and services better. Begin looking online at other business videos and watch what others are doing because this will generate ideas. Don't be shy … just be yourself! If you are not quite ready but want to learn more first, begin watching online videos on Facebook and Twitter and participate in some free webinars online. They are happening just about every day.

YouTube: The Leader of All Things Video

Founded in February 2005, YouTube is the definitive leader in online video. Today, it gets a staggering 1 billion views per day.

YouTube makes it easy to upload and share your videos. You can post your videos on YouTube and even create your own video channel. If you haven't done so yet, go ahead and create a YouTube account. Go to www.youtube.com and click on **Sign Up** at the top right side of the screen. It's easy to do.

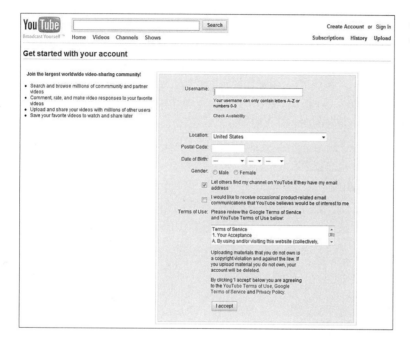

Here's where you create your account on YouTube.

After you get your account set up, sign in, and take a look. Enter a topic into the search bar and look at all of the content. You can subscribe to Video Channels, Search Videos, and more. It's also good to know in advance that viewers cannot download your video from YouTube; however, you will be given an option to allow viewers to *embed* your video when you upload your video file. There is a site called Keepvid (keepvid.com), which allows you to download videos from Youtube.

For great social media marketing, you should upload videos to YouTube. But how do you do that? First, ensure your video is no longer than 10 minutes in length or no larger than 2 GB. This is the maximum time and size that YouTube allows. Next, sign into YouTube and look for the Upload

def•i•ni•tion

Embed means to make something an integral part, such as embedding a video into your website or blog.

def•i•ni•tion

Tags are keywords that describe the content of your video. They are also search words that people use to find content. When selecting tags, think about what keywords viewers would use to find your video.

button (in yellow) in the right corner of your screen. You can upload your video from here or record from your webcam. Click on **Upload** and select your video from your computer.

Now you need a title for your video. Don't spend too much time worrying about the title, particularly when you are getting started, but you do need to title it because you want it to be found. The next step is to describe the video. Write in your *tags*. Then, choose broadcast options: public (with the world) or private (up to 25 people). To upload or select another one, click **Upload Video.**

Here's the Video File Upload screen where you choose your title and describe your video.

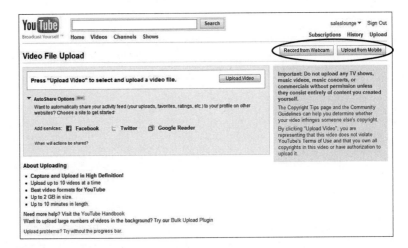

Next click **Go to My Videos,** where you can play the video editor and your video.

Did You Know?

The AudioSwap feature on YouTube allows you to add royalty-free music or permission-free music on top of your video. You can pick the genre of music and publish it to your video. You cannot just use any music or you will be fined. Stick with royalty-free.

Now click **Edit.** Go through all of the areas on the left side of the screen. They ask you about online broadcast options, such as if you want to allow comments, if you want people to vote on a video, and more. You can even add a map for where you recorded the video. You can add annotations or wording on the screen and promote the video. After you've finished, save your responses.

Congratulations, you have a video on YouTube!

This is the final screen that enables you to make some quick changes before the upload.

This screen enables you to make choices about broadcasting options and much more.

To create your own channel on YouTube, go to My Account at the top of the page and click the link to create your own channel. Name your channel and describe it. You have the ability to let people add comments to your channel and check the option that lets others find your channel. After you enable these options, click **Update.** Click **Channel Designs** and **Organize Videos** on the left side of this page. This gives your channel a business look and feel. Note, there are also video tutorials on this on YouTube. Just search for them using the search bar.

This screen enables you to make choices about your YouTube channel.

Other Sites to Market and Share Video

YouTube is the biggest and most popular site for videos, but there are other up-and-coming sites that you should know about. Video is the future, so be sure you're on the lookout for new sites. Next, I review some of the smaller sites that you might find useful.

12seconds.tv

Just when you thought you had the written status update down for Facebook and Twitter, here comes 12seconds.tv. Think of this as a video version of your status update. It's a fun and easy way to quickly share your message (or status) with fans and followers using short 12-second video messages. I like it because it's easy to use and integrates wonderfully with most of the major platforms. It's also another way to use social media to market your business and share your expertise. This site works great with a webcam. You can also easily upload videos from other handheld cameras or mobile devices.

Ready to record a video? Go to 12seconds.tv and sign up for an account.

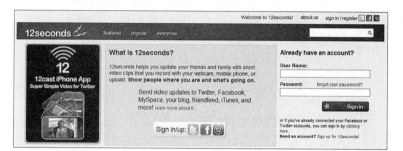

After you sign up, here's an example of your page on 12seconds.tv.

Log in and click **Record.** A screen pops up asking for your *video status* with the question, "What are you doing?" You can add *tags* (or keywords that describe your video) and your location. You can also make your video public or private. Look at the right side of your screen and share your video on Twitter, Facebook, and MySpace. Not sure what to say the first time? Answer the Daily Challenge (just click on it and it will ask you a question). Or do the 12erator, which asks your thoughts on a subject.

This site also integrates with TweetDeck and mobile devices. On your TweetDeck, you will see an icon across the top that reads "12." Here you can click on **12** and record or upload your video directly from TweetDeck. Savvy marketers utilize 12seconds.tv to record thoughts from an event, record before or after an event, share a quick tip, share a client testimonial, and more! The possibilities are endless.

def•i•ni•tion

Video status is just like your written status update, except that it is distributed via video.

Tags in this instance are singular words used to describe what is being discussed in the video. Tags help draw viewers to your video if they are interested in the tags that they read.

Record an update on
12seconds.tv.

Vimeo

Vimeo (vimeo.com) is a clean and professional site where members gather to post and share videos. Their video player has extraordinary quality. You can join groups on Vimeo, create your own group, or even create your own channel. In January 2010, there were 25,740 groups on Vimeo and 57,730 channels. Basic membership is free, but a Vimeo Plus membership will cost you $59.95 per year.

After you create your account, there is a Profile page to fill out before you can begin uploading videos and sharing videos with your friends and network. It's another place to market your videos and your brand and network with others by joining like-minded groups.

The Home page for Vimeo.

Blip.tv

Blip.tv began in 2005 and now boasts over 48,000 independently produced web shows. According to their website, Blip.tv reaches more than 22 million people. A unique component of Blip.tv is that advertisers share revenues 50/50 with the show creators. The site is designed to easily upload all types of video and send them easily to your viewers. When you sign up, you have the option of allowing advertising (which you can make some money from). You still own your own work, but I recommend reading the terms on their site for more information about this. This is great for those who want to create episodic Internet TV shows, not just a one-shot deal. Blip.tv provides a nice user-friendly webpage, which helps users easily interface with the site and quickly upload and produce away. Everything is on Blip.tv, from independent film trailers to video shows from entrepreneurs.

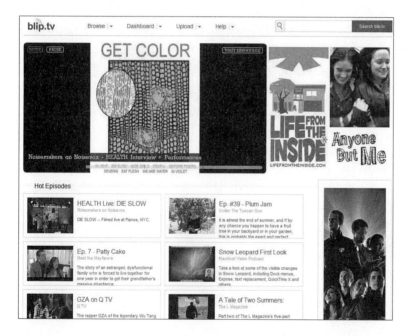

Here's the Home page for Blip.tv.

Viddler

Viddler (viddler.com) is a fun site that enables you to share and optimize your videos for further marketing. The component that makes Viddler so cool is that you can brand your videos with your logo, frame them with your color scheme, and even have the videos link back to your website. What great marketing! You can also post comments and tags at specific points in your video and even share your videos with iTunes or via an RSS feed.

For business use, however, there are monthly fees. But with the fees there are many perks, including dedicated support, so it's definitely worth a look. When you create your account, you'll see the many membership offerings.

The Learn More page for Viddler.

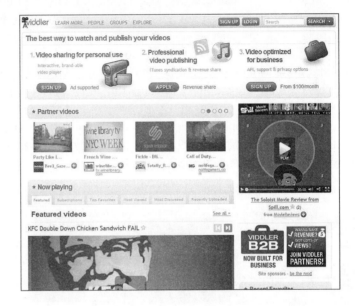

Viddler also has a feature that enables viewers to easily interact with your video by posting comments within the video. The site says it's even possible for viewers to record a video comment. Viddler is hip and popular among savvy Internet marketers—certainly a site to check out.

Learn about building your brand on Viddler.

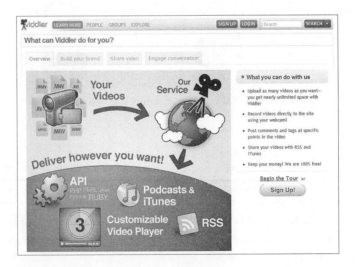

Creating Your Own Internet TV Show

Internet TV is quickly becoming popular among savvy marketers and celebrities. In a medium where people want to see, hear, experience, and engage with the show host or expert, Internet TV with interactivity is becoming the place to be seen.

Ustream.tv

Founded in 2006 as a way to connect U.S. military soldiers with their families back home, Ustream.tv has turned into something with even broader appeal. This site is for anyone and anything that wants to have a live streaming Internet TV show. It provides an interactive video broadcast platform where anyone with a camera and Internet connection can easily broadcast to the world. This site's system encourages two-way communication between on-air talent and viewers. It also offers unlimited possibilities for the entrepreneur and small business owner.

Take a look and explore the site and you will see what seems to be every genre represented, from pets to ponds to politics to people. Yes, it's the one place where people, places, politics, plants, puppies, and even hamsters have their own streaming show. And if you are wondering about plants having their own show, well, there are live streaming shows of gardens.

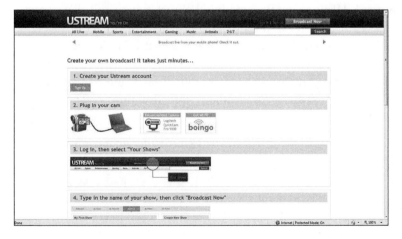

Search for live streaming video on Ustream.tv.

Some creative ideas for you about live video streaming:

- ◆ A pet store runs a live feed from the store window showcasing homeless pets.
- ◆ A retail store can broadcast live.

- A book retailer or book club could stream live book reviews.

- A coach could stream a live coaching session.

- A fitness coach could stream a weekly exercise regimen.

- A sales trainer could stream a weekly class in sales calls.

- Set up a live broadcast from an event and record from a booth or table.

- Host a call-in show and talk about your industry.

- An artist could live stream while they are painting or designing a piece.

- A performance group could stream their rehearsals.

Netiquette

A best practice is not to rant on your Internet TV show. You never know whose eyes will land upon the video. Keep it viewer focused, share value, and entertain (or infotain) people with your knowledge.

Again, the possibilities are endless. Both creativity and reality are what's attracting people to brands and businesses.

BlogTV

You've heard of a blog and you're reading about Internet TV, so let me introduce you to BlogTV (blogtv.com). Want to continue to build your fan base and share your expertise and your business story? You can do it live on BlogTV. Their site reads, "You bring the webcam, we bring the stage." Founded in May 2006, this is a site where you can broadcast your own shows from your webcam and blog. You can chat with viewers and get live feedback while you are recording your show. You can share your show with friends and post it to your blog. You can also upload photos, create events, upload music, and share it with just friends or make it public.

BlogTV also provides a Junior Channel for the 13- to 15-year-old age group so they can create their own TV shows. Once you sign up for the account, you will receive an e-mail confirmation. You can then name your show, gather your audience (send an e-mail to your friends), send an update to your Twitter account, send info directly to your blog, add a custom background to your show page, and more. There is also a pro version for a nominal annual fee that gives you more upgrades, bandwidth, and priority. You may just become the next Internet TV star!

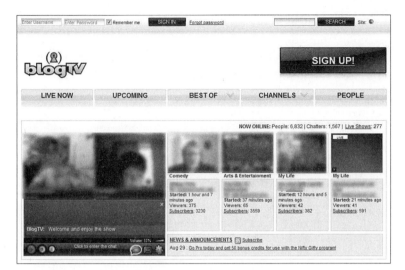

The Home page for BlogTV.

TubeMogul

TubeMogul (tubemogul.com) describes its service as an online video solution for marketers where video is made "actionable." As of August 2009, over one million videos had been deployed using TubeMogul, with over 100,000 users. TubeMogul has a free solution for users that distributes or syndicates your video to a number of sites and also provides you with some light user analytics.

There is also a premium version. For a fee, you can get an incredible array of data regarding your video viewership. A cool feature is that as soon as your video goes live, you can send it directly to Twitter and Facebook. The dynamic thing about the TubeMogul solution is that they make your video actionable—they can incorporate the video description, title, and so on. They can also brand your video display screen.

For example, if you're in the video and the viewer of the video puts the cursor on your face, an information pop-up box will launch that describes who you are. They also provide a dynamic video analytics dashboard of your videos so you can see where your videos are viewed from geographically as well as how often. The rich analytics seem to be a true strength with this solution, along with the way they make your videos come to life, in addition to the actionable links and information that they install into the video.

Instead of uploading your video to all kinds of sites yourself, let TubeMogul distribute it. If you are looking to promote a video campaign or Web series with a wide distribution, TubeMogul can help you by delivering a "guaranteed television-sized audience that is specifically targeted to your business demographic" (on a cost per view basis). TubeMogul provides you reports on viewership so you can really determine who is watching from where. It's worth taking a look for your big video campaign and distribution. They offer free, business level, and gold premium plans.

Here's the Home page for TubeMogul.

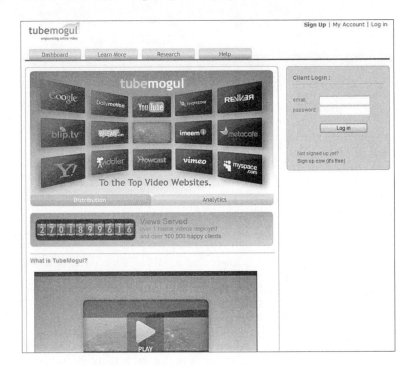

Dailymotion

Dailymotion (dailymotion.com) asks, "What good is a video, if it's stuck on your camera, hard-drive, or mobile phone?" Dailymotion is another site that gets your video distributed. According to comScore (April 2009), Dailymotion attracts 59 million unique monthly visitors worldwide to its website.

The site is about helping you find new ways to see, share, and engage your audience through the power of online video. Aside from uploading your own videos, you can also find videos centered on your interests. Check out Dailymotion to …

- ◆ Share your videos publicly with the world or privately with friends.
- ◆ Discover new videos through channels or keywords (tags).

- Get feedback on your video clips.

- Get your videos across the web by posting them to your blog, website, or other social network profiles.

Metacafe

The Metacafe website (metacafe.com) states it is one of the world's largest video sites, attracting more than 40 million unique viewers each month (per comScore/Metrix). Know, however, that Metacafe is not a video sharing and hosting site that enables any and every video to be posted. Instead, how the website promotes is what makes it different.

- Metacafe specializes in short-form videos averaging approximately 90 seconds long.

- The focus is on entertainment, so you won't find hard-news stories.

- It wants the experience to be audience driven and the videos are user generated, user reviewed, and user selected.

So that's how it differs from the other sites. There's also a community review panel (80,000 volunteers) that reviews the videos daily and a ranking system that identifies the popular videos.

The Least You Need to Know

- Video marketing continues to grow in popularity, and anyone with a camera and a computer can get a video online.

- The new video marketing requires being real, authentic, informative, and entertaining.

- There are many websites to host and deliver your video at no charge, but some sites offer upgrades for a nominal fee.

- Sites like BlogTV, 12seconds.tv, Viddler, Blip.tv, Ustream, and Vimeo are fun and easy to use.

- There are many sites, such as TubeMogul, that help you push your video to many platforms and gather site analytics and viewership.

Chapter 16

Blogs: The Hub of Your Social Media Marketing

In This Chapter

- ◆ Why you need to consider having a blog
- ◆ Tips for writing a blog
- ◆ The top blogging service providers
- ◆ Ways to promote your blog
- ◆ Applications that help make your blog even more powerful

With all of the excitement and newness of social media, is it still important to have your own blog? Absolutely! Blogs are very much alive and doing better than ever. After reading this chapter, you'll understand that your blog is not only an integral part of your social media marketing strategy, but it is, perhaps, the most influential part.

In this chapter, we discuss what blogs are, how popular they are, how to set them up, what makes them successful, and how to tie them into your other social media sites. This chapter puts it all together so you know all the essentials to make your mark on the blogging word.

What's a Blog?

A blog is short for web log. So a blog is sort of a log or a personal writing that's accessible to the world on a web page. The blog is traced back to one blogger (if not the very first blogger), Justin Hall, who began personal blogging back in 1994. Things have evolved since then. Gone are the days of the blog with just text, text, and more text. Today's blog can be just as dynamic and engaging as some of the social media platforms that we've already talked about.

If you want a place to write about your expertise and gear it to your target clients and be easily found on the search engines, a blog is the perfect platform to do just that.

Why Should You Consider a Blog?

Blogging is here to stay, and participation by writers and by readers is on the rise. Technorati.com stated that eMarketer (May 2008) reported there were 94.1 million U.S. blog readers in 2007, which was 50 percent of the Internet audience at that time. And the BlogWorld website stated in August 2009 that over 12 million American adults currently are a part of the *blogosphere*.

def•i•ni•tion

Blogosphere refers to the blogging universe in general. If you blog, you are part of the collective blogosphere.

There are many reasons why you should consider writing a blog. In fact, many would argue that it's essential for someone promoting a business or product. Here's a short list of reasons that might inspire you to start blogging:

◆ You can't control what is going to happen to all of the other social media platforms as they continue to evolve, but you can control your blog. It's your platform to do whatever you want to do with it.

◆ It's a great place to share your expertise, so you'll be seen as a subject matter expert and your readers will begin to see you as an industry leader.

◆ Blogs are a great way to attract clients. Once they find you and follow your blog, they'll learn to respect your expertise and trust your brand.

◆ You can guide your other social media followers from Facebook, LinkedIn, and Twitter to your blog to learn more about you or the subject matter you write about.

◆ You can invite guest bloggers to post on your blog, which is a great networking and strategic marketing tool for you.

- It will give your followers, fans, and prospects a place to leave detailed comments about your blogging posts, and thus become more engaged with you.

- The Internet search engines love blogs. This makes you easier to find for clients, prospects, and strategic partners.

- A good blog can give you great credibility among your clients, prospects, and potential strategic partners.

- Most bloggers agree that having a blog helps you to become a better writer and that it also helps you to clearly define your passions, business direction, and focus.

- For some entrepreneurs, their blog is so alive with information—such as video, Twitter, and other social media links—it actually replaces their websites.

Getting Started

Denise Wakeman, a blogging expert, says, "Think about your purpose, goals, audience, and message" when getting ready to get into the world of blogging. As a business owner, think about who you want to read your blog. But before you jump into the blogosphere, answer the following questions. They'll help you focus and do a better job of crafting your blog:

- Are your readers male, female, or both?

- What age are they?

- What's their income level?

- Are they stay-at-home moms, writers, or entrepreneurs?

- What do readers need to know?

- Why would people want to read my blog?

- What will keep them coming back each week?

- Where can I find these people on the web?

- What should I name the blog?

And here's one more very important question to ask yourself: Are you willing to commit to regularly updating your blog?

Online Cautions _____

Don't start your blog with one entry and not go back to it. As you can imagine, this does not look good. Get three to five posts going and then start promoting it. Experts agree that there is nothing worse than finding a blog that hasn't been updated in three months.

Blogging experts say one post per week is the absolute minimum. But ideally, you want to update your blog two to three times per week to keep things fresh and current and to maintain readers' interest. This may sound like a lot of time, but once you start, your blog must be dedicated to writing new posts and putting new content on your blog.

Tips for Writing Your Blog

A common writing tip given by the popular bloggers is that you need to enjoy, love, and have a passion for what you are writing about. It will come across in your writing and that will attract followers and prospects. Here are a few more basic tips:

- ◆ Along with having a passion for your topic, lists are also good to incorporate into your blog. We'd like to think that people are going to read your blog word for word each time, but people do skim. Lists are great for skimmers.

- ◆ Shake things up a little now and then. Using the same format month after month can get a little stale. So in some weeks, incorporate a list of items. In another week, use a video or have a guest blogger write a post.

- ◆ Your blog is your domain to keep people informed, build rapport, and, here's that word again, "infotain" them. Be sure your posts are informative and entertaining.

- ◆ Use catchy titles, or headlines, for each entry. Great headlines will attract readers and give them an idea of what your post is about. You can also put these headlines in your other social media sites like Facebook, Twitter, and LinkedIn. Be sure to include a link to take readers directly to your blog.

- ◆ When writing, you can put your posts into categories. You can use as many categories as you like, but a best practice is to keep the categories in sync with your subject matter expertise. In other words, if you stray too far off your topic, first-time viewers might get confused because they are going to see a variety of topics and categories that don't have a central theme.

- Make sure you spell-check your blog and, if you're not a strong writer, have someone else proof your blog post for typos.

- Don't forget to have fun. Your blog isn't a doctoral thesis. It's supposed to be a bit more informal in tone. You don't have to get it perfect, just keep evolving and listening to your readers. Keep posts short and engaging. If you are having fun writing, chances are your readers will have fun reading.

Netiquette

Even with your own blog, shameless self-promotion is a turn-off to readers. Sure, if you have an event, product, or service offering, you can promote it. But your blog should be highly content driven and it should showcase your expertise.

Blog Service Providers

Your blog acts as the hub for your company and is the definitive "talking source" for your business. You want to choose your blog service provider carefully. Let's take a look at the current most popular providers. By the time this is book is published, there might be even more options—check the Internet for any new providers on the horizon.

WordPress.com and WordPress.org

There are hundreds of thousands, if not millions, of users publishing their blogs on WordPress. It's a highly respected platform. But there are two WordPress platforms, Wordpress.com and Wordpress.org, and this can be confusing. You can choose to start a free blog at Wordpress.com or pay for hosting and start your blog on Wordpress.org. WordPress.com is also easier to set up than WordPress.org.

I'll briefly highlight the differences between the platforms, but for a more comprehensive explanation, please visit www.support.wordpress.com/com-vs-org. The highlights of that web page are listed here. A few tidbits about WordPress.com:

- Upgrades and security are handled for you.

- The site gives directions for setting up your blog.

- There's no software to download.

- WordPress.com has hundreds of hosting servers, so it's unlikely to go down.

♦ WordPress.com backs up your posts automatically.

♦ You get extra site traffic from blogs of the day and tags.

♦ Note that you cannot upload *plugins* or run your own custom-themed blog. They provide themes, which you can modify to varying degrees.

Here's what you see when you land on the Home page for WordPress.com.

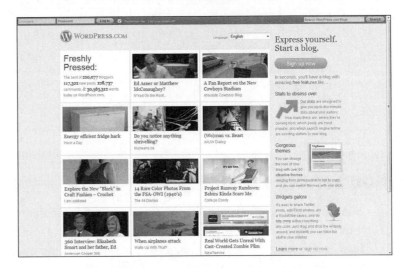

def•i•ni•tion

Plugins are software applications that can be added to blogs to increase the functionality or provide added features.

With WordPress.org, you can upload custom-themed blogs and upload plugins. Here are some tidbits about Wordpress.org:

♦ A great, supportive community.

♦ If you are technical, you have complete control to change the HTML code.

♦ You can monetize your blog and run advertisements.

♦ You pay for your own web hosting.

♦ You must download the software to get your blog set up and running.

♦ You are responsible for stopping spam and backing up your blog.

♦ If you get a big increase in traffic to your site, your blog may go down unless you have a robust hosting setup solution.

With this platform, you have a lot of control, and it's a very powerful solution for your blogging needs. However, it also means you need to back up your blog and beware of traffic issues.

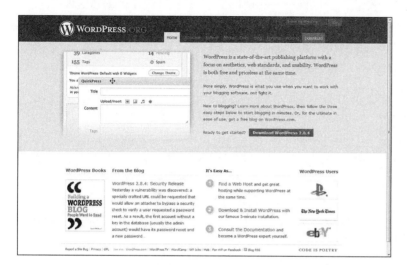

Here's what you see when you land on the Home page for Wordpress.org.

Do some research and think about which platform meets your needs. The WordPress folks suggest setting up a free practice blog on another topic (say a hobby of yours) on WordPress.com. This gives you a chance to check out the features. Then you can decide if you want to stay with that or shift over to the more powerful WordPress.org.

TypePad

TypePad (typepad.com) is another blog service provider, and its strength is that it is easy to use. It also offers the capability to customize the look and feel of your blog. One of its differentiators is that it does charge a fee, but it is minimal. TypePad has several different subscriber levels of engagement and you can easily upgrade to other service tiers without sacrificing your blog site.

TypePad is not only easy to use, but it also incorporates easily with the other social media platforms, such as Facebook and LinkedIn. One can easily transfer or stream their blog to Facebook and LinkedIn as we discussed in earlier chapters.

Here's the Home page for TypePad.

Movable Type

Movable Type (movabletype.com) is a sophisticated blogging service, as the graphics and templates are elaborately designed and colorful. In fact, it refers to itself as "your all-in-one social publishing platform." Brought to you by the same creators as TypePad, this solution is one of the more expensive options, but if you want to use the same provider as celebs such as Britney Spears, leaders such as Obama and Biden, or schools such as Harvard, then Movable Type is for you.

Squarespace

Mentioned in both the *Wall Street Journal* and *Business Week*, Squarespace (squarespace.com) is a site worth checking out for your blog. Priding itself on beautiful nontemplate design and reliability, Squarespace also provides great viewing stats for the business blogger. Their reports will show you where people are coming to your blog from and what keywords they are entering to find you. They do require a monthly fee, but it is affordable and runs across the board from as low as $8 per month. Applications for iPhones and integration to other social media platforms are on the way.

Blogger

Blogger (blogger.com) is another free site where you can get your blog up in minutes. A nice feature is that when you create your blog, you can choose an available URL and later, if you change your mind and want another URL, you can easily make the change. Blogger also has a custom domain option and it'll host your blog there. When you create your blog, you can host it for free on Blogger. Other features include team blogging, which enables multiple bloggers, and blogging on the go from your mobile.

Here's the Home page for Blogger.

Vox

Vox (vox.com) is a free blogging service that is created by Six Apart, the same company that brought you TypePad and Movable Type. This site seems to focus on family and friends, with an emphasis on making blogging "fun." When surfing through the website, you do see family blogs, but there are also up-and-coming musicians, novice travel writers, and other entrepreneurs looking to connect and build their brand. It's simple to use and there are hundreds of designs.

Promoting Your Blog

So you've named your blog, you are clear on your target audience, and you have selected your blog service provider. Now you've got your page set up and you have entered a couple of posts. Congratulations! Now it's time to start promoting your blog to the world.

One of the first things to do is to go back and list your blog on all of your Summary or Informational pages on Facebook, LinkedIn, and MySpace. You can also list it in your bio line on Twitter or put it in the background template on your Twitter page. Secondly, list your blog everywhere else. Put it on your business cards, your e-mail signature, and your website. If you are a speaker or writer, be sure you list your blog in your bio box or signature.

Another way to promote your blog is through the many online communities that offer a place to list your blog. And consider going to blogging conferences. BlogHer (blogher.com, a blogging community for women) holds an annual conference, and BlogWorld Expo also has an annual conference and a new media tradeshow worth checking out. You will also want to begin keeping your eye out for strategic partners so you can link your blogs on each others' websites and/or blogs. For many, self-promotion can be uncomfortable. But remember, if you don't promote your business (particularly in the beginning), no one will.

Here are some other ideas to promote your blog:

◆ Get listed with the blog directories or catalogs. BlogCatalog (blogcatalog.com) and Technorati (technorati.com) are two very popular ones. BlogExplosion (blogexplosion.com) and Blogged (blogged.com) are other all-around directories to take a look at. If you Google blog directories, you will find more.

◆ Also, try to find blog directories in your industry. For example, if you are a writer, check out Red Room (redroom.com). If you are a mom blogger, look at Real Savvy Moms (realsavvymoms.com).

◆ Do a video announcing your blog and put it on your other sites, such as Facebook. Remember 12seconds.tv? Do a short clip announcing your blog.

◆ Do you publish a newsletter or e-zine? In the next issue, write about your blog and tell everyone about it.

◆ Incorporate your blog into Facebook. Use the blog applications to feed it directly into Facebook.

◆ Look for interesting people to do a guest post on your blog. Ask your guest blogger to promote it to their network.

◆ Comment on other blogs. While I don't recommend spamming or making inauthentic comments just to get publicity, strategically comment on certain blogs that interest you and that may also interest your readers. You never know who may find your comment and check you (and your blog) out.

- Write an article. At the end of your article give your name, business name, and blog information.

- When people leave comments on your blog, respond to them. Remember, people want to feel connected.

- Be patient. Building a large following is going to take time. Just know that if you post good content, people are going to find you. Content is king and it will help you build your credibility.

Applications for Your Blog

One of the methods for distributing blogs to others or "feeding" it to them on a regular basis is called a web feed. People will come to your blog and sign up for a subscription to your blog to get it "fed" or sent to them automatically. You will want to encourage readers to subscribe to feeds so you can build your readership fan base. Let's review some of the websites that allow you to feed your blog to millions.

FeedBurner and FeedBlitz

FeedBurner (feedburner.com) is a news feed management tool brought to you by Google. If you already have a blog feed, you can run your feed through FeedBurner and get access to stats that will help you understand your readers.

FeedBlitz (feedblitz.com) is also a popular site to feed your blog directly to folks who want to receive it. Some people would like to get your blog via e-mail versus RSS. Here's how it works: you sign up for FeedBlitz, which provides you with a "widget" to place on your blog or website. This widget gives readers an opportunity to sign up for an e-mail to see all of your latest posts and the post headlines. Start looking at the popular blogs and noticing if they use FeedBlitz.

> **Did You Know?**
>
> Unless your blog currently produces a feed, FeedBurner cannot generate feeds. However, virtually all blogs created by systems like Blogger and TypePad create their own standard feeds, which FeedBurner can locate and then use. Check with your blog service provider to see if it provides a standard feed.

*Here's the Home page for
FeedBlitz.*

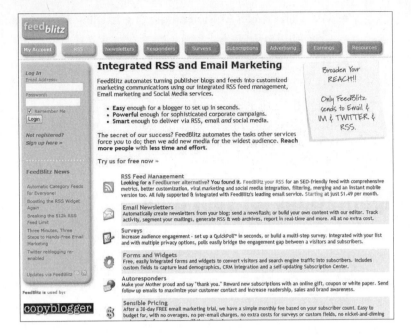

Widgetbox.com

Speaking of widgets, if you still aren't clear about what they are, go check out
Widgetbox (widgetbox.com). This is a great site that enables you to create and import
widgets that link to specific sites. These are kind of fun and you may find some that
you want to put on your blog.

MyBlogLog

MyBlogLog (mybloglog.com) is a fun visual component to add to your blog. Want to
see who is visiting your blog or see their photo and where they are from? MyBlogLog
allows people to say they've stopped by. This tool adds their photos to your blog in
an organized box on your blog page. You can stay connected with them and then they
might become part of your community.

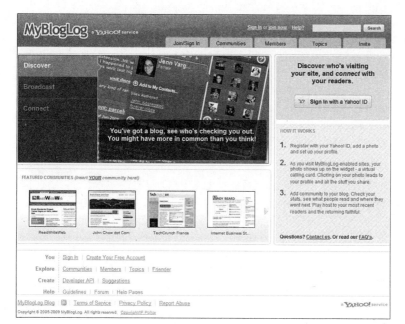

Here's the Home page for MyBlogLog.

Technorati

According to their site, Technorati (technorati.com) collects, organizes, and distributes the global online conversation. Is there any doubt that you need to get your blog listed with Technorati? Just in case you still have any doubts, their website says they are the third-largest blog media property and the sixth-largest social media property.

Simply join their site, "claim" your blog, and include a personal profile so readers from around the world will be able to find you. Did I mention their site is free? Well, it is!

We see the term *RSS feeder* all the time, but what does it mean? Basically, this is a method that allows for really easy distribution of your online content, called a web feed. The technology that enables the feed is called an RSS.

def•i•ni•tion

RSS or **RSS Feed** stands for Real Simple Syndication or Rich Site Summary; it enables you to "feed" your blog automatically to other sites after you've completed your blog update.

Bloglines

Bloglines (bloglines.com) is a news aggregator that collects the RSS feeds from online content. Bloglines then makes this content available to you online at their site for free. First you'll create an account, and then you'll decide on your blog subscriptions and news feeds. You can then sign up and get your favorite Bloglines sent directly to your e-mail inbox. Check it out, because this is one site that is gaining in popularity.

Here's the Home page for Bloglines.

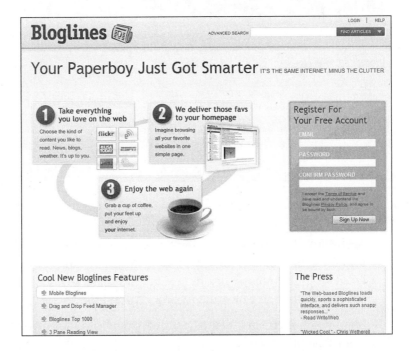

AddThis

AddThis (addthis.com) is something you simply must have for your blog. You may have noticed on a lot of blogs that they have a Share link at the bottom. (If you don't notice this on your favorite blog, tell the writer … they will love you for it.) This link also has other social media site icons listed on it. How do they do that? Go to www. addthis.com. According to their site, this feature is served over 20 billion times per month! So run (don't walk) to add this feature to your blog today so it will get shared around the world. One of the most powerful things you can do is to add a sharing tool to your blog. This sharing tool will help your readers share your blog with other platforms and networks. The reader simply clicks on the Share button, selects where they want to share it to (Facebook, Twitter, LinkedIn, etc.), and boom … it's been sent.

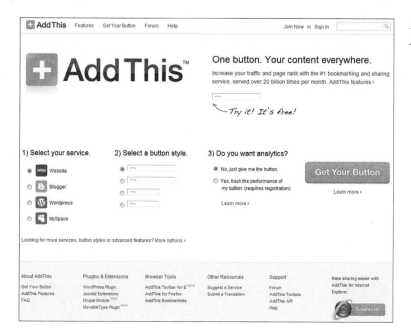

Here's the Home page for AddThis.

Alexa (alexa.com) offers many powerful tools, but one that I've noticed on a lot of blogs is Traffic Rank. This is Amazon's search engine and it ranks every website according to the amount of traffic (or views) it receives. If you want to tell the world your traffic rank, sign up with Alexa.

After reading this chapter, I hope you're excited about getting your blog going. Or maybe you have a blog that you've been neglecting? Either way, the tips in this chapter will get you on your way to becoming a successful member of the blogosphere.

The Least You Need to Know

- Your blog can be one of the most powerful tools of your social media marketing strategy.

- Your blog is your own branding platform, and you can link it to the other social media platforms.

- Before you start a blog, know the who, what, where, how often, and why of your blog.

- There are many blogging service providers for you to use, and many of them are easy and free. You can also choose blogging software that's more technical and requires a hosting fee, but that offers more powerful features.

◆ You can't expect the masses to just come to your blog, so you'll need to promote it everywhere, such as getting it listed in directories and promoting it on your other social media platforms.

◆ There are many applications to help market your blog, such as RSS feeds or using sites like FeedBurner, FeedBlitz, and AddThis.

Part 5

Streamlining and Expanding Your Program

New social media sites and tools are introduced each week, and it can be overwhelming to learn how to manage it all. This part shows you some shortcuts to take so that you can effectively handle all of your social media.

Additionally, you are introduced to other tools and sites to help you further expand your marketing efforts online. From the simple to the more creatively complex, this part will have you imagining new and even more savvy ways to connect, reconnect, and share information with your clients, prospects, and business referral partners. As you are reading, try to imagine how you could use these products to support your business. Have fun exploring!

WE HIRED HIM BECAUSE HE'S GREAT AT SOCIAL INTERACTION. AND, IF WE LOSE SOME OF OUR FILES, HE'S ALSO A TALENTED RETRIEVER!

Chapter 17

Using Social Media for Meetings and Presentations

In This Chapter

- ◆ Discover the new world of webinars and teleseminars
- ◆ Get tips for hosting webinars and teleseminars
- ◆ How to promote your events using social media
- ◆ Discover webinar/teleseminar service providers
- ◆ Get introduced to podcasting and 3-D animation technology

We've covered the new networking online with social media platforms such as Facebook, LinkedIn, and Twitter. Now you understand the importance and impact of video and a blog, and how they can also drive people to you and your business.

So how does all this technology impact how you have meetings? Well, if you haven't participated in an online meeting lately, this chapter should open your eyes to new possibilities. Webinars, teleseminars, podcasting, and 3-D animation sites are all great tools to combine with your social media marketing.

Today, you can meet in your office with a group of 2 to 10 employees, but online you can meet with a group of 2 to 2,000 people from around the world. Come and explore the new world of online meetings to network, collaborate, and grow your business and brand.

Webinars and Teleseminars

The term "webinar" was derived when someone had the idea to give a seminar over the web. These days, with the cost and inconvenience of air travel, webinars are not only an increasingly popular way to do a presentation, but you can also chat with a loyal following or announce a new product offering to your prospects, clients, and fans. Today's webinars are different than five years ago, and there are some great sites to take a look at. Entrepreneurs and small business owners are saving time and money by delivering webinars to their clients and prospects.

Teleseminars are similar to webinars, but without the computer. A teleseminar takes a phone plus a seminar (or discussion) and it becomes a teleseminar. Participants are given a number to dial in to and the facilitator leads the call. The audience is typically muted so the facilitator can speak without interruption. No business is too small to host a teleseminar. You can even have one with no one on the line but still reach hundreds (if not thousands) of people.

Let me explain. I know many people who have done teleseminars with no one on the receiving end by prerecording it, and then posting it on a website or blog, or e-mailing it out to intended recipients. You can also turn it into a product, but that's for another book. For teleseminars, you will still need to plan in advance, but you can promote the same way you do webinars. For topics, you can pretty much host a teleseminar on just about anything. People like teleseminars because they are easy to participate in—you just need a phone. They typically are free or for little cost, and participants can still get a lot of information without investing a lot in travel time driving to and from the event.

Try This _____

Are you an entrepreneur? Host a webinar or teleseminar about the state of your industry. Share the top three things your target audience needs to know about your industry and how it affects them.

Think you need to be a large corporation to host a webinar or teleseminar? Think again. Today's entrepreneur and small business owner are successfully using today's amazing technology to talk with prospects and clients and educate fans on what they do. It's another way to stay connected with people and share your expertise. Still not convinced how you could use a webinar or teleseminar?

Here are some ideas for webinars and teleseminars:

- You want to announce a new product line at an upcoming conference. Have a webinar so you can show slides and talk about the event. A teleseminar can do the same thing, but without the slides or video.

- Participants love to hear from the owner or from the business itself because they hear your energy and enthusiasm.

- Webinars are a great way to show some statistics or pictures of a new product. In teleseminars, you can talk about the statistics and invite listeners (who are your prospects) to a website to see pictures.

- The visual part combined with the audio part is what makes webinars great. Plus with many of the new systems, you can even give clients or prospects control of the screen so they can collaborate and share from their end. Teleseminars are good, too, particularly when you don't necessarily need the visual.

- Are you an artist and have an upcoming show? Host a webinar/teleseminar and talk about where, when, and why you are doing the event.

- Are you a charity or an association? Have a webinar to talk about your organization. Show photos with statistics. Remember, people want to feel connected. Teleseminars can actually have the same effect because you can simply send them an e-mail document afterwards with photos and information.

- Do you own a winery? Or are you a photographer? Host a webinar/teleseminar showcasing your vineyard and upcoming events. Photographers can talk about upcoming specials, or what companies and entrepreneurs need to know about how photography can really impact marketing.

- Are you a real estate agent or broker? Host a monthly webinar/teleseminar on "Seven Things First-Time Homebuyers Need to Know." Or do a quarterly webinar on the state of the market in your region of the country. Share statistics and show photos. If it's a teleseminar, you can e-mail the photos or drive listeners to a website at the end of the call.

- Are you a speaker or an author? Speakers can hold a webinar/teleseminar talking about their expertise and how someone can go about hiring them. Authors can talk about their background and discuss three takeaways readers will get from reading their book. Both could talk about upcoming speaking dates and promote their blog.

Tips for Hosting a Webinar or Teleseminar

When hosting a webinar or teleseminar, you must first be prepared. Know how much time you have to speak. Have a timer or clock in front of you and make sure you don't go over the time. Everyone now wants succinct to-the-point events. If targeting a variety of time zones, ensure you are specific about which one is being used (for example, 9 P.M. Eastern Standard Time). However, do list all time zones and state what time the meeting starts in each one.

Other points to consider in order to lead a successful webinar or teleseminar program are:

- Make sure you have the ability and know how to mute the phone so listeners can't hear, um, distracting noises. Hearing dishwashers, phones, talking, and yes, toilets flushing will ruin your call.

- Have a slide on the screen (if it's a webinar) when they arrive. If it's a teleseminar, have some music playing.

- Be enthusiastic (or at least warm!) and smile. The listeners can tell if you are bored and don't care.

- Start on time and end on time or a few minutes early.

- Offer a special or incentive to participants for taking time out of their schedule to attend the webinar or teleseminar.

- If you can, record the event. Most services today have that option. This gives you the option to replay it later or send it as an *MP3 file*. (Note: if you record a webinar with video or slides, it saves it as an *MP4 file*.)

- Take the opportunity to promote your other social media sites. Ask participants to follow you on Twitter. Connect on LinkedIn and Facebook and let them know about your blog.

def•i•ni•tion

An **MP3 file** is a computer file that's created with compression technology. The files are small and often used to make digital audio computer files that can be easily transferred over the Internet.

An **MP4 file** stores digital video and digital audio streams along with images that can be easily transferred over the Internet.

Promoting Your Webinar or Teleseminar

After you decide that you are ready to do some webinars and teleseminars to grow your business, you need to go back and promote them on all your social media sites. There are arguments for how much time in advance you need to promote, and the bigger your webinar/teleseminar, the more in advance you want to promote. For our purposes here, let's say you want less than 100 people on a webinar/teleseminar. You will want to start promoting about two-and-a-half weeks in advance. Avoid holiday weeks or weekends.

The best times will vary, depending on your audience and industry. Some webinars are done first thing in the morning, at noon, in the afternoon, and even during evening hours. Know your audience and what time they will respond. You might have to either experiment or offer a few different times, or give people a survey to see what time most people respond to. A lot of these webinar and teleseminar companies offer the capability for you to record your webinar so people can play it back at their own convenience.

Promoting It on Twitter, LinkedIn, and Facebook

Even though I don't advocate constant self-promotion on Twitter, you can certainly promote your webinar or teleseminar there because there is something beneficial for those who attend. Typically, participants are going to learn something that is going to help them in life or in business. So promote your webinar on Twitter by providing a link to sign up for the webinar in a tweet. Ask staff members, your PR person, or your clients if they would promote the webinar or teleseminar. Typically, if you are connected to them via Twitter, they will retweet your tweet and spread the news to their network.

You can also promote your webinar/teleseminar in the events area on LinkedIn. If you are in groups on LinkedIn, let your groups know and also promote your webinar in your status update section. This way, the word will get out to everyone in your network when they get the weekly updates from LinkedIn. Do a SlideShare PowerPoint presentation of one to three slides on your LinkedIn page to promote the webinar/teleseminar and the benefits of attending.

To promote your webinar/teleseminar on Facebook, click the **Events** icon at the bottom left of your Facebook Home page. Here, create an event promoting your webinar/teleseminar. And mention it in your status update, too.

Also, write about it on the walls of the groups you are involved with on Facebook (if that group would benefit from the webinar or teleseminar). For example, if you are a nutritionist, you might write "Hi friends, you are invited to attend my special good health webinar program on Tuesday at 5 P.M. Eastern. Our topic? Three things you must know about vitamins to get the best health result. You can register today at (give website or link to register.) Look forward to seeing you at the webinar!"

Promoting Webinars/Teleseminars in Other Ways

Here are a few more ides to get the word out:

◆ Promote it at the top or bottom of your blog a few weeks out. Add a link to where people can RSVP.

◆ Promote the webinar/teleseminar in your e-mail signature.

◆ Promote it on your voicemail and website for the week or two prior to the event.

◆ If you are at a speaking engagement, promote it there.

◆ If you are at a networking event, ask the host in advance if you can leave flyers about your webinar/teleseminar on a table.

Webinar and Web/Video Conferencing Service Sites

Here are just a few companies that can help you host a webinar; if you do a search on the Internet, you'll find plenty of others.

GoToMeeting and WebEx

I like GoToMeeting (gotomeeting.com) because it's easy to set up, install, and get going. They offer service for those having phone/web meetings of up to 15 people. Then, they offer GoToWebinar for those who need more space (up to 1,000 people). They also offer a larger solution for large corporations. There are monthly fees, so check their sites for a variety of programs.

WebEx (webex.com) is very popular within the corporate world for large formal presentations, but it still can be used by the entrepreneur or small business owner for groups of up to 25. It has a few more bells and whistles and there's a bit more technology involved, but it's another solution to possibly consider. WebEx also has a video conferencing service online.

InstantPresenter and Dimdim.com

A webinar, web, and video conferencing site, InstantPresenter (instantpresenter.com) is neat because of the video collaboration component. Say you begin talking and then want to introduce someone else, such as a strategic partner, collaborator, vendor, or another employee. The attendees to your webinar will enjoy seeing who is talking. You can also share screens and chat live (via text) on the site.

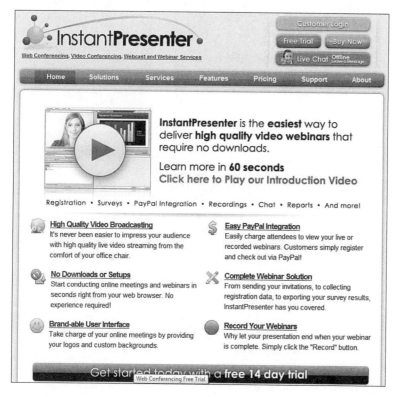

InstantPresenter has a video collaboration component.

Dimdim (dimdim.com) is another neat service you can look into. One standout feature is that after you create your event, the service provides a widget that you can use to promote your event. There is no downloading involved and Dimdim has affordable programs for the entrepreneur and small business owner.

Here's the Home page for Dimdim.

ooVoo

ooVoo (oovoo.com) is another great video chat and video conferencing site for your webinar or video conference. Let's say you want to have a web meeting with your team. With ooVoo, a webcam, and a microphone or headset, you would all be able to see and hear each other.

> ### Did You Know?
>
> The difference between a webinar and a video conference is that on the video confer-ence participants can see you and the team of speakers speaking live on the screen, movements and all. On most webinars they may see your still photo in a slide and hear your voice, but not the live video of you.

Here's the Home page for ooVoo.

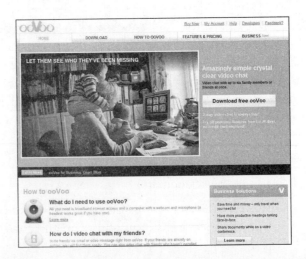

Teleseminar Providers

When starting out on your first teleseminar, know in advance it can be a little awkward. You will be talking and not hearing anyone responding back to you. Even simply getting used to talking without a live person in front of you is a bit uncomfortable. There are many teleseminar companies to choose from, so first ask yourself what you can afford. Then ask friends and associates what they have used. Ask your Twitter or Facebook friends which services they recommend.

After you find one, see if you can do a trial run. An important question to ask yourself is if you just want to speak or if you want to open up the lines to get others talking. This is important because if you want to open up the lines and ask questions, you might need specific types of providers. Also, determine if you want to record the teleseminar and learn how to do this in advance. You don't want to end the call and then realize somehow it didn't get recorded. The recording functionality is also important to know in advance when selecting a provider, because some offer it with their service, but for some it's an extra charge.

Next, get comfortable with the teleseminar setup and features. Learn how to mute callers. Again, do this so you don't hear unflattering noises in the background. Before you do your first one, log in at least 15 minutes early to get it set up and going. Just before you begin, send out a tweet (if it's a public teleseminar) and invite folks to join in. Have fun!

> **Did You Know?**
>
> Telegathering, telesiminar, and teleconference are interchangeable words—all imply that you are gathering a group of people together via phone.

Here are just a few of the teleseminar service providers:

- **Maestro Conference (maestroconference.com).** This is a really neat conferencing service for your teleseminar. It gives you the ability to put your teleconference listeners in individual chat rooms so they can talk among themselves or brainstorm about a project. This keeps your audience members more engaged by participating.

- **FreeConferenceCall (freeconferencecall.com).** This takes minutes to set up. It provides you with a conference bridge and pass code so all participants can dial in.

- **InstantTeleseminar (instantteleseminar.com).** You can create an opening page for your teleseminar and a reminder page so participants can listen through a stream on their computer or by dialing in.

- **InstantConference (www.instantconference.com).** This is another phone bridge line service that's easy to set up and good for your teleseminars.

Podcasting

If you haven't done a podcast before, it can seem a little daunting. Don't despair; after you've done it a few times, it's not so bad. The word "podcast" is the word "broadcast" combined with the word "iPod." However, you do not need an iPod to produce a podcast. What you will need is a microphone and computer audio editing software, an RSS feed, and a website or hosting service that you can upload your podcast to.

When you create a podcast, you will want people to get it delivered to them automatically via an RSS fed. When you download a podcast, it's in the form of an MP3 file.

One option is to use an audio editing program such as Audacity, which has a free audio editing program (www.audacity.sourceforge.net) that works with both Macs and PCs. To learn how to create a podcast using Audacity, view an easy-to-understand video on YouTube. Go to www.youtube.com and search for "how to create a podcast with audacity," and watch the video produced by Tinkernut (tinkernut.com) to actually "see" how it's done. When you have created your podcast, you can upload it to the Internet using www.podcastalley.com or www.podomatic.com. To create your podcast on other sites, you can go to www.blogtalkradio.com and your radio show can be used as a podcast.

Podcast.com is a hosting provider that can help you create a distribution format. If you have a WordPress account, use Podpress.org. Another company, Easypodcast (easypodcast.com), allows you to create your own RSS feeds. It's a great all-in-one site to help you through this process as well. Still another firm, podcast411 (podcast411. com), allows you to submit your podcast to a number of site directories.

After you complete your podcast, remember to market it and upload it onto your social media sites. Facebook has the My Band application, so you can upload it there. Also, put it on your blog and on your website.

3-D Animation Technologies

This is not your Saturday morning cartoon, or sci-fi 3-D movie with the red-and-blue glasses that you remember as a kid. With the emergence of all this new technology, people are meeting, mingling, networking, and teaching in virtual worlds. If you haven't participated in a meeting this way, you must try it. You will not only meet amazing people from around the world, but you just might decide this is something you want to try for your business.

Large Fortune 100 companies are using and experimenting with this technology for collaborative meetings and some of their training. Instead of having employees fly in, they can go to these virtual sites, meet with co-workers, and learn and collaborate there. You can make your meetings as imaginative as you desire. A headset and a high-speed Internet connection with a relatively new computer is all you need. Note, a computer that's older than five years might not have the speed or memory to use this technology.

Running the viewers or 3-D "browser" for virtual environments involves your Internet connection, your video card, and processor speed. If your video card is older, you can upgrade it or add an additional card. Most computers made after 2005, however, have processors and video cards made for video gaming, which is perfect for VW.

Second Life

Many people call this site another type of social media marketing, but with a twist. Second Life (secondlife.com) calls itself "the Internet's largest user-related, 3-D virtual world community." Why do you need to be aware of 3-D animation, you ask? Because as time goes on, more often we are going to see virtual world invites to seminars, conferences, and networking events on sites like Second Life. Secondly, with this social media revolution (as many call it), it is highly important to keep an open mind about all new emerging technology.

One downside is that Second Life can be a bit technical, but there are several folks out there who give Second Life tours and orientation sessions on how to get started. One site is Synapse3Di (synapse3di.com), so check them out.

Even more than Twitter and Facebook, the social communities found in virtual worlds like Second Life become very close and supportive. These are not just gaming or dating sites. There's a whole lot of learning, networking, and training taking place on Second Life.

A unique bonding seems to take place when you meet in virtual worlds; this bonding is tough to explain. One of the outcomes when engaging on this type of platform is that the professionals in Second Life are a supportive community, and as a result, participants are getting answers to their questions about all kinds of business tools, trends, and applications.

Netiquette

Even though you are in a virtual world, this shouldn't give you permission to be someone you are not. There are highly educated professionals on these sites and you still want to leave a good impression.

These types of environments are especially great for busy entrepreneurs and professionals, because they can attend conferences and seminars and grow their skill set directly from their home office or business location—or even from a mobile location, for that matter. Where else can you practice your elevator speech in a virtual elevator, talk about your business goals while riding an elephant, or practice your negotiation skills at a car dealership? In Second Life, that's where. This is the new world of networking, learning, and branding within 3-D animation sites.

Here's a networking event on Second Life.

This technology enables you to engage just the same as if you were at a regular networking event—it's just virtual instead of in person. All you need is a Second Life account, a headset/microphone, and a short tutorial, and you're ready to go.

Some other virtual world platforms include TelePlace (formerly Qwaq), Protosphere, Open Sim, and Olive. Like any of today's hottest technology tools, there are new virtual environments popping up all the time.

The Least You Need to Know

♦ Webinars and teleseminars are amazing ways to connect to individuals or groups of people around business.

♦ Today's technology lets you see, hear, and chat with people from around the world.

♦ Webinars, teleseminars, and podcasts can all be tied into one's social media marketing strategy.

♦ Podcasting is relatively easy to do and it's another marketing tool to get the word out about your expertise and brand.

♦ The 3-D animation sites, such as Second Life, are worth taking a look at.

Chapter **18**

Social Media: Tying It All Together

In This Chapter

- ◆ Basic networking skills that help you effectively grow your list
- ◆ Examine today's new business card as well as the virtual business card
- ◆ The importance of your e-mail signature and how it helps you market your social media sites
- ◆ Time-saving sites that distribute your status updates to your social networks
- ◆ Learn about a news aggregator that collects it all in one place
- ◆ Creative ways to market your social media usernames or sites

By now, you should be social media savvy. You've read about all the platforms, sites, and services. However, how does this all tie together? There are many ways to cross-promote your social media presence, and they've been mentioned throughout the previous chapters.

In this chapter, we go into a bit more detail about how you can create a fluid social media marketing campaign that will make you more findable, more visible, and make your life a bit easier. After all, what good is a great blog, Facebook, LinkedIn, MySpace, and Twitter page—not to mention all those wonderful videos—if no one knows how or where to find you?

Networking in Person

We talked about how social media marketing is a networking tool. You can meet other people around the world, get to know them, and they, in turn, will get to know you. However, let's step back just a little bit. Now that you are setting up your sites and deciding which ones to start with, you also need to begin doing one more key thing: network in person.

Yes, in-person networking is not dead. You still need to get out there, particularly now that you are still building your following and connections online. So while this isn't an in-person networking book, it does play a role in your social media strategy. Let me share a few networking tips.

Survey your current customers, clients, and prospects. Where are they networking? What social media sites do they use? Start attending some of those events (even if it's every other month). After all, if you simply had all your clients following you on Twitter, that would not be so bad. It's a great way to communicate with them.

More importantly, you want to start finding out where the people that you want to target are online. You might hear that they have a blog. Or you might find out they are all on LinkedIn, and that's great. Now you have more information than you did before. And chances are, if your clients are using these sites, then most likely your prospects are as well.

When networking in person, know it's just as uncomfortable for other people in the room as it is for you, so stay outwardly focused. When engaging in conversation, keep the focus on the person you are talking to versus worrying about what you are going to say next. Ask questions and learn how you can possibly help them in the near future. Don't offer a business card until they ask. If you really want to get their information, then ask if you may have one of their cards. They, in turn, may ask you for yours.

Online Cautions

Be careful about putting exact details of where you are going, how long you will be out of town, and where you are staying on your social media status updates. Do you want the world to know you are away from your home for days or weeks on end? Experts predict that would-be criminals will soon begin scouring the status updates to look for those who are not home or who are traveling to specific locations.

Ask people what social media sites they are using. Start getting a feel for what is working for others, but also know at the same time that what works for one person might or might not work for you. At least you will start getting a general sense of what folks in your network are doing.

Here are some additional networking tips:

♦ Be early. Some of the best prospecting and conversations happen before the event starts.

♦ Bring plenty of business cards and carry them in a business card holder.

♦ Bring your BlackBerry, iPhone, or texting tool, and tweet from the event.

♦ Have your Flip video camera or other digital video camera handy for spur-of-the-moment video clips.

♦ Carry a digital camera. Remember, you now have a blog and several social media profiles that you can upload information on.

♦ Wear your name badge (if they give you one) on your right side. This way, when you shake hands, the recipient's eye goes directly to your name tag.

♦ If at a large convention or conference, ask if there is a Twitter hashtag for the event so you can put that in all of your tweets. Some people are now wearing shirts with their Twitter username on it preceded by the @ symbol.

♦ See if you can view a guest list ahead of time and try to meet one to three people intentionally.

♦ For people you exchange information with, ask them how they prefer to be contacted (text, phone, e-mail, and so on).

♦ Remember, you are there to network, not sit. Eat beforehand so you don't gorge on food. You are there to make an impression. Be yourself, be authentic, and listen.

Your Business Cards

Okay, so you've got a basic primer on networking. Now let's move on to that all-important business card. The etiquette around business cards is changing quickly, depending on your generation. For the paper business card user, the new business card should include, obviously, your name, phone, and e-mail.

Next, be sure to list your Twitter username. Ask people to "follow me on Twitter @yourtwittername," or you could simply have Twitter @username. Also put your Facebook information and other social media platforms on there. Have a blog? Put the name of your blog on your card. Remember, we are trying to tie all of this together. Have a Facebook Fan page or LinkedIn group? Put it on your card.

You don't want your card to be too wordy, though, so use your best judgment. Perhaps you just want to mention your Fan page on Facebook, your blog, or your Twitter name. Start paying attention to the business cards you get and see what others are doing. If you are a retailer, have your cards at the checkout counter with all of your social media addresses on it. You could have a sign above that reads: "Follow us on these sites and we'll follow you back."

This will start the engagement and the conversation between you and your followers. There is a great debate about whether to include information on the back of your card. Some say leave it blank so people can write notes, others say that is valuable marketing "real estate" so use it. I say use it—more people don't write on the back than do. On the back you could remind folks of the best way to reach you, explain in a line or two how you can help them, ask a question that addresses a certain business or personal pain that you can help with, or invite them to subscribe to your blog or e-zine.

Honestly, there is no right or wrong answer. However, many people feel it's important to put information on the back of the card because more times than not, people do not write on your cards. The back can be valuable marketing space where you can further communicate how you can help professionals.

Did You Know?

There is a trend now among busy entrepreneurs to not put their direct dial information on their business card. They are putting an e-mail address or a number to their virtual assistant or personal assistant. Also many Gen Xers and Gen Yers prefer not to use the phone anyway, so this could also be the reason why this trend is catching on. The point is: learn how your prospects and customers want to be reached.

Now for the other type of business card: the electronic business card. The day has arrived when many people, particularly the Gen Xers, do not carry business cards. They will carry their BlackBerry or iPhone and put your information directly into their database as soon as they connect with you.

Another product you might see is called Mingle360. I attended an event featuring this product and it was quite the conversation starter. When we arrived at the conference, at check-in we were given a MingleStick (the way you might at tradeshows with your badge). Everyone interested in connecting was instructed to point their sticks at one another and exchange identity information with that person with a single click of a button.

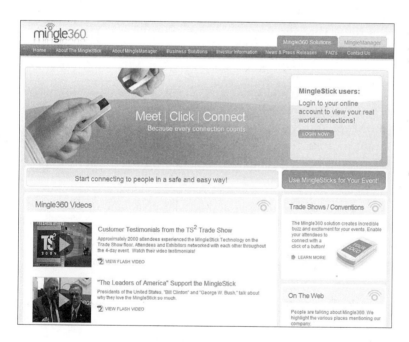

Here's where you learn about the MingleStick on www.mingle360.com.

At the end of the event, conference organizers took back the tool and then they sent me an e-mail listing everyone I connected with at that event.

Another site, www.contxts.com, lets you easily send your contact information via *SMS*, which is built into every mobile phone device. As Contxts claims, "Business cards are so 2007," so they've created the virtual rolodex.

Basically, with this site you can use your mobile phone to easily distribute your contact information from one phone to another. I believe we'll see a lot more of this in the future, but if you are a heavy mobile user now, check out Contxts.

def•i•ni•tion

SMS, the acronym for Short Message Service, is the connection between the phenomenon of text messaging and the underlying technology. In some parts of the world, SMS is used as a synonym for a text message or even for the act of sending a text message (even when a different protocol is actually being used).

Your E-Mail Signature

How many e-mails do you send out each day? Did you ever think of your e-mail as a marketing tool? Well, it is. In fact, your e-mail signature (the text at the bottom of an e-mail below your name) is the perfect place to list the social media sites you belong to. Savvy social media marketers utilize the e-mail signature as a place to give the recipients more ways to reach you. By putting these links in your e-mail signature, the recipient can click on them and learn more about you.

The most common links that you see are Twitter, Facebook, LinkedIn, and blogs. However, also look out for Skype, YouTube, Second Life, and links to online videos. Think about where you want to drive your readers. You can also put a live link to a client testimonial or a link to your book on Amazon.com. Or you can promote a special event.

Obviously, you don't want it to get too busy-looking, but take advantage of this prime "real estate" for your social media marketing. You've done all the work creating these amazing profiles, so now you want to drive as many people to them as possible. This way, you can stay connected with them, build stronger relationships, and continue to share your expertise.

There are many sites to get the buttons from to put on your e-mail signature (buttons are the logo or icon from popular social media sites). Simply Google "social media buttons" and you will see many sites that provide downloadable buttons.

One site I want to bring your attention to is WiseStamp (wisestamp.com). The only downside to this site is that as of August 2009, it only worked with the web browser Firefox. However, please check the site because by the time this book is published, it might work with Internet Explorer.

This site lets you easily share and add the logos and links to your e-mail signature for all the major social media platforms. It even has fun additions, such as adding a motivational or inspirational quote to your signature. It will also automatically include the title of your latest blog post in your e-mail signature. All you have to do is add your blog feed site to your WiseStamp feed account. You can share your latest status updates in your e-mail signature, too, and so much more.

Here's the Signature Gallery on WiseStamp.

I hope you are seeing a common theme throughout the book. E-mail signatures can be a highly personal choice. Use your own style and be creative. There is no box you have to stay in any longer. There are amazing tools and services that are available to you for free to help you become much more findable and visible and marketable to the world.

Another service that provides interesting e-mail signature templates is Email Ideas. This site (emailideas.com) allows you to create your own personalized e-mail signature (called a Bojo) with clickable tabs, a texting feature, your headshot, and contact information. It also provides many already designed templates for a variety of industries like real estate, automotive, corporate, broadcasting, education, and modeling, to name a few. Email Ideas also offers a custom development template program.

Try This

Begin looking at e-mail signatures that you receive each day. Start examining what you like and what appeals to you. Think about what you can incorporate into your e-mail signature that will showcase your brand and identity and make you more findable and visible to others. Now try it on your signature.

Your Website

On your website, you need to have all your social media marketing sites either listed with an icon or with a link. Many people put the links for Facebook, Twitter, LinkedIn, and RSS feed logos across the top or bottom of their Home page, so people can click and directly follow their companies. Also, have a link to your blog so people can start getting that as well.

A trend recently is that many businesses are using WordPress.org to create their websites, with WordPress serving as both a website and a blog with live feeds from Twitter and Facebook. Start looking at other websites to see how they market their social media marketing sites.

Ping.fm

How do people seem to update all their sites so easily? Many of them use a free service called Ping.fm. Ping.fm allows you to update all of your social media sites through one entry point. Sign up and simply type in your status, check which sites you want to update, click on **Ping it!,** and you have updated your networks.

Here's the Home page for Ping.fm.

At this writing, Ping.fm has over 40 social networking sites that you can send your status update to, but they are always adding more.

One recent update is the Ping.fm toolbar, enabling you to "ping" your updates more easily directly from your workspace.

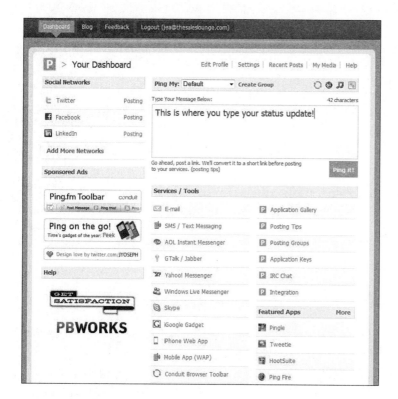

Here's the Dashboard for Ping.fm.

As you can see from the previous figure, after you create your account, you can select which networks you will be sending updates to. On the left side of the screen shot, you will see Twitter, Facebook, and LinkedIn, but if you want to add more, you could click on **Add More Networks.** In the message box, you can see the words, "This is the where you type your status update!" At the bottom right corner of the box, you see the words "Ping it!" Click on that and it will send your message to all of your sites. Hint: The first time you try it, go to your selected social media sites to verify that your message was sent there. If not, you'll need to go through the process again. Make sure to save your changes.

Online Cautions

Ping.fm is a great tool to use, but strongly consider how often you want to use it. Many feel if you put the same updates on Twitter, Facebook, and LinkedIn all the time, why should people follow you on all three places? Good food for thought. Each social media site has its own culture and personality. It's good to chime in live more often than not.

You don't want to lose followers. People seem to like to know that you are "there" on the other side of the site. Even if it's automated or done by an assistant, they like to feel you are really there and not just sending automatic pings to every site every day. So although Ping.fm is a great way to tie it all together and save time, my advice is don't ping to all your sites, 100 percent all the time.

Netvibes

Netvibes (netvibes.com) is an amazing site that claims to save you 30 minutes a day in Internet time. And I believe it's true. Go to www.netvibes.com and create an account. After you do that, you will have a blank landing page. You will want to perhaps make this your Home page. With Netvibes, you can have your Facebook status updates stream into this site along with your Twitter and LinkedIn feeds.

Here's the Welcome page for Netvibes.

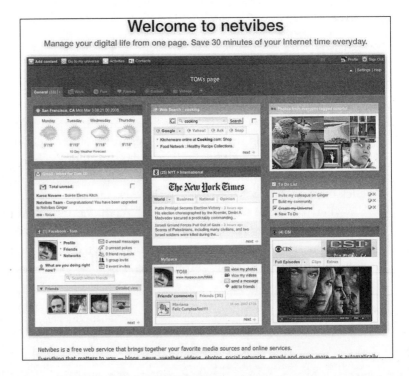

You can also include your hometown weather report and current to-do list. You can even include news feeds from online industry magazines or newspapers that you choose. You can also include blogs that you subscribe to within your industry. It's a custom page with all of your social media and news feeds coming directly to you through Netvibes.

Netvibes calls itself a "news aggregator," enabling users to aggregate their desired information into one place. This is another place where you can tie it all together.

Clever Ways to Market Your Social Media Sites

What is beginning to happen is that people are networking, socializing, and growing their business and branding nationally by connecting to people on sites such as Twitter and Facebook. They're creating new and different ways to communicate their brand.

Here are a few more ideas to put in your social media marketing toolbox:

◆ Have a shirt created with your Twitter username (@_____) on it. Then ask your staff to wear the shirts at events or at your retail location. If you're an entrepreneur and don't have employees, wear the shirt yourself and/or have your family wear it.

◆ Have pens made with your Twitter name or a "Connect with me on Facebook" message.

◆ Have coffee mugs made with a quote or saying with your Twitter name and/or blog name. Send them to clients and prospects. Another idea: have an open house with coffee and give out the mugs.

◆ Have custom Christmas or holiday cards made that have all of your social media contact information on the back.

◆ Do a video of the month (or week) and remember at the end to ask viewers to follow you on Twitter, Facebook, and so on.

◆ Send your top clients, prospects, or business champions a great book, and include custom bookmarks that have your social media information attached.

◆ Change your answering machine so that you mention your social media platforms during your message to "follow us on Twitter, join our Fan page on LinkedIn, and view our channel on YouTube.

◆ Put your Twitter name and other social media links in your newsletter and/or e-zine.

♦ In all of your publicity, whether it's an article, a seminar promotion, or phone interview, ensure that at the end you mention one or several of your social media sites. Blogs and newsletters are the number-one things to mention because you want to begin capturing names and e-mail addresses.

A last but important tip: from this point forward, start connecting with fellow Twitterers, Facebook friends, and LinkedIn connections and see if you can do some strategic cross-promotion. Here are some examples: be a guest blogger, be a guest on each other's teleseminars or webinars, or do a seminar together. In other words, make a pact to promote each other's social media sites. It's networking at its finest.

The Least You Need to Know

♦ In-person networking is not dead and is, in fact, a great way to grow your visibility and to begin building your social media connections.

♦ Some say the paper business card is a thing of the past; products such as Mingle360 allow us to electronically share contact information.

♦ Be sure to include your social media sites information in your e-mail signature, because it makes you easier to find and increases your visibility.

♦ There are timesaving sites like Ping.fm that enable you to update your status to Facebook, Twitter, LinkedIn, and 37-plus other sites all at once.

♦ There are many creative ways to market your social media sites, including T-shirts, pens, and e-zines that include all of your social media contact information.

Chapter 19

More Ways to Wow Your Audience

In This Chapter

- Join other social networks on a particular topic to meet and network with like-minded people

- Create your own social network and learn which sites can help you do that

- Learn how social networks are becoming more customized

- Learn about great social networking platforms specifically for entrepreneurs and small business owners

- Creative ways to engage your audience

Are you feeling like a social media marketer yet? No doubt you are familiar with and have most likely joined several social media networks, such as LinkedIn, Facebook, Twitter, and MySpace, just to name a few.

In this chapter, we explore other ways to impact your audience and look at the tools and websites that can help you do that. If you have ever thought about creating your own social network and weren't quite sure how to do that, this next section is for you.

There are many additional ways to impact your audience, so let's continue on. Who knows? Perhaps your own social media network could be the next one to have millions of members.

Creating Your Own Social Network

You might not have realized until now that you can have your own social network—literally within a few minutes. If you have a lot of customers or clients and are looking for one portal where you can post questions and share information, then you might want to create your own social network.

Think about it. If you can create a place to listen to your customers, view discussion boards, and read what's on their mind, this would empower you and get you better connected. There are several sites out there that make it easy to create your own social networking platform. Let's look at two of them: Ning and SocialGO.com.

Ning

Founded in 2004, Ning (ning.com) is now an ever-growing platform enabling anyone to create his or her own social network. As of January 2010, Ning had more than 1.8 million social networks with more than 39 million registered users. If you want to create a forum for your customers or create a community for your clients, followers, and fans, Ning may be for you.

With Ning, you can create your own custom social network with your own page design, name, member profiles, photos, event calendars, and more. You also have the ability to make your network public (so anyone can join) or private. You can really create a great sense of community with Ning because you can observe what discussions are taking place. When taking a glance at the Ning network, you will see a multitude of small businesses, entrepreneurs, and special interest groups. You will see Twitter groups, Mom groups, coffee groups, and entrepreneurial groups. And you'll see highly focused groups like fitness, foodies, realtors, and private entrepreneurial groups for their members.

To get started, join the network. Give your name, e-mail address, and other requested information. Then, like the other platforms you have registered for, you will get a confirmation e-mail and you are in. Before you create your own social network on Ning, look at the others that are out there. You can search by name, by subject, or topic. Some are private and you cannot get in unless you are invited or are a client of that person's network, but there are thousands of open networks as well.

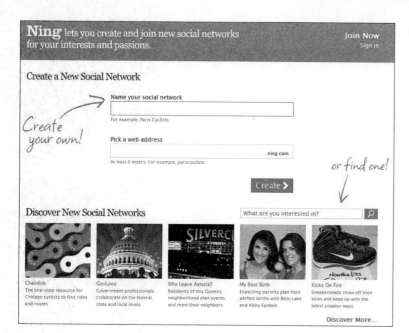

Here's the Home page for Ning.

Type in a word to search. Pick your favorite hobby, like fashion, antiques, or books. Type a word that represents that hobby in the box that reads, "What are you interested in?" and look at all of the forums.

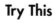

Try This

Log on to Ning and type in a keyword of a topic, subject, hobby, or area that interests you. Then find a social networking group in that area that you are interested in and join it. Practice creating an amazing profile. Remember to participate, give information, share tips, and, basically, be a connector. As you participate, think about whether it makes sense for you to create your own public or private network.

For example, I typed in the word "books" and more than 2,500 social networks on books popped up. See if there is one that meets your needs. The reason why I suggest typing in your hobbies as keywords is because you can also simply join these other social networks. You'll be with like-minded folks and begin building relationships with them. Ultimately, they will get to know you and your business and support and refer you. That's one way to utilize this site to add impact to your business. When you join these networks, you will list your website, blog, Twitter username, Facebook page, and other social network information.

You also will most likely meet new people that you haven't met on the other social media networks. Here's another example: let's say you speak as part of your business. Type in "speaker." More than 250 groups pop up on a page that looks like the following figure.

Here's a list of social networks for speakers on Ning.

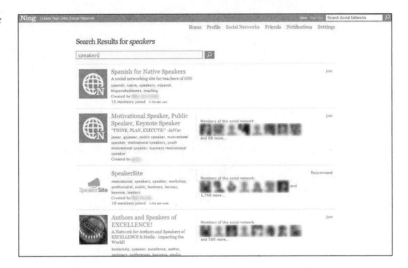

Next, you would pick one—say, SpeakerSite, because it has 3,700-plus members. You can either click on the SpeakerSite wording or click on **Join.** Now you will see an entire social network just for speakers. Join the group, create an amazing profile, and impact this audience with your information and knowledge.

This is how strategic alliances and partnerships are born. Perhaps you want to begin speaking in your town. Find other speakers on this network who are near you. Connect with them and then arrange an in-person meeting. Perhaps you can develop a joint venture together.

That's one way to use a service like Ning. Want to do business locally and become a connector in your area code? One social network on Ning that you should know about is Inside Area Codes, a social networking site for every area code in the country. Go to www.insideareacodes.com and click on your state (yes, they include Alaska and Hawaii) and then find your area code.

When you find your area code, click on it and you will be driven to a social networking page. Every small business owner or entrepreneur who wants to do business locally should be on local social networks like this. It's a great way to get on a social media network and meet people in your area code so you can network, get involved, and become known. Check out area code 919 and look at their site. This was amongst the first on Inside Area codes and they have a great network of members.

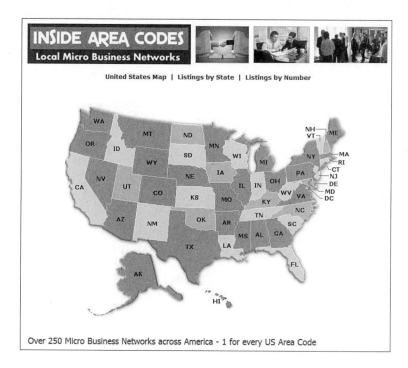

Inside Area Codes has a social networking site through Ning.

Seek out other social networks and join them. Contribute to the conversations. Share information. And consider the idea of creating your own social network.

SocialGO

SocialGO (socialgo.com) says it's the "social network maker." It's based in the United Kingdom, and in August 2009 this site had more than 2,000-plus social networks. Although it is smaller than Ning, it has some of the same features as well as additional ones.

One of the cool features is the live video chat sidebar where you can "dial up" a member and chat live with them through the site. Another good feature is that you have the ability to "white label" your site. This means that no one would know it is a SocialGO platform because people see only your business's branding. Note: both of these features are available at the premium level, which requires a small monthly fee. Also, at the fee-based levels you can accept advertising and actually make money from your site. However, at the free level you can still create forums, groups, events, photo sharing, member profiles, and some branding.

Here's the What is it? page on SocialGO.

Another interesting component of SocialGO is that participants can create their own blogs, which can be placed on a SocialGO magazine portal where they will be displayed with other bloggers on the platform. They have multiple templates to choose from and you can fully interact with your blog readers.

CrowdVine

At CrowdVine (crowdvine.com), many entrepreneurs create their own networking group or even produce a conference. This site allows you to communicate information with your group or conference attendees through an organized portal, which is basically a social network. Founder Tony Stubblebine said his site "helps people get rid of the social anxiety of knowing beforehand who they can connect with at [a] conference."

It also helps promote your conference because would-be attendees get "social proof" of who is attending, and they want to be a part of the event. The other great feature around this site is that when you create your account, you give your Twitter, Facebook, and other social media information. When you register for a conference that is using CrowdVine, the site will tell you who in your social media communities (or even your Google Mail or your Outlook contacts) is attending the same group meeting or conference. The site is also user-friendly.

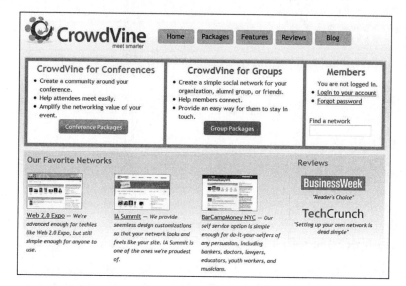

Here's the CrowdVine Home page.

More Reasons to Create Your Own Social Network

You already probably realize that having your own social network is a great marketing tool. But just in case you need more reasons why you'd want to do this, here are a few:

◆ You want a private community for your clients or customers.

◆ You want to create a public community for your fans.

◆ You want to further establish yourself as an expert in your industry.

◆ You want to easily communicate with your clients in an organized way.

◆ You want to create a membership portal for your business.

◆ You want use the latest technology to further market your brand.

◆ You want your customers to be able to communicate with each other.

◆ You want to expand your reach nationally or globally and combine those folks in one portal.

◆ You want to use a site like CrowdVine to allow your group or conference attendees to meet and socialize beforehand.

◆ You want to create a site that is a central hub for discussion in your industry or around your business.

Other Social Networks to Consider

You're probably quite surprised at just how many social networks there are. Well, we're not done yet! Here are some more social networks that you might find useful for your social media marketing efforts. So take a little time and review each of them.

PerfectBusiness and StartupNation

PerfectBusiness (perfectbusiness.com) is the place to be seen for serious entrepreneurs, investors, and experts in a variety of industries. Here, you might just meet potential strategic partners, mentors, and advisors. There's a video center and a nice learning portal that provides resources for you. There are also free and additional services for a fee at upgraded levels. It's a rich and robust platform.

StartupNation's tagline reads "by entrepreneurs, for entrepreneurs." Check out this social network (startupnation.com) for new entrepreneurial startups and small businesses that want to grow and connect with others. On this site, you can connect with other entrepreneurs and learn from experts and their blogs. There are many blogs, articles, and podcasts, as well as many forums and groups for business owners to participate in.

They have a great dashboard that is easy to use. If you are a first-time user, take the tour of StartupNation from the Home page. It's a very rich site with incredible tools, resources, and a community feel. Also, check out the Community tab, which is a great place to find local connections forums and even classifieds from your area.

Netiquette

Most of the sites featured in this chapter are getting very serious about spamming. They encourage their members to report spammers and will not tolerate it. Don't lose you memberships on sites because you want to sell, sell, sell. Sales success will come naturally as you continue to participate and share.

PartnerUp and Meetup

There are two additional social networks to examine: PartnerUp and Meetup. PartnerUp (partnerup.com) is for entrepreneurs and small business owners who are searching for specific business resources. You can find commercial real estate for your next big move and find both professional service providers and vendors who will help keep your business on track. Just like on the other sites, you'll also find a personal Profile page, forums, and a place to ask and answer questions.

Are you looking for new ways to meet people to network with and grow your business and connections? Or do you want to create your own live group or "meetup"? Meetup (meetup.com) does just that. No longer will you have the excuse that you can't seem to find networking groups to attend or that you can't afford them. Many on Meetup are free. Claimed to be the "largest network of local groups," Meetup has thousands of "meetups" based on hundreds of topics happening all the time.

With six million monthly visitors and nearly 60,000 meetup groups, you are bound to find something of interest. Whether you're a book lover, wine enthusiast, or entrepreneur, at Meetups there is something for you. Consider going to meetups that are not in your industry. You might meet interesting people this way. Sure, an entrepreneurial or small business marketing meetup is great and good to attend, but also consider a sports car meetup, a movie enthusiasts meetup, or a book lovers meetup. Again, you never know where your next business partner, client, or business supporter will come from.

Another creative way to use Meetup for your business is to create your own meetup. By creating your own, you set yourself up as a leader, and you will start to become a power networker.

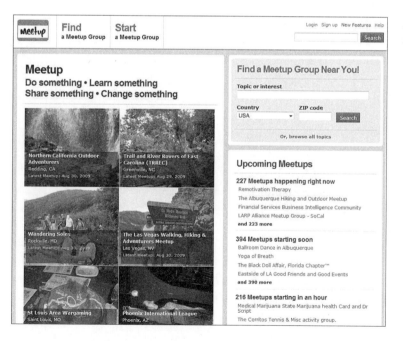

Here's the Home page for Meetup.

Entertaining Ways to Engage Your Audience

The world of social media gives you unique opportunities to be creative with the ways you engage your clients, customers, or followers. You're only limited by your imagination. Take a look at the following sites and you'll probably get some new ideas.

UserVoice

UserVoice (uservoice.com) allows you to really monitor and listen to what your customers are saying. You can get them to vote on ideas, share, and give new ideas. And you can respond to all of them in one "uservoice," or forum. You can integrate this product into your website by installing one of the widgets (by copying and pasting code into your website). If you need to have your webmaster install it, that's okay, too. You can now capture feedback and ideas directly from your clients.

Remember that people want to feel connected, so this might be another tool to consider when trying to engage and listen to your audience. Note that there are many tiers to this service, ranging from free to upper-tiered pricing, so be sure to read about the pricing structures and consider the costs and benefits.

Here's the Home page for UserVoice.

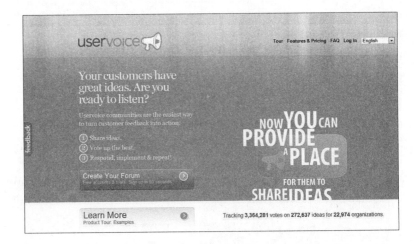

TriviaonTwitter

People love contests, and TriviaonTwitter (triviaontwitter.com) reflects that. Your company can participate in or sponsor trivia contests on this site. In exchange, you'll get to promote your product and brand in the various trivia rounds. This is another creative way businesses can market themselves with interactive contests all while using the power of social media platforms.

Here's the Home page for TriviaonTwitter.

Many adults and teens use social media, and it was just a matter of time before they partnered with the world's largest gaming networks. Probably by the time this book is published, both Facebook and Twitter will be on Xbox 360 and PlayStation. Imagine being able to interact with your friends online while you are gaming!

I've included a demo screen shot from a site I found online—a screen shot of Twitter on Xbox 360. This might be a very innovative and creative way to reach this audience with a contest.

Here's a sample screen shot of Twitter on Xbox 360 from 2009.

Using Social Media for Contests

Contests involve fun interaction. Here are additional ways to engage your audience on a variety of social media platforms:

♦ Create a link that promotes a sale or a special promotion. Tell your Twitter followers that the first 30 people who retweet that link will get a coupon or a prize.

♦ Have people send in a video (with their digital camera, Flip cam, or through 12seconds.tv) as to why people should use your product or service. The top video gets a great prize from your business.

♦ Tell friends and followers that the next 10 new clients will be featured in your blog.

♦ Have an Internet radio show? Tell your audience that your next big referral partner or next new business client will get 20 minutes of airtime on your next radio show to talk about his or her own business.

♦ Have a dental office or restaurant or photo studio? Get out your digital camera and get a video testimonial. Post it on video sites, Twitter, Facebook, MySpace, and LinkedIn. (Note, if you're a dentist, make sure the patient's mouth isn't still numb!)

- Work with teens or tweens? Have them do an online video as to why they like your business. Post it to your social media sites. (Remember, if they're under 18, you need parental permission.)

- Post a status update on Facebook and ask a question. Tell them the first 20 people who reply will get placed in a drawing for a free certificate to try out your service.

- Are you an author who just published your first book? Ask readers to send in a video or comment on your blog as to what they got out of the book or why they liked it. Take your best testimonials and interview them as part of your blog, radio show, or e-zine. Ask them to tweet about your book.

- Create a meetup and the first 10 people who arrive get a coffee gift certificate, a prize, or a discount on your fees. Or even feature them as guest bloggers on your blog.

You've gotten some great ideas in this chapter and I'll bet you come up with some creative ones on your own. Have fun with it!

The Least You Need to Know

- Social networks are becoming more individual and industry-specific to their audiences.

- Many social networking companies allow you to both join individual social networks and create your own.

- Many social networking sites are rich with content for the entrepreneur or small business owner.

- Your followers, fans, and clients want to be entertained, so get creative with the social media sites by using polls, contests, and trivia challenges.

20

Writing and Marketing Your Articles, E-Zines, and Books

In This Chapter

- ◆ How to build an "expert" mind-set
- ◆ Learn that published articles, whether online or in print, are one of the best ways to build instant credibility
- ◆ Ideas on how to begin your first article
- ◆ Companies that can help you with your electronic e-mail/newsletter marketing
- ◆ Ten creative ways to build your e-zine subscriber list

One of the best ways to build credibility for your business is to begin writing so your customers and prospects can begin reading about you. I often tell my clients that one of the first things people will do when they consider working with you is Google your name.

Before you read this chapter, Google your name. What pops up on the screen? Are there articles, stories, newsletters? If not, read on as you will discover easy and effective ways to get yourself published online.

You, the Expert Author

Most people don't necessarily think of themselves as an expert, but as a business owner, you need to begin believing that you are. You are an expert in your industry. You are the expert in what you do, whether you are an architect, Realtor, coach, actor, financial planner, artist, speaker, chef, mom, lawyer, interior designer, consultant, or car salesperson.

People want someone they can rely on, and that is why they will pay you for what you do. More importantly, from a business development standpoint, the more people read about your expertise, the more they'll be attracted to your business. This leads to your website, subscribing to your blog or newsletter, and then, perhaps, ultimately hiring you.

One way to build instant credibility is to get an article or two published. If you write an article, it could potentially be read by hundreds, if not thousands, of readers. And it's easier than you might think.

If you are not sure what you could write about for your first few articles, let's do a little brainstorming. Ask yourself the following questions:

- What three tips can you share about your industry?

- What three things can you share with people to help them avoid a certain pain in their life? Can you help them with financial, job, health, home, car, travel, legal, business, or real estate pain?

- What three questions should people consider before hiring someone like you? In other words, what are prospects looking for? Are they interested in credentials, testimonials, or examples of your work?

- What are the latest trends in your industry?

- What are the five biggest mistakes people make when hiring the wrong _____ (fill in the blank with your industry/title)?

- What experience have you had that would benefit others if you shared it? Share a big learning experience.

- Five ways to _____ (you fill in the blank). Examples: five ways to change your home, five ways to have better fitness, five ways to a better job, five ways to a better vacation, five ways to upgrade your home for under $1,000, and so on.

These are just some examples of what you can write about to highlight your expertise in your subject or industry. Smaller articles of 300 to 600 words are easy for readers to quickly digest, so that might be a good starting point.

Okay, let's get your article online. This way, when people Google your name, your article will pop up as an "expert author" in your industry. One site I'd like to direct you to that will do this for you is EzineArticles (ezinearticles.com). Through their website, you can submit up to 10 articles for free, then upgrade to a Platinum member status.

To create your account, click on either **Join Now** or **Submit Articles.** You can click on the audio links to get detailed instructions. After you're done, you will get a confirmation e-mail. If you have questions, review the editorial guidelines. They also have a good video tutorial and provide newsletters to assist you.

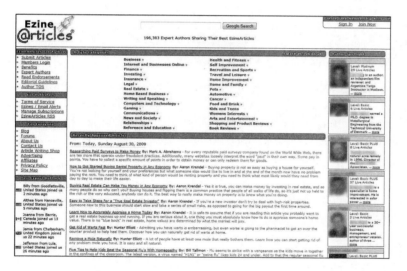

Here's the Home page for EzineArticles.

Be sure you select a category that is closest to your article content versus your business. The title is key, so make the first three words in your article title very strong. Search engines love the first three words and the keywords. Your article content is where you share and give information. There's no selling here.

After your article has been accepted (and it will only be accepted if you are giving information

> ### Did You Know?
>
> What is WYSIWYG? It stands for "what you see is what you get." In other words, the way your document is displayed on the screen is the way it will look when it's printed.

to help people, not shameless self-promotion), try to submit another. Remember, you have up to 10 to submit before you can be upgraded to a platinum member. You can also go back into the site, click on your article stats, and see how many people viewed your article and how many people clicked on your website.

Another way to get an article published online is to be a guest contributor to another person's blog or newsletter. This is a great strategic marketing strategy. Let's say you own a dog-walking business. You could approach a local veterinarian and see if he or she has a newsletter; if so, ask if you can be a contributing writer. Chances are the answer will be yes.

Another option is to check with a neighborhood newsletter or even a small-town magazine. In exchange for submitting an article, ask if you can put your name, website, and e-mail address at the end of the article. Oh, and don't forget to add your Twitter username, too.

Newsletters, E-Newsletters, and E-Zines

There was a time when print newsletters were all the rage. Now it seems everything has gone online. But the counter viewpoint is also true. Because there's so much online, if you did mail a newsletter, chances are pretty high that it will at least get looked at ... and maybe even be read.

What many entrepreneurs are doing now is publishing their own print newsletter quarterly to save a bit of money. If you can do one monthly, that is great. But printing a newsletter and mailing it can get expensive, so let's examine some additional options.

E-Newsletters and E-Zines

An e-newsletter is an electronic or digital newsletter. An e-zine is really the same thing. The "e" stands for electronic and the "zine" is last syllable of magazine.

Many define it as an electronic magazine because an e-zine should have a more visual component, such as color, art, and photographs. In contrast, an e-newsletter is more like a newspaper with more words and fewer graphics. The line can be easily blurred for some, but it's important to know the two terms and how they differ. We examine the e-zine in the next few sections.

As you get into social media marketing, you might get asked if you have an e-zine or e-newsletter. Earlier in the book, I mentioned several times that building your list is important. One of the reasons is that you will want to stay in touch with your customers, clients, and fans from your social media sites by publishing a regular e-zine.

By regularly communicating with your followers, you continue to build credibility by sharing your expertise. Another big bonus is that if your e-zine is good and you truly give great information, over time you are not only building credibility but you are creating loyalty. There is nothing like a loyal fan of your business—they'll stick with you.

When you offer a 30-percent-off special, a two-for-one promotion, or want to promote your book, chances are loyal readers of your e-zine will either buy it, or at least tell everyone in

> ### Did You Know?
>
> Sending out an e-newsletter or e-zine is also referred to as e-mail marketing. To find additional service providers to help you distribute your e-newsletter or e-zine, you might want to look under e-mail marketing solutions. If someone asks if you participate in e-mail marketing, you now know what that is.

their network that they should buy it. It's better for you to keep your name in front of people and stay on the top of their minds—otherwise your competition will.

Resources to Help You Create Your E-Zine

These are not all the resources that are out there, of course. But in the next few pages, you will find samples of very reputable e-mail marketing solution providers. These providers will help distribute your e-zine or e-newsletter. Most will also provide you with amazing analytics so you can see how many people opened the e-mail, how many opted out, how many forwarded your e-zine, and so on.

Constant Contact and VerticalResponse

Founded in 1998, Constant Contact (constantcontact.com) has thousands of devoted subscribers. It provides great templates, wonderful training, and powerful customer service. Free customer support is another benefit that comes with this site.

VerticalResponse (verticalresponse.com) calls itself the "self-service direct marketing" program. You get your first 500 e-mails free and then there are no contracts or commitments. You pay for only what you send. It also has a great tracking component to its system.

MailChimp and iContact

With over 225,000 users as of January 2010, MailChimp (mailchimp.com) has a lot of features, including great e-mail design templates, free usage for up to 100 receivers, and great reporting. An interesting feature with its reports is that you can find out not only who received your e-mail (as you most likely will not know everyone who is receiving your marketing piece), but where the recipient is located geographically.

With low monthly fees and more than 560,794 users as of January 2010, iContact (icontact.com) is a powerhouse, working with small business owners as well as Fortune 500 companies. It has more than 250 template designs for you to choose from. This site is worth a look.

1ShoppingCart and Infusionsoft

1ShoppingCart (1shoppingcart.com) not only allows you to integrate your direct marketing, but provides a whole host of other service offerings. It has e-mail broadcasting, autoresponder e-mail services, ad tracking tools, shopping cart links, online payments, affiliate program tracking (for those of you who want affiliates to resell your services), and so much more. 1ShoppingCart is one of the top-rated total solutions for Internet marketers.

Infusionsoft's (infusionsoft.com) tagline reads "Double Your Sales" and on the Features page they say it helps you "close more leads, get repeat sales, and grow your business fast." How do they do all this? By automating your follow-ups, managing your contacts, and helping you send targeted e-mails.

A glance at their August 2009 press sheet reveals that Infusionsoft facilitated more than $1 million in e-commerce sales per day and delivered more than two million e-mails per day. This is a very sophisticated and robust e-mail marketing system that integrates many top features into one system and another good one to consider.

Tips for a Successful E-Zine

Keep the tone of the e-zine conversational and write as if you were talking. How often you want to send your e-zine to people is up to you. Some people send e-zines quarterly, monthly, bimonthly, or weekly. I deliver mine weekly. It builds loyalty and people look forward to it. And maintaining a weekly schedule keeps me on my toes because every week I need to communicate good information that will help businesses grow.

An e-zine, whether weekly or monthly, allows you another forum in which to communicate with your friends, fans, and followers. While this is not a general Internet marketing book, I will review just a few of the many pointers that will help you produce a successful e-zine. Here are a few tips to get you started:

♦ Promote it everywhere—in your e-mail signature, blog, website, letters, and business cards. The point of the e-zine is to build your list or subscriber base.

♦ Whichever service you use to deliver your e-zine, make sure you have a good thank-you message that is automatically sent to them when they sign up.

♦ Write as if you are speaking to them. Keep it conversational, less formal, and use real-world scenarios. Include photos and color, if you can. Put a copyright notice at the end of each issue.

♦ More and more e-zines are including video in them, so put a video in your e-zine.

♦ Look at your stats. What you can analyze, though, will depend on the service you're using. If possible, find out if people are subscribing regularly. Are they unsubscribing? Remind readers your e-zine is subscription-based only.

♦ Put your social media links and sites in your e-zine. Example: follow me on Twitter, connect with me on LinkedIn, join my group on Facebook, and so on. Remember, everything is circling back around to each other.

♦ Look at other e-zines that you receive. What do you like most about them? Dislike? Try to deliver something you would read and the followers will come.

♦ Have a great subject line in your e-mail so recipients will open it! Keep it short yet strong, and include the name of your e-zine in the subject line as well.

♦ End your e-zine with an author's box describing who you are. Include the name of your business and a short bio.

One cardinal rule about sending your e-zine: it should be sent only to people who subscribe. You should not be a *spammer* and send your e-zine to people who have not asked for it. Send it to people who want the e-zine, not to those whom you happen to sign up only because you have their business card.

def•i•ni•tion _____

A **spammer** is one who sends spam (unsolicited e-mail) to people.

And one more tip: take a look at e-zine directories. Early in this chapter, it was mentioned that you should get your e-zine placed into certain directories. This will help you become more findable on the Internet. A great website that provides a list of directories is www.ezines.nettop20.com. This top 20 list provides a rich selection of the highest-rated and most popular e-zine directory sites.

Ways to Build Your E-Zine List

Now that you have a terrific e-zine, you want to get it out there and grow your subscriber list. Here are a few ideas for you to consider:

♦ On your website, put your e-zine/e-newsletter sign-up box preferably at the top of the page.

♦ When first starting out, ask colleagues and friends to subscribe. Ask them if they'd like to forward to people whom they think will benefit from reading it.

♦ Tell all of your new customers and clients that they will get a complimentary subscription to your e-zine.

♦ Offer new subscribers a free gift such as a CD of tips, a discount on one of your products, a free report of some kind, advanced news on new releases or products, and so on.

♦ Look at online forums where people who are similar to your subscriber base hang out. Participate in the forum and list your website and e-zine information.

♦ If you are an independent professional, put your e-zine info on everything. Put it on cards, invoices, and promo material. Example: for weekly (your industry) tips, get my content-rich e-zine.

♦ Get with other business alliance partners and agree to cross-promote each other's e-zines. You can recommend their e-zines in your e-zine, then they can return the favor.

- If you do any speaking, offer a giveaway when you are done speaking. Tell everyone in the audience as they pass around the card for the drawing that they will also get a complimentary subscription to your e-zine.

- If you have a reception area or checkout counter, put a bowl or a booklet out that reads, "We want to stay in touch with you. Sign up for our monthly e-zine for specials and great information."

- Mention it in your blog and YouTube videos, and tweet about it from time to time. Also, remember your Facebook page? Remind people about your e-zine in that box below your photo or in your information summary page. Invite people to become subscribers on your LinkedIn page as well.

Self-Publishing a Book

Want to take your writing to another level? How about considering self-publishing? Of course, if the big publishing houses come calling along with an interested literary agent, that's great. However, many entrepreneurs don't know that they can still get a book published without an agent or signing a six-figure book deal.

You can self-publish your own book. This means that you write it and get it published or printed on your own and then market it yourself. There are many publishing resources out there to help you. Although this isn't a book on becoming an author, I thought this might be good to mention because writing is a big part of social media marketing. And if you have a book, you can promote it on all of your social media sites.

Imagine, now that you have all of these great vehicles to share your expertise, what it would be like to capture your expertise in your very own book. By self-publishing a book, chances are you will gain expert status in the eyes of your clients and prospects. And you will also establish greater credibility and generate a lot of publicity for yourself and your business.

You might be thinking that you could never write a book. Well, did you ever think you could write a blog? What many self-published authors are doing is taking their blog posts and turning them into chapters in their self-published book. Another idea is to take articles that are in your e-zine or newsletter and use those as chapter guides for your book.

Imagine, if you are a dentist, doctor, lawyer, artist, fitness coach, chef, business coach, speaker, photographer, or decorator, how great it would be to hand your book to new or prospective clients who are looking to work with you. For example, one time I visited a new dermatologist, and as part of the welcome kit, I received a copy of her book. I was very impressed, because not only was it a great book, but no other doctor had ever given me a book as part of a welcome package.

Book Coach Sam Horn, www.samhorn.com, who's also the 17-time Maui-Hawaii Writers Conference emcee and author, has helped thousands of entrepreneurs become authors. She's fond of saying, "I have never met any authors who were sorry they wrote their book. I've only met authors who were sorry they didn't write it ... *sooner!*"

Donna Kozik, who helps professionals write and self-publish their first book through her business, www.mybigbusinesscard.com, says, "Self-publishing a book is a great way to capitalize on your message and business or life philosophy." And it's one of the best business cards you will ever have. So consider self-publishing. There are many businesses that will help you get your book published.

The Least You Need to Know

◆ Writing articles on sites like EzineArticles will help establish you as an expert author in your industry.

◆ If writing articles seems daunting at first, try simply writing about three to five things that people need to know about your industry.

◆ There are many e-mail service providers that make it easy to help you electronically gather e-mail addresses and deliver your e-zine/e-newsletter to subscribers.

◆ Your electronic newsletter or e-zine should be professional, conversational in tone, and include links to your other social media sites.

◆ E-zine directories are a great way to get the word out online about your e-newsletter or e-zine.

◆ Use every opportunity you can to promote your e-zine, whether it's on your business cards or at speaking engagements.

Chapter 21

Time Strategies to Get It All Done

In This Chapter

- ◆ Learn about mind-set strategies
- ◆ Learn about time-saving tools and ideas
- ◆ A timeline to help you manage your social media time
- ◆ Discover the world of virtual assistants

Okay, so now you're on your way to becoming an expert on social media marketing. You've learned a great deal and now you're probably wondering, "How do I manage my time on so many different social media networking sites?" Well, this chapter is here to show you how.

Mind-Set Strategies

Let me just say this: don't panic. You may feel you have to do it all and know it all today, but you don't. You have this book and now you are in the know. You might be thinking, "I've got to get a headshot, video camera, set up a Twitter account, consider a Facebook Fan page, produce videos, and, oh yeah, determine my strategy."

Just step back and take a deep breath. Think about what you want to get out of social media. Start with one site, get comfortable, and then try another. Remember that we talked about mind-set in previous chapters. Well, having the right mind-set as you become involved in social media is key. Stay focused, but don't worry about the number of friends you have online or the number of followers you get the first week. This isn't a race, it's your business.

Focus on Sending Out High-Quality Messages

Remember, people don't necessarily care about what you had for breakfast. Share tips and tell them what you're working on (without giving away your trade secrets). Give them a glance inside your business. You'll be amazed over time what that will do. And don't forget to share useful links and highly relevant updates.

Ask yourself before hitting the send button, "Is this something that people might want to hear? Will they pass it along and/or will they find it valuable?" If the answer is yes, then you are on the right track. It gets tempting to vent or express what you are feeling at the moment, but if you focus on quality relevant updates, you will have nothing to worry about.

Watch Your Time

Be selective about how you spend your time. Many people put a timer next to their computer so they don't get drawn in. Sometimes, before you know it, an hour has gone by. After you have your social media sites set up, log on to Twitter, post an update, and check your Direct Messages.

Then, log on to Facebook and post a status update and check your inbox. Next, log in to LinkedIn and post a status update and check your inbox. Time spent so far? About 5 to 15 minutes.

Now if you are really in a pinch, you can save time by using Ping.fm to shoot out messages to all of your sites. Check into Ping in the morning and again at night when you are first beginning.

Have Realistic Expectations

Many people set up accounts on these platforms and expect the cash register to begin ringing within the first 30 days. It doesn't really happen like that.

Review your experience either monthly or quarterly. Think about which social media sites you are getting the most value from. Look at your web stats from your website hosting provider to see where people are coming from, but don't give up any of them yet. Give it a good three to six months to see where you are most comfortable. You might be comfortable with one form of social networking or you might feel at ease on several.

For example, you might find that having a blog is working well for you. However, you are not quite ready for video yet. And that's okay. Be realistic and take it slow if you need to.

Learn to Skim

After you have TweetDeck, Facebook, and LinkedIn running (and you are participating in groups and Fan pages), you just can't read it all or it will turn into a full-time job for you. Over time, you will know your favorites and the people that you want to follow. These are the sites or the people who provide you great value. Focus on them.

Don't feel you need to read it all. The same advice goes for videos. Over time, you will begin getting a lot of videos. After a while, you will start to learn which videos from certain people provide value to you. Focus on these videos and don't worry about the rest.

Reach Out

Some amazing alliances will be formed, but you will need to reach out. Reach out to people you seem to enjoy following, those you have something in common with, or those you just want to get to know better. That's what a lot of this is about. You're expanding your network of influence.

Arrange a time to speak on the phone with one of the followers you feel comfortable with. Ask questions about this person's business and where he or she is trying to take it.

Time-Saving Tools and Ideas

With all of these Internet tools to help you market your business and expand your networks, you might find that you are busier and more overwhelmed than ever. Here's a tip for you: the more you can consolidate or leverage your time, the better focused you will be.

Try This _____

Sign up for a bit.ly account. This is a URL shortening service that tracks all of the links you create. This way, if you have a long link, you can shorten it through this service. It also keeps all the short links you create to save you time in the future. Try it! The website is http://bit.ly.

Here is a list of ideas to help you manage your social media marketing time:

♦ When scheduling a meeting, think about whether it makes sense to meet in person or if it would be more efficient to schedule a web meeting or teleconference. If you're a home-based business owner, don't be a hermit. At least get out one time per week for a networking event or an in-person meeting.

♦ As mentioned previously, when you want to update your social media networks quickly, use Ping.fm. Another site that simultaneously updates social networks is hellotxt.com.

♦ Use news aggregators, such as Netvibes, to combine all your feeds and news into one landing page. Make it your Home page. This way you can easily scan the news, your incoming blogs, and your social media messages.

♦ If it is possible, check your voicemail only three times per day: morning, noon, and evening. This will allow you to focus on your business.

♦ Update your Twitter, Facebook, LinkedIn, and MySpace sites in the morning and at the end of the day—20 minutes in the morning and 20 minutes in the evening.

♦ Automate your welcome message on Twitter so that all new followers will get an automated greeting. Use SocialOomph.

♦ Make three appointments with yourself each week to post on your blog. Or write three blog entries at one time and then post them on three different days.

♦ Get an intern to help you with posting information, answering friend requests, and uploading videos.

♦ Write a week's worth of blog posts at one time. Tweet about the topics with a link to your blog. Post a link on Facebook and LinkedIn as well.

◆ Get a *virtual assistant* to help you with your social media marketing. While the tone and the wording should come from you, an assistant can help you implement your strategies. An assistant can also provide you with weekly reports, such as how many new followers you have, the number of retweets, how many joined your Fan page, and so on. We'll talk more about this later in this chapter.

def•i•ni•tion

A **virtual assistant**, known as a VA, is a person who provides professional support to assist their clients. A VA is usually someone who works from home for an entrepreneur or a small business owner and can provide many services, such as social media marketing and web development.

Did You Know?

Do you like those little yellow Post-It notes? Do you have them on your desk or computer right now? Well, they've gone virtual as well. Check out Zhorn Software (www.zhornsoftware.co.uk/stickies). It's a cute time-saving utility tool that allows you to post notes on your computer screen. You can pick the color and size. After trying this, you can say you've gone green.

Jott

On the road often? Jott's service (jott.com) converts your voice to text allowing you to send messages, via e-mail or SMS text, to any distribution list you set up ahead of time including to your own e-mail. You can also get your voicemail received as e-mail—it's a real timesaver. You can forward and reply to them, screen calls when you're in meetings, set call-back reminders, and more.

A new service that was announced in Summer 2009 is called Jott Links. It is called this because they will "link" Jott with some of your other social media services. For example, you can call Jott and say the link name "Twitter" and then say your tweet and it will post in on Twitter. You can send a Jott message to "Outlook" and have your appointment posted directly to your Outlook calendar before you are back in your office. Pretty neat, huh? If you are a mobile entrepreneur, Jott just may be the tool to help you save time and get it all done.

TrafficGeyser

You've worked hard to start your business, and you may offer the best service and most unique product that everyone should have their hands on. You want to get the word out quickly to a lot of people. Obviously, by now you know social media marketing can truly help you get the word out. There are many products that can help you accelerate getting the word out.

We know now that the more findable you are and the easier you make it for people to get to know you, the greater the chance your business has of being successful. That said, it takes a lot of effort and time to manually distribute your information on the Internet, and we've mentioned several sites throughout this book that will automate the process for you.

TrafficGeyser (trafficgeyser.com) is a service that seems to solve the distribution issue. It charges monthly fees, but there are a variety of affordable price levels to choose from. This solution helps entrepreneurs and small business owners save time by helping them distribute many of their social media marketing products to various online channels.

With over 20,000 members as of Summer 2009, this site is worth a look. In speaking with TrafficGeyser's Mike Koenig, he reminded me of some interesting points about what his system does. Here is a sampling: the product submits podcasts to directories and social bookmarking sites. It also submits articles to article sites and submits your video content to Twitter and Facebook. It also has a service that schedules and resubmits your content a number of times, and a host of other timesaving services.

Sample Social Media Marketing Timeline

By no means is this the only way to manage your social media marketing when you are first starting out, but it's a sample timeline to give you an idea how to organize your time. You want to get the benefit of marketing your business and brand using social media without it taking over. One could obviously take this to higher levels, but here is a "basic" starter timeline. (Note that times will vary depending on how big your network is.

- ◆ Monday morning: Send out a Facebook, Twitter, and LinkedIn status update. Check your inbox on Facebook and LinkedIn. Time: 10 minutes

- ◆ Monday afternoon: Post a previously written blog update. Time: 5 minutes

- ◆ Monday evening: Check your Facebook inbox and Profile page for comments. Respond to comments. Check friend requests. Check Twitter for retweets and direct messages. Post a new update. Time: 15 minutes

- Tuesday morning: Send out updates to all sites via Ping.fm. Check direct messages on Twitter. Time: 5 minutes

- Tuesday evening: Check inbox on all sites (Facebook, LinkedIn, and Twitter). Time: 10 minutes

- Wednesday morning: Send out Facebook, Twitter, and LinkedIn status updates. Check your inbox on all sites. Go onto LinkedIn and look at discussions within the groups you are a part of. Add to the discussion. Time: 10 to 20 minutes

- Wednesday afternoon: Post a previously written blog update and respond to comments on your blog. Send a tweet. Time: 10 minutes

- Wednesday evening: Check friend requests on Facebook. Look at inbox and respond to wall comments. Check direct messages on all sites. Time: 15 minutes

- Thursday morning: Update status on all sites via Ping.fm. Check Twitter direct messages. Look at blog comments. Send out your prewritten newsletter. Time: 25 to 30 minutes.

- Thursday evening: Check your inboxes on all sites. Respond to Twitter direct messages. Send out a tweet, look at blog comments, and check the discussions on LinkedIn. Time: 20 minutes

- Friday morning: Update your status on all sites. Get out the Flip cam. Record a 30-second tip. Post to Facebook and YouTube. Time: 20 minutes

- Friday afternoon: Post to blog (prewritten). Respond to blog comments. Send a tweet and respond to direct messages on Twitter. Log in to Facebook and LinkedIn to review comments and direct messages. Run a report on your newsletter to see the open rate. Time: 30 minutes

- Friday evening: You've connected to a lot of people this week and many people are receiving your branding messages and understanding your expertise. Check direct messages and update status via Ping.fm. Time: 15 minutes

- Weekends: Post a tweet and update your status each day if you can. Stay visible. And unless you choose to write it during the week, one idea is to try to write your blog and newsletter/e-zine over the weekend so you can simply post it during the week. Time: 30 to 45 minutes

Congratulate yourself! And take note: it's good to alternate your times that you post your status updates. You will reach different people by doing so.

Virtual Assistants

Never heard of a virtual assistant? No, it's not a robot. The virtual assistant industry is still an emerging industry, but the entrepreneurs and small business owners who use them say it's one of the best investments they have ever made for themselves.

When you Google "virtual assistant," you will see virtual receptionist, virtual phone assistant, and virtual office assistant. With all of this technology available to you, it's important to know that you can have real people help you with your business. They just won't physically be in your office; they work virtually for you from their home office, whether it be 5 minutes away or 5,000 miles. There aren't many official statistics, but my Internet research shows that as of August 2009, there are anywhere from 8,000 to 35,000 worldwide.

Perhaps you have been looking at the previous timeline sample for social media marketing and saying, "How can I do that and get my job done?" Consider investing in a virtual assistant to help you with your social media marketing and other duties. This will free up your schedule to work on other aspects of your business.

A virtual assistant can help you respond to e-mails, post your status updates, and create your social media sites. He or she can also schedule meetings, plan events, maintain records, schedule appointments and interviews, and so much more. Many entrepreneurs have a VA do most of their administrative tasks so that they themselves can manage the social media.

Some entrepreneurs ask their VA to do both administrative duties and help run the social media. Many power social media users who have tens of thousands of followers claim that they have a virtual assistant (maybe plural!) to help them manage the administrative side of their businesses behind the scenes.

To find a virtual assistant, you can check out the International Virtual Assistants Association at www.ivaa.org. You can also check out AssistU at www.assistu.org. There is also oDesk (www.odesk.com), where you can find a variety of freelance assistants from around the world for very competitive rates.

Virtual Phone Assistants

There are many of these types of services out there that help with your phone issues. As an entrepreneur or small business owner, your phone presence is key to your overall marketing, and having a virtual phone assistant should not be overlooked as another place to market to clients. For example, your voicemail greeting is very important.

In the spirit of getting it all done, you might consider a solution like this if you are a one-person show or you run a small business office. Consider a phone service that will automatically answer your calls, particularly if you travel often or are in frequent meetings. Services like this will give the caller prompts as to what the call is in regard to and then direct that call to the appropriate person (or line) based on what the caller is looking for.

While this really doesn't have much to do with social media per se, we would encourage you to make the most of your voicemail. For instance, mention one of the following: "Follow me on Twitter @_____," "Join our fan page on Facebook," or "make sure you see our blog, called _____."

Having an automated system that will track you down to deliver the call either by text or by voicemail will certainly help save time.

Password Management

Not all of us are gifted at organization. How many times have you had to ask the system to retrieve your usernames and passwords to certain websites? Well, sometimes it was because you simply couldn't remember the password. Now that you're involved in social media, it can be a real problem—you have been introduced to so many social media marketing sites, and all of them require usernames and passwords. It's no wonder that you might get confused. RoboForm (roboform.com) is a tool that can help you manage it all.

Here's the Home page for RoboForm.

The tagline for RoboForm is "Remembers Passwords So You Don't Have To." Sounds good, right? This password management software not only manages all of your passwords, but also fills in all those site registration forms, backs up your passwords, and more. I'm sure there are other programs out there, but this seems like a good one to at least check out.

The Least You Need to Know

- Try one social media site at a time so you don't panic or feel overwhelmed.

- Set realistic expectations for the amount of time you spend on sites and try to use timesaving shortcuts and tools to help you.

- Schedule social media in the morning and evening and write blogs in advance, if you can.

- Automate as much of your distribution as you can by using sites like TrafficGeyser.

- Consider using a virtual assistant to help you with social media or with other administrative tasks.

- Ask your networks what other tools they are using to aggregate or automate tasks.

Glossary

blogosphere   The blogging universe, in general. If you blog, you are part of the collective blogosphere.

business champions   People who will always give you a great reference and are high-powered networkers who will sing your praises. They can also serve as your strategic partners, so that no matter who they are talking to, when the opportunity arises they will bring up your name.

embed   To make something an integral part, such as embedding a video into your website or blog.

MP3 file   A computer file that's created with compression technology. These small files are often used to make digital audio computer files that can be easily transferred over the Internet.

online reputation management (ORM)   The process of monitoring online references to a person, brand, company, product, or service with the objective of minimizing the damage of online negative feedback and defamation.

plugins   Software applications that can be added to blogs to increase functionality or provide added features.

RSS   Really Simple Syndication, or Rich Site Summary. It helps create website feeds that enable you to publish frequently updated texts, such as from blogs.

SEO   Search engine optimization, which describes various techniques used to improve your website's search engine rankings.

SMS   Short Message Service, which is the connection between the phenomenon of text messaging and the underlying technology. In some parts of the world, SMS is used as a synonym for a text message or even for the act of sending a text message (even when a different protocol is actually being used).

spammer   One who sends spam, or unsolicited e-mail, to people.

status updates   Updates that are posted on the social media sites. Your status update answers the question "What are you doing right now?" or "What is on your mind?" Think of your status update as your marketing message on social media sites.

sticky   A social media site where one can easily write/post (or paste) information on the page and then replace it with something else is said to be "sticky."

tags   Keywords that describe the content of your video. They are also search words that people use to find content. When selecting tags, think about what keywords viewers would use to find your video.

Twitter cloud   A cluster of single words or a (visual) written description of words that you have tweeted most often.

video status   Like a written status update, except that it is distributed via video.

viral marketing   A marketing technique that encourages users to pass a marketing message to other users or websites, which can create an exponential growth in the number of people who see the message.

virtual assistant (VA)   A person who provides professional support to assist his or her clients. A VA is usually someone who works from home for an entrepreneur or a small business owner and can provide many services, such as social media marketing and web development.

wall   A feature found on everyone's profile page, fan page, or group page. This is where visitors can write a message and it stays on the profile page, or wall.

WAP   Wireless application protocol, which enables users to access information via handheld wireless devices, such as cell phones.

Additional Resource Directory

These following websites are great resources for your social media marketing efforts. Some are mentioned in the book, while others are not. These sites offer valuable information and resources that can help you stand out in the crowd of millions online! Here are some of my personal favorites:

The Sales Lounge (www.thesaleslounge.com)—Learn the hip, fun, and conversational way. This site brings you programs, workshops, and mentoring on success, sales, and social media. Learn from award-winning sales and success expert and million-dollar producer Jennifer Abernethy. It's a three–tiered ultrahip success club with virtual learning, mentoring, seminars, and annual success conference.

TweetDeck (www.tweetdeck.com)—This site is an absolute must for managing your Twitter account. Set up your TweetDeck account and then create custom columns based on your areas of interest.

BubbleTweet (www.bubbletweet.com)—Incorporate video into your tweets—it's a great way to be innovative. Change your video greetings around the holidays, an event, or company special promotion, or just before a product launch.

12seconds (12seconds.tv)—A great site to use to create 12-second video clips. Post on your blog or website, or incorporate into Twitter.

Animoto (animoto.com)—This one was not mentioned in the book, but it is great! Create MTV–style videos for your blog, Twitter, or Facebook page to promote you and your products or services.

TubeMogul (www.tubemogul.com)—Use TubeMogul to distribute your videos to sites across the web.

TweetPhoto (tweetphoto.com)—TweetPhoto is a platform that enables your photos to be discovered, published, and shared easily using popular social media tools, and encourages viewer interaction with your photo and push marketing.

Blog Talk Radio (www.blogtalkradio.com)—Thinking about an Internet radio show, or want to create podcasts? Look into BlogTalkRadio.

Viddler (www.viddler.com)—Create and share great marketing videos using this tool. There's lots of customization potential.

Ustream (www.ustream.tv)—Create your own streaming TV channel or watch many content-rich (or just plain fun) shows. Lifestreaming (or just streaming) is going to become ever increasingly popular.

Ning (www.ning.com)—Create your own social network around your industry, brand, or business. Create a custom-looking social networking site and make it private or public with just a few easy steps.

AddThis (www.addthis.com)—The site is the number-one bookmarking and sharing site (ComScore July2009). Place it on your blog, e-zine, or newsletter. Let the world share what you have to say—it's a great way to encourage viral marketing.

OoVoo (www.oovoo.com)—Use this great timesaving tool to conduct live meetings, see each other, and collaborate. I use this tool all the time and just love it. It's free, fun, and very professional.

Ezine Articles (www.ezinearticles.com)—Article marketing is here to stay. Use EzineArticles to showcase your expertise. When someone runs a search for your name on the Internet, your expert article will appear—remember, though, no selling. You'll find great information and tips and your article will get published online on their site.

SecondLife (secondlife.com)—This site is great for virtual meetings, networking, and presentations. More and more events, meetings, and gatherings will be taking place using this tool, or others similar to it.

VideoTrio (www.videotrio.com)—This site is an online video production from Hollywood insiders. This group unites professional video production expertise together with the power of online marketing and your business expertise and messaging.

bit.ly—Shorten your links, track your links, and collect a history of your links and how often they are clicked. It's a great tool to use to provide links in your social media marketing.

Tiny URL (tinyurl.com)—Shorten that long URL or link, and make it tiny. A must for your social media updates to make space for your content links.

Mashable (mashable.com)—A news resource site with everything dealing with social media. I mean everything: articles, updates, statistics, and so on.

StumbleUpon (www.stumbleupon.com)—This site will help you discover great websites that are matched to your personal preferences and have been recommended by others with similar interests.

Twellow Directory (www.twellow.com)—Be sure to get listed in the Twellow directory. Want to reach other journalists? Type in the word "journalist" and see who pops up. This is a great way to connect and follow like-minded folks! It's search based on your Twitter bio line that you fill out on Twitter.com.

FeedMingle (www.feedmingle.com)—Combine all of your RSS Feeds into one with this site.

audioboo (www.audioboo.com)—A cool audio blogging application, this site is neat for audio messaging on Facebook.

VideoTrio (www.videotrio.com)—Use this site to combine video and stunning professional production expertise together with the powerful online marketing.

Index

video, 142-143
  webinars, promoting, 261-262
  Xbox 360, 291-292
Twitter Gallery, 156
Twitter Grader, 158-159
Twitter Toolbar, 155
TwitterBerry application, 131
TwitterCounter, 159-160
TwitThis, 153-154
TwtBizCard, 157
Twtlong, 154
Twtpoll, 156
TwtQpon, 157
Twtvite, 156-157
TypePad.com, 245-246

U

unwritten rules of engagement, 25
updates, Twitter, 112
usernames, Twitter, 115-116, 121
users
  Facebook, demographics, 8
  LinkedIn, 10
  Twitter
    following, 130-131
    locating, 125-126
    managing, 146-148
    obtaining information, 151-153
UserVoice, 290
Ustream.tv, 233-234

V

VAs (virtual assistants), 309, 312
VerticalResponse, e-zines, creating, 299
Viddler.com, 231-232

video
  equipment, 224
  Internet TV shows, creating, 233-237
  marketing, 222-223
    12seconds.tv, 228-230
    Blip.tv, 231
    Viddler.com, 231-232
    Vimeo.com, 230
    YouTube, 224-228
  online audience, 223
  tags, 226
  Twitter, 142-143
  written permissions, 222
video cameras, 32
Video Channels (YouTube), 225
video conferencing, service sites, 262-264
Video File Upload screen (YouTube), 226
video status (12seconds.tv), 229
videos
  embedding, 225
  Facebook, uploading, 97-98
  MySpace
    recording, 213-214
    uploading, 211
Videos application (Facebook), 66-68
Vimeo.com, 230
viral marketing, 38-39
virtual assistants (VAs), 309, 312
virtual phone assistants (VPAs), 312
virtual world platforms, 267-268
Vox.com, 247
VPAs (virtual phone assistants), 312

W-X-Y-Z

Wakeman, Denise, 241
walls, Facebook, 44
WAP (wireless application protocol), 201
Web 2.0, 31